# LETTERS FROM THE WILDERNESS

## (SPIRITUAL SURVIVAL FOR GOD'S REMNANT)

## HENRY A. WASHINGTON

Copyright © 2005 by Henry A. Washington

*Letters From The Wilderness*
by Henry A. Washington

Published by Henry Washington Publications
Mailing Address: P.O. Box 94, Mastic, NY, 11950
Website: henrywashington.com

Printed in the United States of America

ISBN 1-59781-801-1

Unless otherwise indicated, Bible quotations are taken from *The King James* Version of the Bible.

www.xulonpress.com

# For Diddi

I could not have written this book without you.
I see more of Christ in you than anyone I know.

# *Acknowledgements*

Thank you to Glenn and Shevaun: for giving me life and good principles.

Thank you Jim: for giving me the essential basics of Christ with fear and trembling.

Thank you Clare: for truly being a **man** of God.

Thank you Mae Gillespie (Mom): for being pure and loving me with all of your heart.

Thank you George Gillespie (Dad): for teaching me the value of prayer.

Thank you Alex: for teaching me how to 'go for it'.

Thank you Bev: for teaching me the beauty of elegance.

Thank you David, Glenn, & Kailee: for exposing me to myself; and your love.

Thank you Pastor Pendray: for showing me what a Pastor is.

Thank you Pastor Fricker: for showing me what a preacher is.

Thank you Vern: for showing me the heart of a missionary.

Thank you Jim and April: for being my friends.

Thank you to all of my congregations for believing in my ministry.

Thank you Donna: for the rough critique and editing.

Thank you Jules: for reminding me what I am all about.

Thank you Fran: for being my New York mom.

Thank you Diddi: for making me smile every day.

Especially: thank you Jesus for rescuing such a man as I.

# *Contents*

# *Introduction*

The truth is that I wanted somebody well known to write my introduction. This was not because of an inflated ego but because it might lend some sense of endorsement to my first published book. I contacted the office of a man I look up to quite a bit. After many attempts to contact his office I received a recording on my answering machine telling me that he had received many such requests and did not have the time to do them. It was just another reminder that I am just a 'nobody'. This fact does not bother me since most followers of Jesus spend their lives in relative anonymity.

The record of Jesus is that He deliberately came to earth as a 'nobody'. I have this picture of God planning Jesus' entry into the world and saying to Himself, "We'll have to make sure that there is no external appeal to this man" (Isaiah 53:2). In His infinite wisdom God obscured Himself in this world from those characteristics that would most naturally produce awe in His creatures. John made it very clear that Jesus was such an unassuming man that neither the world He entered nor the people He went to recognized Him (John 1:10-11). We are, as He is, in this world with both Kingdom authority and parallel worldly obscurity (1 John 4:17). In His own ironic way God veils His Kingdom in the 'earthen vessels' that only have appeal when His Kingdom is somehow displayed.

Being a 'nobody' places me in a unique position to speak to a large cross-section of American Christendom. Most of us are nobodies. I have been the Pastor of two churches but have done little to distinguish myself in such a way that I might put it in my 'Bio'. I have started no profound movements. I have not produced a famous or a large church. I have not managed to compose a program that will, "Change the face of the Church in America." I am definitely not a gifted Christian recording artist. Except to the small circle of people that love and know me, I am relatively unknown. In other words, I am a simple traveler in the byways of God, just like you.

I know quite a few spectacular Christians. They are also relatively unknown. Most of the outstanding examples of Christian living that I have seen have not been 'Stars' but anonymous persons. Each one was glad for the privacy. I am married to the most generous person that I have ever met. The best preachers I have ever heard were in small churches where their congregations little appreciated the privilege they enjoyed. The best people of prayer are even more obscure—their services are not booked three years in advance. In fact, although they are one of the most valuable assets to the Body of Christ, they are rarely even discerned or sought out.

This book is a series of letters written to you by me. They constitute the core of simple realization and living that God has brought me to over the last thirty-one years. These letters reflect my tiny, puny, personal experiences that have proven true in relation to the Word of God. I have no 'new revelation' to bring. I point to life lived in relation to a very old and dear revelation; the Bible. These letters will not appeal to those seeking new things. Rather, I find myself pointing to a life that has been profoundly obscured today because of this present spiritual wilderness we find ourselves in. This is the simple life of God that we can partake of as we abide in His Word and His Holy Spirit. Won't you come aside to a quiet place for awhile and read these Letters from the Wilderness?

# *Prologue*

*T*his book is a series of letters. The physical wilderness (Chapter 3) is used as a metaphor for the current spiritual environment we live in. We present the comparison between the two as a parable. No new truth is being presented here. Instead I am presenting what I regard as very simple old truth. As with most of the Bible, I believe my letters will not be hard to understand. At times, the Bible can be hard to take. I will present some essentials of the Christian life. These truths are as essential for our spiritual survival as their physical counterparts or skills are in the wilderness. All of my Biblical quotes will be from the Authorized King James Version unless otherwise stated. The truths I am examining are so clear that any good translation will do. When I use the term America, I am including Canada by extension and all countries that have been profoundly influenced by American-style Christianity.

My motive for writing is encouragement and edification of the people I call the remnant (Chapter 2). I indulge in no direct criticism of individuals. There are already plenty of people who spend much of their lives critiquing every prominent believer, preacher, and teacher. What I do wish to impart is discernment. Avoiding the general errors and practices of the 'Brick and Steel' churches will help you to prevent personal error. More importantly, I hope to assist you in adjusting your focus (if needed) about what you regard as central to your faith and walk with Jesus. Some people have some very good theology but struggle with personal practice or what I call 'Applied Theology'. Jesus made it clear that we must not just assent to His truth but that we must obey it.

You will see a lot of the term 'religious'. What I mean by this term is not what the traditional meaning has been. In times past, being religious meant being dedicated to the things of God. When I use the term I am referring to the use of human effort to bring about God's results in the Church. As well, I am referring to all of the extra-Biblical practices that different groups use in their particular approach to Christianity. I am not speaking of the true and unde-filed religion of the Bible (James 1:26-27).

This is not a scholarly work but a personal work. I am not trying to prove my point. I love the Bible and I love God. I am sharing what I have learned and seen. You will either accept the picture I paint or reject it. You will either receive the truths I present or you will not. I have been pretty clear about what I see, what I hate, and what I love. If I trouble you, look to the Scripture I give. If you see truth, ask God to make it real in your life. Each of us is so puny and helpless that we need to appraise ourselves properly and throw ourselves on the mercy of our Adversary (Luke 12:58-59).

I want to assure the skeptical person that I have no desire to start some kind of movement. Neither do I represent any group using the term 'remnant'. I especially want to separate myself from any group that is militaristic for Jesus. As I will later share, the beauty of God's remnant is that they are found all over. Their placement transcends earthly organization because they are placed by the holy genius of God. The real question to answer is, "Are you part of what God is doing in America today?" I hope that question will be easier to answer when you are done.

Your Fellow Traveler,

Henry

P.S.: I have used some wilderness authors to document my basic information. I do not recommend any of the religious practices or associations that may be represented in their books. There is only one way of salvation: Jesus Christ (John 14:6).

# CHAPTER 1

# *A Suspiscion*

Dear Fellow Traveler,

My name is Henry. I have been on The Way for just over thirty years now. I am writing you this series of letters to share some of my discoveries along the way. It is my hope that my discoveries will help you with your walk with God. In this letter I will give you a little of my background and a few of the experiences that have formed me. These experiences have also confirmed a suspicion that I have had from almost the beginning.

Jesus encountered me in quite a profound way. During the summer of my seventeenth year I started to have a feeling that if there was a God in heaven, I was in real trouble. I had been awakening to my need for God for about a month. I was spending the summer working at my father's service station when a new fellow came to work for my Dad. He spent the whole shift 'Bible-thumping' me. In my heart, I knew that what he was sharing was what I needed. I received Jesus into my heart on the front lawn of his boarding house the next day.

Later the same week the man who led me to Jesus, with the assistance of his friend, gave me a thorough background on the need to be baptized in water. I had been baptized as a child but they taught me the necessity of being baptized as an adult. I had come to Christ of my own volition and baptism was an expression of my new-found faith in Jesus. These two goofy guys took me to a busy beach on a lake and baptized me by immersion in water, in the name of the Father, the Son, and the Holy Spirit. I was not really that concerned about all of the doctrine they taught me. I just wanted to be baptized and obey the Lord. What a new and joyful experience my baptism was for me!

The next weekend we went to a coffee house of the kind that was very popular in the early seventies. Many young people were there. Two young men approached the table where I was sitting and asked, "Have you received the Holy Ghost since you believed?" I said, "What's the Holy Ghost?" They said, "It's a gift that God gives you where you speak with other tongues." This, of course, is not who the Holy Spirit is or what His work is all about. I responded, "If it's from God, I want it!" They prayed for me and I had a sensation like a laboratory burner flame coming up out of the floor which engulfing me! I was aware of a new Power and Presence permeating my being. I knew I would never be the same again.

In looking back, I am amazed that none of these events happened in a church. There was no Pastor to supervise what was happening. There was no kind of religious service with the traditional tools of music, altar call, or human influence. God wanted me to see that my personal relationship with Christ was clearly initiated by Him. He used His people but everything unfolded according to His plan. I see now that the Lord did things this way to show me that none of the ordinary trappings of organized religion were needed for Him to initiate His approach to a human being. God could bring any person to a decision to enter His Kingdom all by Himself. In fact, no one can come to Jesus unless the Father draws them (John 6:44).

I was immediately taken out on the streets to share my faith with strangers of all kinds. The people I was with were street preachers and they used a very forward approach. They taught me that preaching to others was a normal thing for Christians to do. As I went back to school in the Fall I got the impression that I was a rare bird. Although I knew one very brave boy who was teased for loving Jesus, I didn't know any other students who were Christians. Later I discovered a Christian club and was astonished by who was there! I treated school like my street-preaching friends treated their street ministry. I was very aggressive in sharing this wonderful salvation with everyone. Over the years I have met classmates who still ask, "Are you still going on with You-Know-Who?" as they point upwards. Today I look back on that naïve time of my life with great fondness. God gave me a joy that insulated me from resistance to the Message and the natural persecution that followed my very vocal presentation.

As the year came to a close my life took quite a turn. It was graduation time and it became clear to me that I needed to strike out on my own. My parents were quite distressed at the change that had come over me. Looking back I think I was probably far too aggressive and not respectful enough at home. I really can not blame them for asking me to leave. I had no job and no place to live. God used a series of events that caused me to end up at Jim's house. Jim was a praying man. He was very prophetic. He ministered and shared in power. Jim brought home to me, in no uncertain terms, the claims of the Gospel and the cost of discipleship. Jim showed me the power and persistence of faith-filled prayer. He provided a place to live and training in a trade. I left Jim's house eighteen months later.

I made friends with another man who would be my mentor for many years and started to attend his church. I became involved in the life of that church. I taught Sunday School and attended the youth services in addition to the weekly services. After I had attended the church for a few months I became aware of the vast difference between someone my age who had grown up in the church and someone who had not. This church was a pretty nice church, with a very good and stable Pastor. Nevertheless, there was a definite **interior culture** which I have since observed in many forms in many different churches over the years.

In fact, the youth of this church became my teachers about the unwritten rules of what was and was not acceptable in that church culture. Sometimes, what was and was not acceptable had little to do with the life of Christ. It had much more to do with the particular social and religious dynamics of the group. Kids are very quick to figure out the rules. Although these were great kids, they were a little confused about what Christianity was all about. They were very clear on what the church rules were. Perhaps in our quest to keep our children from evil, we inadvertently instill another, more insidious evil—rule-keeping. If you want to know what a church is really like, talk to the kids.

Over the subsequent few years I got nicely cleaned up. I went to church and had many adventures. I met and married a great girl named Bev. I had a decent job and worked hard. I loved the Lord and grew up. I listened to hundreds of sermons and Bible lessons, attended church parties and socials, participated in the choir, went to pray, attended men's meetings, and generally participated in the life of the church.

One morning I was sitting in the balcony of the church with my wife Bev and a light turned on in my head. It was like the previous few years had passed before my eyes and I said to her, "I got religious, let's get out of here." We immediately left the service and went for a cup of coffee. I can only remember that I was racking my brain about how I could have become so 'religified'. Over coffee, and for the next few days, we discussed ways and means of correcting that malady. Somehow, I had allowed the religious life of a 'good' church to seduce me into becoming a very good (religious) churchgoer. In some ways I had become very small in my thinking and had let an 'I'm OK, you're OK' attitude lull me into a 'trying to be good' kind of Christianity. I have since observed that this outlook pervades so much of the religious landscape in North America.

Twenty-five years have passed since that time. God has given me a host of mentors and teachers in succession, each for their season. I have attended different churches, been the pastor of churches, started churches, and restarted churches. I worked as a lay person in just about every capacity that you could serve in a church before I went into full-time ministry. I have had three children with my wife Bev, raised them with her, and saw her unexpectedly leave me for heaven at the age of thirty-eight. God sent my present wife Diddi to be my blessing and participate in raising our children. I have nursed a chronically ill wife for ten years, nursed my own broken back, been well off, and been poor. In the midst of these and many more events, no more or less important than the events of your life, I have walked in The Way. Occasionally, I have failed in The Way.

That morning in church, I became aware of a **suspicion** that would grow into an understanding. Finally this understanding demanded a response from me. It seems silly now because the truth is so obvious to me. The truth is obvious to many in the Church and very many outside of the Church. The truth is what we call 'church' and do in 'church' often does not really reflect what the Bible says **the Church** should do or be.   Over the years I have realized just how far the professing church is from God. It has been profoundly difficult to face the magnitude and scope of the problem.

Let me be rightly understood, my friend. I am not here to critique the American, Canadian, Australian, and probably the whole First-World Church. Many great authors have come before me to point out, in general and specific ways, the sins of America and the errors of different teachers. There have been abundant critiques by people, both of a Biblical and personal nature. I suppose the idea of such correction is to heal the ills and inconsistencies of the church. Some people feel if we only had a better theology or thought about the Bible in their prescribed manner that everything would be fixed. Some authors named people, movements, leaders, and churches. Others were more general in their scope. Some assessments were right and fair and others were not.

Correction is not the purpose of my letters. **Spiritual survival** is. I have both recognized and faced the desperate state of the American Church. This low spiritual ebb has left many people I have met feeling as if they were wandering in a spiritual wilderness. I am much more interested in helping people to live within the environment of this present spiritual wilderness. Through these letters I will give general assessments of what I see. I then hope to show some personalized responses that may be helpful to you.

My suspicion that all was not well did not lead me away from my church. Instead, my initial recognition of the problem drove me to serve. Bev and I chose more direct ministry work and sought to enhance the fellowship that we attended. Later, we joined another church that allowed us more opportunities for leadership and diverse service. Our new Pastor had been a missionary in Africa. He had a very mission-minded approach for his ministry and outreach into the community. In looking back now, I can see that this was a small taste of how church could be. I saw that a church fellowship could have life and love, reflecting the indwelling Christ in its members. The main reason for this life and love was that we focused upon the conversion and growth of individual people.

After a couple of years my new mentor suddenly resigned. I was surprised and devastated. It seemed so very untimely to me. By the time the Pastor left I had become a deacon and the search for a new Pastor had begun. We finally invited and certified a Pastor. To my astonishment, the deciding factor for the congregational vote was that an elderly lady in the church had known him as a little boy. She said that he was very nice. In many ways he was a man who would epitomize a lot of denominational and institutional Pastors today. I believe that he did the things that he did because he truly believed they were the right things to do. The emphasis was placed on the things which make many institutional churches run: nickels and noses, control-style leadership, programmatic effort, and religious service.

Religious programming produces religious behavior which always brings about religious consequences (Matt. 15:1-9; Mark 7:8-9). The vibrant life of the corporate fellowship in the church was sucked dry. The astonishing thing to me was the swiftness and thoroughness of the process. The petty concerns of men replaced the over-riding question of corporate fellowship: "What saith the Spirit?" (Acts 13:1-5; 15:18). Human understanding supplanted the excellence of His Word. Political machinations tempered the climate of planning and leadership. The fire, life, and power of our fellowship were quelled. There was no great dissatisfaction with the process. Many people just saw the changes as a natural consequence of a change of leadership. People wanted to support their new Pastor. I believe these types of circumstances are repeated with alarming frequency in many denominational churches.

The beauty of every crisis that God brings into our lives is the perfection of the timing and His foreknowledge of the results. My suspicions were confirmed! The whole realm of the institutional church must be wrong! I might be forgiven the radical nature of my conclusions at the time because of the ego-centric nature of being a Christian who was, spiritually, a teenager. Just as the teenager in the natural realm can come to sweeping conclusions, I have observed that this also is the case with the Christian who is a teenager in the spiritual realm. There was nothing wrong with my facts; I was right about much of the church world without really knowing it. God was leading us to leave the 'brick and steel' church for a season. My differences with the Pastor's approach came to a head. I could have caused a split. I could have headed a departing faction. I could have stayed to 'improve' the church. Instead I just left. By God's grace, at least I got that part right.

My departure heralded a whole new phase in our lives of the kind that most nice church-going people can hardly imagine. We lived outside of the institutional church setup. We fellowshipped with other Christians, prayed, and read the Bible. For three years we never went to a church building. It is clear that many people have made this choice in America. Some people would rather quit than fight. I did it as one propelled by conviction. I believed that it was a sane response to the very difficult conditions I had found in the churches that I had attended. I am not persuaded that it is not a sane response to this day.

The problem many people have when they leave an institutional church is that they do not initiate fellowship nor do they gather together with others for prayer and the Word. I have observed that the great majority of those who leave fail quickly because of neglect of fellowship and disobedience to God's Word. It all comes down to conviction. Many people have no conviction about where they are fellowshipping. Others leave a fellowship without the Holy Spirit's guidance to do so. If they have not sought the Holy Spirit's conviction, both those who stay in a church and those who leave, will fail where they are. Folks will often quit going to church for good as an angry response to one or a series of hurtful events that convinces them that 'church' in general is not for them. That is no reason to leave.

During those three years I found out that I needed the Body of Christ and they needed me. God has outwitted any of us who wish to be Lone Rangers. He uses metaphors such as the human body, living buildings, and agricultural crops to illustrate a massive interdependence upon each other. If we do not seek and find our living place in the Body of Christ, we rob others of a blessing. If members of the body fail to recognize their function the rest of its members are not built up and replenished. I suddenly realized that I could never be the 'me' I was supposed to be without the Body of Christ. After three years, I became aware that the Lord was sending us back.

I want to pause here to make a few observations. My suspicion that something was woefully wrong in the institutional church had blossomed to a full understanding during my time away. I realized how religious I had become. There were times where I had measured my life by church attendance and a sense of being 'good'. I needed to use a different measurement: obedience to the Holy Spirit's leading. Living by the leading of the Holy Spirit is the central focus for living (Gal. 3:3; 5:16, 25; Romans 8:9). A great deal of inquiry, through prayer and Bible study, is required to dwell in the will of God. The distractions from such a life are manifold. I knew how to live in the Spirit but sometimes ignored His promptings. Part of the reason for this was because of the foreign interests that had presented themselves inside of the fellowship such as friendships, politics, and situational ethics. These foreign interests can often become the main foci for people who are nice churchgoers.

People's reactions to my departure were a study in themselves. Even today, to hear some people tell my story; those three years were the years that I 'fell away' from God. What fascinated me was how weak the rescue effort was! If I had left Jesus, how far was my 'family' willing to go to rescue me? Not very far. After all, people would say that, "It was my life." How often we sheath our indifference in a libertarian phrase. There are many believers on the outside of our religious mills who can identify with this reaction from church people. They are saved and moving on without the administration of their consciences by a formal tax-deductible charitable group's help. I was no longer a part of the **vested interest** of that particular church so most of the people broke fellowship with me. I could habitually sin and be part of their group but if I committed the ultimate sin of not coming to 'church', they wanted nothing to do with me. How fascinating that we tolerate the traitor against

Jesus within but reject the brother in Christ who is outside of our own vested interest.

God had drawn me apart to open my blind eyes. One of the challenges of living during our modern times is responding to God's call while facing a time of unprecedented apostasy, error, and imbalance (1 Tim. 4:1ff; 2 Tim. 3:1ff). It is not just that many do not have the truth but that those who do stress the wrong things. The people whom I had fellowshipped with were orthodox. God wants much more than right thinking. God wants us to be sanctified. Once we have dealt with ourselves, whatever God allows to happen will not swerve us from our convictions. Jesus still wants us to come apart into a quiet place for a while. He wants us to let Him balance us out and strengthen us to do his will (Mark 6:31).

During my first eight years in church I had started to measure myself by what I did. This is the commonality in the diversity of all world religions. The individual adherent must do something to bring favor from God. It is human nature at its worst. The whole Bible from beginning to end draws a line between human effort and God's 'graced' reality. The line is between doing and being. The religionist in any form 'does' to win favor and reward from God. This 'doing' may take the form of good deeds or religious rites. The point is that all religion leaves individual salvation to the behavior of the religious devotee.

The believer is created by God. They offer no human work but trust in Jesus' substitutionary sacrifice alone for their salvation. The deeds the believer does result from their relationship with God as adopted children (Gal. 4:6). This **New Life** is the central theme of the whole Bible and the glory of the Gospel. Yet many of those who are supposed to teach how to live this new life cop out to lower interests. They define themselves by distinctives and doctrines, beliefs and values. They split into groups, divide over practice, and teach to the intellect rather than the heart. Many groups think of themselves as 'right'. They become defenders of the faith but are really just defending their position. The battle to keep it all going consumes most of the time and means of the religionist.

The honest adherents know there must be something 'more' but have divided loyalties. They read the Bible and see life but 'go to church' and see death. The 'more' these adherents seek is quite simple, my friend. As stated above, it is the life of grace. We exchange our life for the life of Christ in us, the hope of glory (Co. 1:27). Jesus challenged His detractors to take a peak in the volume of the Book that spoke of Him (Ps. 40:7; Heb. 10:7). Jesus challenges us to understand that the Bible is not just an instruction book but a book to be experienced. The Bible tells us what we can **be** as much as it tells us what we should **do**. It reflects what God will do in us that we could never do in ourselves.

So, after three years God sent me back... to the most religified church I could imagine. I fought and fussed and He sent me back. He sent me back against my human reason, to where I would never have gone myself. It just didn't make any sense but I knew it was right. So off we went.

The very first Sunday our family went back to church, we met a man who I had heard about a couple of months earlier. I had been told by a friend that the man's father had accidentally cut down a tree that hit the poor fellow on the head. I had images of this poor family man lying in bed, addled. Imagine my surprise when we providentially met the first morning our family returned to the brick and steel church. He had been injured but was recovering. He lived not five minutes from our house in a village that was forty-five minutes away from that church. He was a Pastor and was planning to start a church in our little village. He and his wife had been praying for another couple to help them. Soon, Bev and I figured out that we were to be that couple.

The next two years were taken up with home groups and teaching. We had good fellowship and were able to witness about Jesus to the community. It was an easy transition because we were far from the hotbeds of organized religion. We simply invited God's presence and taught His Word as we found it. It was at this time I was to recognize my own particular call to ministry. I do not use the term full-time ministry anymore because everyone who meets Christ is called to full-time ministry. My call was to stop the secular work and move into Biblical leadership. How in the world would I do it? The truth is I never could. I was going to become more acquainted with the truth, "Without Me you can do nothing" (John 15:5).

God pointed me toward a denominational Bible College. He spoke to me that I should quit my job, sell my house, and go to College. I cannot express to you what a horror this was to me. Selling my house and leaving didn't bother me but to go right into the midst of a place that trained institutional ministers scared me. While I believe that people in leadership need Bible training I was very concerned about what many Bible schools were producing. It was a paradox to go to a place that taught so many to be religious professionals. I was worried that I might lose the ever-increasing freedom that I enjoyed day by day.

I shared the idea with my best friend and spiritual brother. He and I had learned all of our most important spiritual lessons together. His response was, "There is no way, Hank." I said, "Amen." God said, "Go." I sold our home on the lake, packed up our family, and left Vancouver Island. We moved one hundred miles away, east of Vancouver. The day that we left, my best friend came and said, "You're doing the right thing." It seemed a strange way for God to confirm my decision.

I had made a deal with myself that I was not going to be one of those guys who attended a Bible college with a chip on his shoulder. I was sure that God had not sent me there to be a reformer. I was there to just get through. There are all kinds of aspiring reformers in the church today. People stay in churches in the hopes of reforming the church. Others stay in denominations to try to reform the denomination. I think there is an arrogance that goes with a lot of these efforts. According to the Bible, individuals, churches, and denominations have as much light as they desire to have. Unless God has convinced you otherwise, my friend, don't be a reformer. It is more likely that God will call His remnant out from that which is dead. God makes all things new. He does not put new wine into old wineskins (Matt. 9:17).

In choosing to attend Bible College I was afraid that I would hear things I didn't agree with and have to make a stand. Of course, I did choose a college that was very respectful to the Scripture. Still, I was afraid that I would have some sort of problem. After two weeks I realized that I was wrong. The teachers were generally very good at teaching their respective courses and showed great respect for the Bible. In fact, the years I spent in college made me look at the Bible with a broader view. I learned the basic skills of hermeneutics, exegesis, and historic background. It was one of the best experiences of my life. It was more gratifying still because I had the maturity to appreciate the experience.

In retrospect what does shock me is that there was no School of **Applied Theology**. I wonder if one exists in any Bible college or university in America? I received a lot of relevant and true information. Still, other than the parameters of the school code of conduct and dress, little of the truth was pressed upon me with any vigor to apply it. I mean no offense to my alma mater because I think that this is largely true of all Bible institutes. Aside from what the denomination or group think is important, either Biblically or extra-Biblically, applications of truth are left up to the individual. We have designed the education of our leaders as an academic exercise. Unfortunately, we will produce only what we teach. One does not become a spiritual giant by acquiring information but by encountering the Living God in the lives of their teachers and by protracted seasons of prayer.

Don't get me wrong. I ran into the constraints of my particular denomination. These constraints did not bother me since my only concerns were about how we apply truth. I had no problem agreeing with the core values of my group. I am sure that many different denominations would have little problem with me. Many of our denominational differences are so ridiculously small that they have little meaning to me. What does matter to me is applied truth. How do we live the truth? Does God dwell in our midst? I have been in churches where the charismatic Pastor screamed, "God is here!" and I sensed that He wasn't. I have been in churches where people stated, "God is here because we believe the right things!" and I sensed He wasn't. God will dwell with any individual or group who will meet His terms of total surrender, love His Word, and invite God to dwell with them. Jesus will still take care of the rest. The indwelling Christ is the only genuine center for any Christian fellowship.

The twelve years I have spent in ministry since my training have matured my understanding of my first suspicion. In America there is a systemic problem within the 'brick and steel' professing church. Even when their doctrine is right there seems to be a disconnect between belief and Applied Theology as enabled by God's Holy Spirit. There are some wonderful exceptions out there, both in the realm of church fellowships and individuals. Unfortunately, the vast majority are content to grind along with a form of godliness that denies the very power that it professes to have (2 Tim. 3:5). Our critics are often justified when they call us 'a bunch of hypocrites'.

I have learned that every individual, church, denomination, and religious or para-church organization has to make a decision at the very core of their beings and stay true to it. How can Christian groups have so many mission statements when the Bible is uniform in the main mission of the Body of Christ? The question for every church or individual should be, "Are we going to be organic or organizational?" or "Are we going to be a machine or a body?" No one has ever built a body because it would be just too hard to do.

Men make machines. God makes bodies. Machines are temporary. Bodies are eternal. Machines are amazing and help us with all kinds of tasks. Bodies are miracles created by the infinite Mind of an all-wise Creator. They house the souls and spirits of eternal free moral agents. The glory of the metaphor of the Body of Christ is its nerve-center and brain, Jesus Christ (Eph. 1:22-23 4:15-16). He is revealed to us and in us by the Holy Spirit (John 16:13-14; 1 Cor 2:10). Without the Holy Spirit we can do nothing (John 15:5). When men try to substitute **their** best for **His** best the result may resemble what God **would** do but is only a **pale facsimile** of what God could have really done. Thus, without God, human organizations and efforts constitute mere machinery.

I have learned that you hardly need to fight about anything in a church. If we take our mission from the Bible, things become astonishingly simple. The really important activities for people in a church are prayer, the Word, fellowship, and evangelism (Acts 2:42). Leadership must lovingly guide people toward these activities. Every other interest will compete with these four essentials. The building, the money, the furniture, the tax exempt status, politics, and the programs can be profound distractions to having our eyes signally on Christ. I have learned from my own walk that human carnal nature loves to substitute just about anything for the rigors of the disciple's life. Ninety-five percent of what people fuss about in church should never even be spoken about because it is of such a minor and petty nature. All 'organic' gathering invites the very presence and power of the living Christ.

The challenge for me has been how to present the reality of the God-centered community to the people within my sphere of influence. I have been the Pastor of two different church fellowships. I have since realized that Pastoral ministry is not my main calling. There were some similarities in the churches. Both churches were almost fifty years old when I took over. Both churches had their traditions and power-brokers. Both had seriously declined and were ready to die. Both had either moved from or never had an organic living fellowship. The challenge was the same, to re-tool for the present working of the Holy Spirit. The answer was simple and up to the group: "Will we say yes or no to what God wants us to do?"

There were also profound differences between the churches. One had a very healthy history and one had a very unhealthy history. One was born of revival and one was born of demographics. One church had people who were born again in the fires of revival. Its members knew when the Holy Spirit was moving and would not get in the way when God was speaking to the body. The other church had many people who had remained profoundly carnal and self-motivated for years. Although they were very nice, they really were unable to hear what God was saying to them as a group. One group responded positively to Applied Theology and the other negatively.

I think it is shocking for church people to find out they have been doing it wrong for twenty or thirty years. I can remember specific moments when I realized that the simple truth of death to our selves was hitting home. This is the unhappy news ministers often have to deliver today. I know I was not pleased when, as a younger Christian, I found out I was not living a Biblical Christian life. It hurt my pride but it was good medicine. The truth is that there is a profound need to return to the simplicity of faith in Christ. Unfortunately, people often won't face the scope of repentance and change that are required to return to the simplicity of faith.

One of the most important discoveries that a few of my friends and I have made is that praying in the Holy Spirit is doable in a corporate church setting. There is a real art to allowing the Mind of the Spirit to rule a prayer meeting. People can learn to invite His presence, with power, into their midst. It is clear that we have profoundly underestimated the power and usefulness of corporate prayer. The Acts of the Apostles relates to us the power of the single-minded devotion of the group at prayer, with immediate and powerful results (Acts 4:24-31; Acts 12:1-17). I have seen God's Spirit take control of a meeting when there have been only a few keen and sensitive participants. What prayers are prayed then! What prayers should be prayed whenever God's people gather together! Jesus said that His house was to be a house of prayer (Isa. 56:7; Matt. 21:13); not of worship, praise, preaching, or fellowship. These other activities are all birthed in the place of prayer.

C. G. Finney said that to speak of revival presupposes a declension.[1] I have grown tired of what people mean by revival. What people have done is put 'revived' spirituality just out of reach, for later. They may put it this way, "Some day I will be the Christian I should be or we will be the church that we should be." Others go a step further and believe we can never clean up the mess of human sinfulness. They believe that we just have to learn to live with our wickedness somehow. This idea brings a false tolerance for evil that is often misnamed love.

I can have revival now! If I am saved and Christ is dwelling in me now, I have revival! Most folk who talk of revival really mean they feel insufficient. They feel that they or their group are lacking something but some day, by and by, a revival will fix it all. I learned revival is **NOW**! Many people could be revived after a couple of hours of true heart-searching and repentance. If enough of those of us who are revived get together, the fire will set off the fireworks! It only takes a few individuals who are completely sold out to obedience to God to make a profound difference for God.

I believe that if Paul the apostle was around today and came to many of our churches, he would give us about three weeks to respond to his teaching. Paul would be run out of a lot of the churches today. Other churches would have many members who would become offended and leave. The problem would be with Paul's Applied Theology. He didn't just write those letters down, he lived them. He would not bring us to a new set of rules or tell us to try to be good. He would call us to yield to the indwelling Holy Spirit and let Him call the shots. He would root out sin and evil and send the devil packing. Now as then, it would be the religious pretenders who would persecute and resist his ministry.

In both churches, we did see some people respond to the surrendered life. As we pressed the simple truths of the Spirit-filled life, people were transformed. Many more people chose to live religiously rather than yield up control of certain areas of their lives to God. This is prevalent in both the ministry and laity that I have both met and heard of. As much as I wish it otherwise, my suspicion that all is not well in the North American church has proven to be true, most of the time. The fact is that we are in great danger because many are 'falling away' from the truth.

Truly, perilous times have come because we are living in the last days (2 Tim. 3:1-7). We find ourselves in a kind of spiritual wilderness. My suspicions have turned out to be true but what can one individual do? Perhaps more than you know. The rest of my letters will all convey themes essential to surviving in the wilderness of today's very religious landscape. Throughout history God has always reserved a people who are at His beck and call. Like Jesus, they seek to always do the things that are pleasing in their Father's sight (John 8:29). These are the people these letters are addressed to: **the remnant**. My next letter will talk about today's remnant.

Your Friend,

Henry

# CHAPTER 2

# *The Remnant*

Dear Fellow Traveler,

*E*ach letter that follows will contain a metaphor relating to the basic skills of surviving in the wilderness. In my next letter I will give a thumb-nail sketch of my perception of the spiritual wilderness in which we find ourselves. In the letters following, I will proceed to make some helpful parallels between survival in the physical wilderness and survival in the spiritual wilderness.

It is interesting that there is a remnant of those who are experts at living in the physical wilderness today. Most of us would be lost and helpless in the woods. We would regard living in the forest as a difficult task. The wilderness wayfarer is very able to live and even thrive in the natural beauty of their surroundings without many of the tools that the average city-dweller would need. In the same way, there is a remnant of people who are learning to live in the present spiritual wilderness in America. In fact they are even thriving there.

These letters will have special meaning to those who are called to be part of God's remnant in America. The term remnant refers to any group who remains from a whole. The whole would be 'the masses' in the professing church and in the world system at large. The masses in the 'brick and steel' church are those who participate in the general established order but do not participate in God's Kingdom in any meaningful way. Albert J. Nock puts it this way:

What do we mean by the masses, and what by the Remnant? As the word masses is commonly used, it suggests agglomerations of poor and underprivileged people, laboring people, proletarians. But it means nothing like that; it means simply the majority. The mass-man is one who has neither the force of intellect to apprehend the principles issuing in what we know as the humane life, nor the force of character to adhere to those principles steadily and strictly as laws of conduct; and because such people make up the great, the overwhelming majority of mankind, they are called collectively the masses. The line of differentiation between the masses and the Remnant is set invariably by quality, not by circumstance.[1]

I am using the term 'remnant' to specifically refer to those who are growing both to understand and practice Biblical Christianity in our day. The remnant does not just know **about** Jesus, they know Him. They crave to share their experience with others but find many in the church do not relate to them and their journey. They are a minority, hidden away in society. The remnant is not discernable as we understand discernment. Again, Albert J. Nock states:

> ... in any given society the Remnant are always so largely an unknown quantity. You do not know, and will never know, more than two things about them. You can be sure of those dead sure, as our phrase is-but you will never be able to make even a respectable guess at anything else (sic). You do not know, and will never know, who the Remnant are, nor where they are, nor how many of them there are, nor what they are doing or will do. Two things you know, and no more: first, that they exist; second, that they will find you.[2]

Friend, you may need to recognize that you are part of something unseen—the remnant. Then you may appreciate that you are not alone. In spite of external evidence God still has plans and He still has his chosen ones. The question that I would ask you is, "Are you part of God's last-day remnant?"

Most of us only have a small sphere of influence. We may only have a few people that we truly relate to or maybe, none. We have a voice to speak truth to others but may see only occasional results. Often, we may not see 'results' at all. We may be walking intimately with Jesus but feel very alone. Some people in the church have realized the way that they view the world, as well as their practical spirituality, is profoundly different than most other people they know. They are starting to realize that they are part of a vast minority within the professing church. Members of this minority may know a few people who are really sold-out to the things of God. Fellowship with such people will produce healthy results in their lives. Some know more than a few sold-out people. There are a privileged few who belong to a fellowship of people who are still functioning in the Body of Christ and understand the times that they are in. The question is: what do we do once we realize we are part of a minority in the professing church?

I want to be clear that I am not advocating some particular 'chosen' group, organization, or denomination. These letters are not motivated with any desire to advocate or start another group. Sectarianism is already one of the shames of the institutional church and is abhorrent to our God (1 Cor. 1:10-18; 3:3-7). There is only One who has chosen us for His own unsearchable reasons through Jesus Christ our Lord. What I am talking about is a group that Jesus knows. It is one thing to say that you **know** the Lord. It is much more important to have the Lord **know** you, especially on Judgment Day (Matt. 7:21-23). Jesus knows who His remnant is.

This remnant that I am speaking about is of a spiritual nature. The remnant has been created, not by God, but by the 'Great Falling Away' of the last days (1 Thess. 2:3; 1 Tim. 4:1). The professing church's continuing move to apostasy was predicted by the apostles Paul and Peter (2 Tim. 3:1-9; 2 Pet. 3:3-6). This apostasy is forcing the hand of those who wish to remain true. A lot of commentary has been given to the subject of error in the professing American church by other authors. There have been some very accurate warnings of the consequences of apostasy by some very reputable and godly men. As a fellow traveler I am hoping to give you some answers to successful living as you face the circumstances and difficulties that we all find ourselves facing. I want to help you in identifying the faithful and give you tools to survive in this present wilderness landscape. I have walked in this spiritual wilderness. By God's grace I have survived to this point and hope to give you some of the tools to both survive and thrive.

In many parts of the world the church has been purified by persecution. In most Islamic countries and in places of political despotism the church is persecuted. The remnant are dispersed and hidden. To belong to this group takes supernatural bravery, even to the death. The persecuted Church exists because of the power of God and is sustained by the power of God. In many places Christianity is an all or nothing proposition. Obviously there are still problems, disagreements, and schisms but persecution will most often refine and define the genuine. When external religion is no longer profitable or ego gratifying, many of the pretenders quickly abandon it. It is very clear that when faith is a matter of life and death, those who love this present world will retire from even appearing to practice true Christian spirituality.

In America and the First World this process of persecution is just beginning. Most Christians have only had minor resistance to their beliefs. In fact, much of secular America will still commend you for having religious beliefs and morals as long as you do not shove your beliefs down their throats. They may even admire you. However, if a person gets a little too zealous, a little too outspoken, or a little too joyful, at church or among their religious acquaintances, he may well receive correction. The same thing may occur to the leader who pushes too hard upon his people with the cost of discipleship, the rigors of spiritual exercise, or to have a great concern for the lost. The common wisdom is that it is fine to bring change but let it be at a snail's pace over a period of years. Then it will not arouse the hackles of those adherents who may be smug, satisfied, carnal, or suffocatingly indifferent.

What is behind these attitudes? In my lifetime I have observed a decline of morals in the church. From all accounts this decline has been well underway for forty or fifty years. All of my mentors and my spiritual parents have observed this decline during their lives, as well. It seems that much of the protestant church has forgotten what they were protesting about. The evangelical branch of the American protestant church has, in many quarters, become fraught with compromise. As different sins are tolerated and the general spiritual temperature of the church has declined, hardness of heart and indifference have gripped the hearts of many of God's people. In the last three decades I have watched many of the professing conservative or so-called Bible-believing groups change their stands on many major moral issues. Are we more enlightened now than our forefathers? Are we now wiser than they were? Has God changed His mind or did we? Like Samson we shake ourselves for battle once more and do not realize that the Spirit of God has departed from us (Judges 16:20). After all, the Holy Spirit only dwells in the midst of people committed to holiness.

The principles of Balaam have been repeated over and over again in history (Num. 22-24; 31:16). If you can seduce the people of God to knowingly sin against what God has proclaimed, God will curse His people Himself. So we see in our day that compromise and even sin, in the name of Jesus, is accepted and condoned by many. The Scripture clearly teaches that if you do not love truth you will be turned over by God to believe a lie (2 Thess. 2:9-12). So much of the professing church **sympathizes** with the sinful situations of friends and loved ones. They turn a blind eye to evil because so many of their acquaintances have not repented of their sin. I am not talking about caring for others. I am talking about looking the other way when we need to say or do something to rescue the wandering brother. The Bible clearly states that if we can rescue a brother or sister that is overtaken in sin that we are doing God's work and saving them from eternal death (James 5:20).

To resist such compromise as we see in this day, in the midst of an institutional church family, will single you out to the religionist as unloving. To speak up about the evil you see, even in the most polite terms, will identify you to many as an intolerant judge. "It is not our place to judge," the teachers of tolerance will intone. In fact, this is a misapplication of the teaching of Matthew 7. Jesus does not prohibit judgment. He does prohibit hypocritical condemnation of sin while you still practice sin. Many times Jesus demands that people use righteous judgment (Luke 12:57-59; John 7:24; 12:47-48). It is not for us to pass sentence but it is for us to look at evil and call it evil. No matter how politely and gently you may point out evil, you will join Jesus in His reproach (Heb. 13:13). Jesus was very clear that if religious leaders called Him the devil that His followers should not be astonished if religious people associated them with the devil as well (Matt. 10:25).

One may observe that there are times of increase and times of decline for the followers of God. Men are sinners by nature and we see that most will choose to live their own lives on their own terms, even when presented with the claims and benefits of the Gospel. The history of Israel is replete with the ups and downs of God's people. It seems that there were more downs than ups. The Bible records some beautiful exceptions where many followed God and His name was glorified. These righteous examples serve as a contrast to the times of repetitive backsliding and degeneration that occurred under Israel's wicked kings.

Such a king was Ahab. In contrast to the evil of Ahab and his wife Jezebel, God had raised up a prophet named Elijah. We see his story in 1 Kings 17-20. Apparently, Elijah burst on the scene from a life of obscurity. His powerful ministry is a type of the powerful ministry of both Jesus and His forerunner John the Baptist. I love to read about Elijah's story and never get tired of the details. The supernatural provision that God made for him shames many who claim apostolic and prophetic power today, without much consequence. He spoke boldly and turned the nation of Israel to God for a season. Elijah gets all the great sermons preached about him because he was like a spiritual action figure. He was the prominent righteous person of his generation. That is why he got all the press.

As a remnant man, Elijah had a problem with his basic view of the world and himself. He had started to believe his own press. He had met Obadiah and heard about the one hundred prophets that Obadiah had hidden (1 Kings 18:4, 13). Later, Elijah seemed to forget this fact in the midst of his discouragement. He told God that he was the only one left (1 Kings 19:4). The Lord dealt with Elijah's physical and emotional exhaustion first. He let Elijah get some sleep and gave him divinely empowered food. Elijah traveled for forty days arriving at Mount Horeb for his meeting with God.

Amazingly, God granted his request to leave the earth. God gave him the run down on arrangements for his departure and then revealed a very telling fact. There was a substantial remnant! There were seven thousand other individuals that God recognized as faithful and testified that they belonged to Him. Elijah had missed the correct number of the remnant by seven hundred thousand percent. It is unlikely that any of us would fare any better in our calculations.

I do not have the relish for pointing out the weaknesses of Elijah that some commentators do. Considering the trials he went through and the separation he felt from his whole society it is not surprising that he felt alone. Israel was a society that was a theocracy and should have been serving God. His feeling of aloneness is not the point. The real point is he wasn't alone—just Elijah and God. There were seven thousand others who had to hide and suffer because of the intense persecution of Jezebel. What encouragement and solace Elijah could have had if he had simply inquired of the Lord about fellowship or found out more about Obadiah's one hundred prophets. What is it that could have caused him to become so isolated?

The enemy of our soul loves to divide and conquer us. I think this is what happened to Elijah. He was consumed with God and the task set before him. He had a lot of time alone to think about things, especially in the seasons between God's visitations. This is particularly relevant for the Church. If you are one of the few vibrant believers in a fellowship, it can be easy to get discouraged and focus on the negative. It also can become easy to over-estimate yourself. We can start to believe that we are superior in some way to the indifferent and the carnal. The fact is that if we have anything spiritual, we received it by the power and revelation of God. Since our life comes from God we have no grounds to feel superior or proud (1 Cor. 4:7). We are all very needy, whether we are aware of it or not. We are described in the Bible in the context of the spiritual group because we need one another.

When God gives us light, we have a responsibility to walk in that light and seek to fulfill the purposes of God for us. Any balanced observer of the current spiritual condition of the church in America will not retreat into a fool's paradise of positive confession or denial. Instead, we must face the circumstances that confront us. Although I believe in confessing God's Word it will not change people against their will. Repentance and humility must come first. What is necessary for you and for me is that we be right with God. Then we will be able to identify others who are right with God and be able to partake of true fellowship, prayer, and encouragement. Following are some characteristics that help identify today's remnant people.

The primary and most helpful tool for identifying God's remnant is the **witness** of the **Holy Spirit**. The apostle John boldly states that we have an unction from the Father and we don't need anyone to teach us (1 John 2:20). Of course John is not belittling the ministry of the teacher but glorifying the Holy Spirit's power to lead us into all truth. As deep calls unto deep so men of kindred spirit can identify one and other (Psalm 42:7). The transparency of spirit that comes with total devotion to Jesus' Word and the work of the Holy Spirit are easy, not hard to identify. This is especially true when we have matured to the point of being delivered from the snare of the fear of man (Prov. 29:25). When we do not regard spiritual people as threats we are more likely to be able to discern their spirits.

Next, I have found that the remnant has a **healthy suspicion** of institutional religious authority; whether mainline, denominational, or independent. This has come from the deeper suspicion that all is not well and that the church at large is in a troubled state. The remnant is very aware of the evil of the foreign interests of man and organization that can hinder God's work and grieve His Holy Spirit. As a younger Christian I definitely over-reacted at times to behavior in leadership that was obviously not of the Lord. I have met many other honest believers who have done the same thing. We have become careful.

Jesus did not commit himself to the crowd who wanted to make Him king because he knew what was in man. The remnant have also had it revealed to their spirit what is in man (John 2:25). With the apostle Paul, all believers may testify that in our flesh dwells no good thing (Romans 7:18). The remnant is aware that institutional religious authority often has competing interests with the interests of Christ. This authority can start to aspire to rule rather than serve.

The remnant wants no ruler but Jesus. It is surely true that God is never moved or influenced by men's sectarian interests.

It is possible to find the remnant **everywhere**. They are in all kinds of denominations, non-denominations, and independent churches of every ilk. I have met many that do not have any formal connection to any religious organization. Those that do fellowship within the confines of different denominations or non-denominations have a firm understanding of the limitations of the particular group that they are associated with. Their loyalty to their denomination goes only as far as the Lord will allow it to go. They possess their particular memberships and credentials without the memberships and credentials possessing them. There is almost a uniform dislike for all manner of human political manipulation. They understand that God does not need our help or our wisdom to fulfill His purposes. In fact, the remnant realizes that we must always receive our vision and direction from God, not men.

**Transparent vibrant change** will characterize all in God's remnant. This transparency applies not only to their successes but failures. The remnant understands that falling down is part of the process that God uses to grow us. I have always had to die inside to make the major changes that God has called me to make. As a young Christian I failed hundreds of times in some areas until God finally granted me the victory. My failures as an older Christian are less visible but just as painful. Anyone who knew me at the beginning of my walk can testify of the change that has occurred. Nevertheless, when you meet me it will become clear that God has a lot of work to do yet.

The remnant sees themselves as works of God in progress and their transparency comes from this knowledge. What grows out of this kind of self-perception is what I call **sweet reason**—an attitude that beautifully combines the quest for holiness with the mercy of the soul forgiven. Those who see that they have been forgiven much, love much (Luke 7:40-47). This understanding makes the remnant the most sweetly reasonable group on the face of the earth.

As you observe people who are part of God's remnant you will always observe vibrant growth—over time. I remember an elderly lady who knew me when I was first saved. After I had been in the ministry for a few years I met her at a summer camp. We chatted about the 'old days' and she confided with great conviction, "I always knew you would make it." I know there were a lot of people who would have judged that I would never grow up in God or be of much spiritual use. Nevertheless, His Kingdom was growing inside of me. This old saint knew that God takes the most unlikely persons and grows His Kingdom in them. This is the heart of the parable of the mustard plant (Luke 13:18-19). God's Kingdom starts out undiscernibly small in our lives but soon it takes over everything. If the people of God get out of His way and let His Kingdom grow inside of them there will be unparalleled growth and change in their lives. Over time it is easy to see who is growing and who isn't. Eventually, God's remnant will always grow.

God's remnant will not look at a person just on the basis of where they are in their walk but **what they are growing up into**. Religious people often pick on or criticize new converts because of all the messes that they make. What kind of person criticizes a baby? We coo at babies and love them. We understand that messes, weakness, and dependence are characteristic of babies. Isn't it interesting that many of these same critics have sat in church for thirty years? Many times when these same people answer a religious survey they state that they are carnal or a baby. The central characteristic of God's Kingdom is that it grows. None of the remnant will profess perfection (aside from what they find in Jesus) but they will display profound growth from their starting point. The world will take note when it is obvious that they see someone who has been with Jesus (Acts 4:13).

You might agree with me that human beings are pretty puny. Our capacity to absorb ideas and concepts is limited. As we get older, we tend to want to be more and more settled in figuring out the way things work. In contrast, God's remnant is open to **new ideas** that are outside of the realm of their experience. My mother-in-law tells a story about her smoking when she was first converted. Somebody told her that she should quit. Her response was, "Never! I will never quit smoking—I love to smoke." She paused and looked up toward heaven and said, "Unless of course YOU would like me to quit Lord—then I would quit." It had never occurred to her that God would want her to quit. Her mind could never conceive that smoking could be wrong but she was willing to do whatever God wanted. She never had another cigarette from that day forward and had no sense of ever needing one.

I remember a Pastor who I worked with years ago. He was being assailed by a pretty typical attack on his leadership, style, and character. This Pastor was so sweet and patient about all of it. He just kept talking about love. He was driving me crazy! I thought he should stand up and rebuke them. I thought he was being an idiot. I was the idiot. He was so sweetly reasonable with his love and thus distinguished himself as one of the remnant. He could not be that good or kind on his own. He allowed the sweet reason of Jesus to temper him. He never compromised his principles or yielded to the pressure. Instead, his love heaped coals of fire on his enemy's heads (Romans 12:20). We will meet many difficult and obtuse professors of faith. If we can meet them with the sweet reason of God, what a testimony it will bring. Who knows, we may be able to teach them something.

The remnant is **not prejudice**. The most obvious form of prejudice to most of us living in American society is probably racial prejudice. I have to admit that I am not crazy about the idea of ethnic churches. The simple reason is that when we mix the races we start to resemble heaven. The subtle truth about ethnic churches is that people tend to be more comfortable with their own culture, both ethnically and religiously. The church at Antioch provides some lessons for us to follow today. The Antioch church was on the trade route to the East. There were people of multiple ethnic backgrounds in this church. We see that God caused this blended group to send out the first missionaries to the Gentiles. There were Jewish people helping black, white, and Asian people grow in their faith. Although there is often a need for ethnic outreach with the Gospel, the remnant will be devoid of the kind of racism that keeps ethnic groups apart.

Spiritual prejudice will often go hand in hand with racial prejudice. This kind of prejudice has to do with possessing a superior attitude because a group shares a particular ethnic or denominational background. We see a perfect example of both kinds of prejudice expressed in the story of the woman at the well (John 4). She identified with the historic cult formed by Jeroboam which substituted the worship of golden calves in Bethel and Dan for going to Jerusalem to worship (1 Kings 12:28-29). The people of the Northern Kingdom had the same Bible and same Patriarchs. Their problem was that they mixed pagan practice with Judaism and they had pretty much succumbed to pagan worship at that time.

She also identified with the ethnic prejudice that tainted her worship. In many quarters, denominational people are just as prejudiced and blind as the woman at the well because they are settled religious hobbyists. A lot of attention is given to style and form but these do not make one a worshipper. For this reason the religious hobbyist is the kind of person who cares most for the outward appearance and has no dynamic of personal worship on a day to day basis. This is the natural outflow of spiritual prejudice.

I find it fascinating that Jesus does not point toward the **right** religion but the coming relationship that all can have with God. This relationship would enable His followers to appropriately worship the Father wherever they were. It is interesting that God sent His own Son to move worship out of buildings and into men's hearts. It seems that men have labored ever since to move worship back into buildings and to hallow buildings... "Shhh, we're in church!" The godly remnant has not been sucked into worshipping the worship service as is so commonplace today. Worshippers have a life commitment to worship and their corporate worship is only a small expression of worshipful lives.

Finally, God's remnant will be **holy**. As a term, holiness becomes highly subjective according to who is defining it. Biblical holiness is not defined by people's sin lists. Sin lists refer to what different men or groups think righteousness is. There are over one thousand commandments in the New Testament and I have never met anyone who even got close to obeying them all. We are not rule-keepers.

Neither are we resigned to constant failure at overcoming sin. The remnant doesn't use such copouts as, "We are righteous in Him, and will never attain to His holiness in our lifetime" or "Love Jesus and do your best." Jesus has commanded us to be holy as He is holy

(1 Peter 1:14-19). We do not attain this state by human effort but by the power of His grace. Since He commands us to attain holiness, it follows that we must be able to obey this commandment.

Those who are holy have learned the secret which is not a secret and was never meant to be a secret. In fact, only in times of profound decline do we find that the core of the Gospel is a secret. Holiness is God's distinguishing attribute. Therefore, those who follow Him will be distinguished by His nature. Those who are God's have yielded themselves to the Holy Spirit. The 'Law of the Spirit of Life' has set them free from the 'Law of Sin and Death' (Romans 8:2-4). They are walking in the Spirit (Gal. 5:16) and they are living in the Spirit (Gal 5:25). There is an air of another world about them. God's remnant walk in the light as He is in the light; they don't deny their sin but live in constant cleansing from their sin (1 John 1:7-9). God's chosen are not hard to identify because they are looking more and more like Him.

Loved one—there is a platitude that has some truth to it. You will never find a perfect church. Even if you are fortunate enough to find a small group of believers that are in tune with God, most of your encounters with God's remnant will be chance meetings orchestrated by Jesus. You will find them in the most surprising places at the most astonishing times. To believe that we have found the perfect church or the right group is to fall into a grievous error and distraction. Our gathering is not cultish, proclaiming that we have the right doctrine or the only real truth. God will draw His dear ones together. He will bring His unity in our diversity. His Holy Spirit is the mortar that holds the lively stones together in the glorious Temple of God.

As I mentioned at the beginning of my letter, one of the characteristics of a godly remnant is the difficulty of identifying them as a group. It will be impossible to identify them by their social standing, vocation, ethnic background, or the places that they live. You will not be able to find them through their religious, denominational, or non-denominational affiliation or the lack of the same. The fact is that they will remain hidden from obvious view. The remnant will not receive much attention from the current religious order. The thing that will bring them into the spotlight will be catastrophe. Events such as the fiscal collapse of America, the political collapse of America, gigantic natural disasters, or the outlawing of Christianity as a result of the decadent decline of society will send the pretenders scurrying away and reveal the faithful of God.

When I was first saved my first mentor told me something that changed my outlook. I so wanted to tell everyone about Jesus. One day as I was going out to save the world he said to me, "It is wonderful to save the world but first save yourself." I really didn't understand then as I do now that in each of our cases we have to answer the Proverb that the Pharisees quoted to Jesus: "Physician, heal thyself:" (Luke 4:23). Jesus could blow off the question because He was the impeccable son of God. None of us can. We can only speak from what we have experienced and testify to that which we truly know (John 3:11). God wants us to know Him and be conformed to His will. For this reason He takes His people and His prophets through the wilderness. This is where we come to maturity where the sons of God are revealed.

Now I have given you some clues to identifying members of God's end time remnant. Keep your eyes open because God may plug you into all kinds of unlikely people.

Your Brother in God's Remnant,

Henry

# CHAPTER 3

# *The Wilderness*

Dear Fellow Traveler,

*I* remember an unlikely movie a few years ago where the main character was on a plane that crashed into the ocean. He alone survived and was washed ashore on a desert island. The story chronicled his fictitious battle for life and his amazing return to civilization as one from the dead, four years later. This film was a sort of modern day Robinson Crusoe. It seems modern society has a fascination with these types of stories. Shipwrecks, plane crashes, environmental disasters, and TV reality series raise the same simple question, "could I survive if it was just me alone against the harshness of nature?" The question reveals a modern insecurity. Without our modern tents, equipment, guns, and GPS finders most of us would feel way out of our element if we were forced to survive in the wild. Yet there seems to be an underlying question for many about how they would do without anything but the basics in the wilderness.

Quite a few years before this film I became interested in survival in the wilderness. I had done some reading about wilderness survival and decided to take a basic survival course. As the movie went on I found myself sitting up on the bed yelling at the main character, "No, no, you need to find a shelter!" and, "No, no, you've got it all wrong—you need to build a fire!" It was quite easy for me to feel like I was an expert while I yelled advice at the main character from my bed as he blundered and learned by trial and error. I had learned from my teachers that survival in the wilderness was always a matter of life and death. To survive, you must have an understanding of the things that you must do and the order to do them.

During my instruction in the basics of wilderness survival I learned four basic necessities and the order in which they were to be acquired. As a city dweller I was surprised the first priority was shelter. It now makes sense to me. If you have no place to protect yourself from the elements you may easily get too cold and die of exposure, even in a tropical climate. Conversely, if you find yourself in a desert climate you may die quickly if you do not shield yourself from the sun. Since nature is unpredictable we need to put shelter first or we may never survive to eat or drink.

Water is the second necessity. You may live many weeks without food but it is the rare person who can survive more than a week without water and you will swiftly lose strength without it. It is imperative that you know where in the terrain to look for water. You don't want to drink from stagnant pools but from cool running streams and rivers. Otherwise, you will need to produce water by condensation. It is essential to know how to purify your water so it gives life and not death.

Fire is the third necessity that you need to survive in the wilderness. Fire will keep you warm at night or in the cold. Fire will drive away dangerous animals and the smoke will act as an insect repellant and deodorizer to remove your scent. With your scent masked you can hunt more effectively. You really need fire to purify any water you find. If you don't you may become ill and disabled by water-born parasites and organisms. To possess fire is to possess power. One of the most powerful moments of my life was when I first made fire with two pieces of wood and a bow. I stood holding the fire in my hands and realized that I might just be able to survive in an emergency.

Food is the final necessity in the wilderness. You need to know which plants you can eat and which plants are poisonous. You have to know how to hunt game and how to dress it when you have caught it. There are many primitive tools and weapons you can use and it is important to learn their use quickly. How do I track animals? How do I find animals? How do I get near to them? I realized that everything that looks like food is not necessarily food.

I found out that I was afraid of the wilderness and felt very insufficient to live there. I had not understood or even believed that I could belong there. Although these skills are foreign to many people in our day, they were common knowledge in the ancient world. They continue to be important in many parts of the Third World to this day. There is not much use for these basic skills in our modern cities but they are essential for those who lack our modern infrastructure. After learning the basic skills I realized that God did not create a hostile wilderness after all. It is just that we no longer know how to live in the wilderness.

Many of the great messengers of the Bible went to the wilderness as part of their schooling. Moses spent forty years shepherding his father-in-law's herds. David took care of his father's flocks and fought wild animals in their defense. Many of the prophets lived through the most basic of wilderness experiences and arrived on the scene, seemingly out of nowhere. John the Baptist dressed for the wilderness and ate wilderness fare. Also, consider the amount of time the apostle Paul and his entourage spent in travel. Paul surely had tents, since he made them for a living, yet it is easy to miss the hundreds of miles that he traveled on foot and his many consecutive weeks on the road. It is hard to imagine Paul and his group settling down by the road side and making a fire with a flint—missions for the hearty.

Nowadays, we do not have to have the sense of being alone that the wilderness brings. We have the radio for our car and the television for our house. We can be on the telephone for periods of time that were unimaginable just ten years ago. The personal computer is a remarkable instrument that allows us to communicate with the written word, pictures, voice, and interactively. We can even communicate with groups of people simultaneously. We have cars and can travel long distances at will. We can go shopping.

So much of church fellowship today is taken up with stimulation. Visual effects in worship, real and synthetic music, overhead picture presentations of sermons and announcements, pre and post service video, streaming video, dance, banners, flags and so on, have been neatly packaged into ninety minute segments. I really wonder whether humans were built for such constant stimulation.

If a person was quickly thrust into the wilderness the first thing they would notice would be the deafening silence. All the noise of daily life can leave the average person nervous of silence. I believe many people are addicted to noise. I have been to many homes where the inhabitants feel a need to have the radio or television on from morning to night. Some people will leave this kind of noise on all night. After a person is in the deep woods for awhile they start to hear another kind of noise—God's noise. There are birds singing, waters moving, winds blowing, and the noise of animals. Humans are usually a noisy visitor as they move through the forest. A person becomes aware of their own thoughts in the silence. I have found that in such circumstances that my soul calms and my spirit is able to hear the voice of God. I have found the personal school of silence to be the place where I learn to hear God.

In the wilderness we are confronted with the vanity of 'busyness'. Out there, so much of the activity of city life seems to be such a waste. We are removed from the frantic pace of life and the immediate tyranny of the urgent. The silence can be deafening. I am reminded of a television ad where a fellow and his wife are out camping. His wife checks to see if he is ready to go home. He looks over the hills and sees a bunch of gophers sticking their heads out of their holes and his mind flashes back to the cubicles at his office. He sees his fellow employees sticking their heads up like gophers. He turns to his wife and says, "Maybe we ought to stay out here for a few more days." In the woods or the desert, time will show that many of us are living a Solomon life—wasting our time on grand projects that don't matter. Our addiction to activity is exposed in the wilderness. We can say, as Solomon did of his life's projects and accumulations, *"I have seen all the works that are done under the sun; and, behold, all [is] vanity and vexation of spirit"* (Prov. 1:14).

Another reality begins to surface in the wilderness. We find that we are alone. People who have spent months alone in the wild speak of a profound loneliness that they are compelled to overcome. If they do not overcome it, loneliness will overcome them. It is true that people are made to be with people and even the most reclusive personalities will tend to want to spend some time, with some people of their choosing. The question arises, "Why am I lonely?" The craving for social interaction and acceptance is powerful in many people's lives. They just do not like to be alone. The silence of the wilderness is where we prove the worth of the saying, "God is enough." As we are drawn apart to a quiet place we discover that we are not alone. Our great Friend that "sticketh closer than a brother" reveals His adhesive nature to us by the comfort of His Spirit within us (Prov. 18:24).

Aside from the removal of basic comforts, there is a return to simplicity in leaving behind all of the legitimate modern means of taking care of ourselves. Alone in the wilderness, a person has to face themselves. There is no place like a forest or a desert to expose human weaknesses and limitations. The pretentious façade that is projected by many 'adults' is not really of much use out in the wilderness. I am constantly amazed by the transformation that people go through when they get out in the wild for a little while. Often the toughies turn out to be the wimps and the wimps turn out to be the toughies.

Jesus said that we need to become like little children to enter the Kingdom of Heaven (Matt. 18:3). Many of us need to return to the simplicity of childhood without the pretentiousness of the adult world. There is no place in the Kingdom for the societal-taught nonsense that often passes for acting like sophisticated adults. God has a lot of things for us to unlearn or change our minds about. He wants to bring us to a place of simplicity of life in the Kingdom, so He takes us for a little camping trip out into the spiritual wilderness.

You may possibly be asking, "You're advocating camping for Jesus?" Yes and no. What I learned in the natural from my studies of wilderness wayfaring has become a metaphor for two processes that God has used in my life for transformation. First, the wilderness represents the means that Father has used to break me and to mold me for His purposes. These **means** include trials, troubles, mistakes, and events that are often beyond my control. When I have gone through these circumstances, they have seemed like a wilderness to me. Afterwards I have seen God's use of all kinds of difficulty to cause me to grow.

Secondly, the wilderness represents my journey through different religious landscapes. These experiences have taught me how to function in the brick and steel church world without, necessarily, being part of it. In contrast, I have learned that a person may function outside of the realm of traditional religious administration altogether. All false religion, put forward in the name of Jesus, is a cruel wilderness. This kind of religion uses the ways and means of this world to deceive its adherents into thinking that they have the truth; all the time holding them in devotion to denominations, human authority, or sectarian prejudice. Often, these competing interests are dressed up with a 'great big Christian smile'. Let me share a few examples that illustrate my point.

My first wilderness lasted for most of ten years. It began around the time that my wife Bev became ill and lasted until after her death. The illness itself started the process of education and growth. **Growth** actually comes through **death**. The Bible uses a lot of pictures to help us understand how this process that God uses works. Jesus said that growth starts when a seed is cast off, "dies," and is buried (John 12:24). Of course this refers to His death, burial, and resurrection. It also refers to the life of a believer. We are taken into our particular emotional, physical, or spiritual wilderness so that we may face ourselves, die to ourselves, and live anew through the power of God.

Jesus went on to teach that anyone who wished to follow Him must deny themselves, take up their cross, and follow Him (Matt. 16:24; Luke 9:23). Paul talked about having a sentence of death in himself (2 Cor. 1:9). Very often, people tend to want to make this **dying** process theoretical so that they might continue to satisfy their own desires. Jesus wants to make this dying a reality so that we may live in newness of life. The way to live the life of God is through a practical death to our own soulish desires. Then the motives and empowerment of God will be released in us. We are God's slaves, like Shakespeare's poetic lover who states, "I have no precious time at all to spend, Nor services to do, till you require."[1] This internal work is accomplished by a continual series of revelations of our powerlessness. These are followed by impartations of His deliverance from our own selfishness.

Jesus used another picture to help us understand what He really wants to do. He tells us that we are the branches, He is the vine, and his Father is the gardener (John 15). In this word picture we understand that we draw **all of our life** from another **Source** than ourselves. Through the Holy Spirit we see God's Word brought to life in us. The Bible reveals this source as Christ in us, the hope of glory (Col. 1:27). All of our spiritual life is drawn from the well-spring of everlasting life, Jesus. None of this life is drawn from ourselves because without Jesus we can do nothing (John 15:5). The Father **cuts off** all of the 'branches' of our lives that draw strength from us but are not fruitful. Again, we see the horticultural picture of the central work of death for the believer. The removal of useless branches releases the new life that Jesus brings us by the means of His death and resurrection.

Paul describes the work of God in another way. He refers to us as **living sacrifices** that are made holy by the sacrifice of Christ (Romans 12:1-2). We need to both understand and cooperate with this process. We do not die one time but multiple times as living sacrifices. We are living but we keep being sacrificed to God over and over again. This becomes a central focus for the believer since they see death to their self-life as an open door to receive Christ's life. The death of the Cross was very excruciating for Jesus to endure. I think the role of pain is lost on a lot of people. Death generally causes some pain to the person dying. In the case of a cross, it would be heavy and painful to carry around day after day. It must be even worse to feel the pain of crucifixion.

The seed that dies literally dries up so that only the germ lives. All traces of its former life are stripped away before it springs forth into new life. If the branch could feel itself being pruned, the sharp and harsh pruning shears would feel like knives. What enjoyment can there be in being put to death over and over again? The Bible spends a lot of time explaining and describing this process of spiritual growth. It is not surprising that people want to avoid the pain of death in their soul. This is what they will experience in the process of dying to themselves repeatedly. Nevertheless, the process is essential to their spiritual survival.

At times I felt such a sense of denial during my years in the wilderness. My family's world grew smaller and smaller. I had to economize on my legitimate enjoyment because more and more of my time was devoted to care-giving and raising my children. It also fell to me to be the sole provider of whatever funds I could to support the family. Looking back, I believe nothing special was required of me. I had promised Bev to love her in "sickness and in health, for richer or for poorer..." Nothing special was required in raising my children either. They were good kids. What was demanded by the circumstances was **sacrifice**. Then more and more extreme sacrifices were required. I found out that I really didn't even know how to sacrifice cheerfully for my own family! Over time God changed me.

The pressure of my wilderness showed me what a selfish and really unloving kind of guy I was. There were no tasks that I should not have been glad to do but I found that I could be bothered quite a bit. We had no help from family and little from the church. This was my tutorial on the **way things are.** I was growing up to see that we have little facility in many quarters of the church to give people practical help on a long-term basis. The pressure got so great that there were times where I would secretly pray that God would take me home. When you pray that prayer you are in a good place because Jesus really wants us to die to ourselves anyway. Bev and I often felt very alone. Upon reflection I see that I needed every day of difficulty and every dark night of the soul, to expose me to me. It has been said that, "Before God makes a ministry He makes a man." If you wish to be much for God you should expect that God will allow you to have trouble.

Years before these circumstances developed I had taken a shipping job that provided a good living. I had worked my way from being a pretty mediocre employee to one that was quite helpful to the company. I learned that it takes a long time to build up a good reputation on a job and a short time to ruin one. As I progressed at work, I found myself doing vacation relief work. Because I had become more reliable, I drew a lot of the night and afternoon shifts. Things had to be done and done right because I was usually working alone. Again, this contributed to my wilderness experience because I had time and silence with which to face myself. I learned to pray as I worked but more importantly I learned to hear. I am persuaded that hearing is a much more important part of prayer than speaking because God already knows everything I need and I hardly know anything.

I come from a Biblical tradition of healing. My wife Bev was healed so that we were able to have children. I have seen some remarkable healings and met others who have been healed. I believe that the healing of body, soul, and spirit are available for us in the atonement (Isaiah 53:5; 1 Peter 2:24). I take a very simple approach to praying for the sick. If any person has the faith to be healed, God will heal them. Faith for living as well as unusual interventions of God are not something we conjure up but something God imparts (Roman 12:3; 1 Cor. 12:9). If a person asks me to pray, it then becomes my responsibility to have faith for them (James 5:14-16).

It is amazing how unkind those who believe in healing can be to those who are injured or ill. I was amazed and instructed by the theories that came forth during the time of Bev's illness. Of course, lack of faith was the favorite accusation but there were all kinds of other theories and cures presented by helpful people. These ranged from the cruel to the absurd. There were diets, doctors, faith formulas, and reproofs of all kinds. The reality is that I never met one person to whom God had imparted faith for Bev's healing. Since God is the only One who can impart faith for healing, if He had imparted it to someone, Bev would have been healed. God did not provide anyone with the faith for her healing because it was her time to go to be with Jesus. Nevertheless, her spirit was healed as each or ours will be in their season. The death of any believer is precious in the sight of God (Psalm 116:15). I learned that sometimes God doesn't care about my theology because He has greater purposes that concern our eternal destinies.

As a young man I used to look sideways at people who were always complaining about their backs. There was nothing mean or sinister in this, it was just the beautiful strength of youth. Six years after Bev became ill I suffered a stress fracture in my back. This came after three years of chronic pain. I became so debilitated that I often could not even stand. God turned up the volume of His silence. I have learned over the years that when I do not listen, God may speak with illness. He stops my frenetic life so that I will hear His voice. He used my back pain to change the direction of my life completely. I have since been healed of debilitating back pain.

I had been taught the great Judeo-Christian work ethic. I do believe the Bible teaches work and support of your family. What I had to learn was who my Source was. The way I learned was by being unable to work. Paul said, *"My God shall supply all your need according to His riches in glory by Christ Jesus"* (Phil. 4:19). Suddenly, I was no longer the **great provider**. I found out at a young age what some folks do not learn until they are old. I am puny and weak at my best and Father holds all of my strength. I could not take care of myself, my wife, or my kids. I was crippled for months. God had to use a crowbar to pry off the golden hand-cuffs of my worldly security. He provided. Sometimes His provision was hand to mouth but He has been very kind to me and my family. I quit associating my work with my money. I am commanded to work but God supplies the wages.

In the days after Bev's death I looked at all of her things in the closet and around the house that she would never use again. I had worked twelve hour Saturdays just to meet our needs in the last year of her life. What good had it done? I have always valued people only second to God. I realized that all of our slaving for stuff had robbed me of time for family and friends. Don't get me wrong. I think it is a reprehensible man indeed who will not care for his family—worse than an infidel (1 Tim. 5:8). Still, many of us are on an insane quest to get many things we don't need. You can never get a day back, my friend. So many believers are spending too much time working and planning to live later. First they have to get everything they want. The truth is that today is the only day we have been given to live. If we do not live each day to its fullest when we are young, we will be dead inside when we get to our future retirement.

My second wilderness came in conjunction with the first. At the same time that all of the circumstances of my life were pressing in and teaching me the ways of God, there was the growing knowledge that much of the 'church' that I encountered was also a wilderness experience. I have shared some of this already but I want to get to the root of what has made so much of my church experience a wilderness.

Many people hate what they call politics in the church. Politics really speaks of how people handle and treat people. You can handle and interact with people for good righteous purposes and you can do the same for the most sinister reasons. I think what really does bother people is situation ethics. It seems to cause the same kind of strong emotion as political passion. Somehow, some people can suspend their conscience when they want their own way. This **is** reprehensible because it is at the very times where our passions are most inflamed that we need God's righteous rule the most. We see a picture in the Acts of the Apostles that stands as a stark contrast to this kind of suspension of conscience. Although truly impassioned for God's purposes, the early Church was a praying people who took their council from the Holy Spirit and the Word of God, without reference to their own personal agendas or desires (Acts 13:1ff; Acts 15).

Much of the fighting and situation ethics that I have observed came from a wholesale misunderstanding of Who's in charge. As both a congregate and a leader I have seen people rise time and again and espouse some perfectly plausible piece of man's wisdom that was not God's will for the situation. It is hard to think of fellowshipping with such unrepentant foreign interests when they arise to grieve and foil the interests of the Lord. It is deception indeed to think that our evil deeds or even our own good deeds lend any assistance to God (Romans 3:8).

Further, I started to realize that many preachers and congregants were willing to overlook the mishandling or dead presentation of God's Word. There is an old saying about dealing with errant use of the Bible: "You can eat the fish and throw away the bones!" This well meaning sop is presented to convince us that we cannot really expect a relatively error-free presentation of the truth. When I eat my fish I like them fresh and properly filleted. That way I can avoid eating any bones. I do not find the Bible to be a complex book but it is a hard book. It exposes every nuance of human frailty and evil, as well as God's thoughts on everything that is important to Him. We are to handle God's Word carefully and preach it under the Holy Spirit's anointing. Teaching and preaching without life application is tiresome theorization. Teaching and preaching without the anointing of the Holy Spirit makes the most exciting thing in the world seem common-place. Who wants to fellowship with deadness? Most of us abhor the idea of being around decaying bodies but I have found the same smell of death around much of the presentation of God's Word.

I cannot count the times that I have been in a church service where those leading, whether pastor, worship leader, or lay person, grieved the Holy Spirit. They did this by disobeying His leading, quenching His movement, or speaking outside of the realm of the Word of God. Over the years I have seen this in all kinds of contexts and it seems like a dry wilderness to my soul. It has become more and more tiresome to have people call services and events anointed by God that were devoid of His presence and power. I am convinced in this day that God has departed from many places of worship.

Yet many still loudly claim His presence when He is not really there. Jesus ironically asks, "If the light which is in us is darkness then how great is that darkness" (Matt. 6:23)? Many think they have 'got it' when the rank and file in many places wouldn't know the presence of the Holy Spirit if He came up and introduced Himself. If you find yourself in such circumstances it is appropriate to question whether God wants you to stay. You are more likely to become like the group you are with, than the group you are with is to become like you.

We have come to a place of the perversion of power in many institutional churches in America today. This perversion is two-fold. Jesus presented leadership in the church as a serving competition (Matt. 20:27; 23:11). If you want to lead, become the servant of all. To my fellow ministers and all who aspire to ministry I would say that you are no more ordained than any other member of the Body of Christ. This statement will, no doubt, upset some leaders but we must understand that we are all called together into **one** Body. We are **all** ordained to His service and empowered by His Spirit (1 Cor. 12:27). God has a different function for leaders but it is not to manage or control God's people. Our function is to lead and love His sheep and to feed His sheep.

It is an atrocity before God when ministers strut or display the arrogance of the world system. In fact, a lot of our leadership structures look and function more like institutional Roman Catholicism than Biblical models. I have come to the conclusion that those who participate and those who lead in dysfunctional structures are largely co-dependant. Geoffrey Bull states: "We make the ministry professional and are glad to have it so that we might mind our own business. We let men institutionalize us, catechize us, and proselytize us, control our conscience and consume our substance."[2] Such leadership may have results but it will never produce mature disciples, no matter how large the group or successful the church or its programs. The minister who displays Christ-like servant leadership may be considered a poor leader by American cultural standards. That minister may have a lonely and misunderstood desert trek. I suspect that this is why more do not give it a try.

The polar opposite to the perverting of leadership authority is the growing incivility and lack of submission prevalent amongst church congregants. In his very revealing book *Clergy Killers* [3], G. Lloyd Rediger cites the break down in civility in our society as one of the main sociological contributors to a lack of unity in the church. As well, Mr. Rediger is persuaded that there is a whole class of evil, errant, or mentally ill people who try to destroy and remove ministers. He calls such people "clergy killers."[4]

With so little light, and such an ethical decline in our day that evil dwells within the tabernacle of the Lord, it is a good thing that some people **are** troubled. Many of these are God's remnant. It takes no genius, however, to diagnose these problems. It will take the genius of God's Holy Spirit to bring solutions. It is a shame when people revert to worldly tactics in an effort to cure what the group or church they are associated with may not even see as a problem. One must be called to such a task and should not be naïve enough to think that there will be anything but a wilderness experience in exchange for their efforts.

The stark reality is that today's professing church is in a desperate state. This can lead a thoughtful person to feel a sense of challenge and hardship that can turn traditional church attendance into a wilderness experience of the soul. I cannot cure anything and I know it. I have tried kindly and not-so-kindly and have failed. I have never met anyone who has been able to fix these situations... besides Jesus. In most cases Jesus has not been properly consulted. Each congregate should ascertain that they are where they are supposed to be. Then they can count on Jesus to take care of the difficulties that will no doubt arise. Each minister needs to ascertain where he belongs without reference to income, benefit, children's education, or personal preference. After all, we are sent as servants to His flock.

In spite of the wilderness landscape I see in the institutional church, there is hope. The hope is in the purity and power of God's remnant. We cannot do much about others but we can certainly allow God to make **us** the best **us** that we can be. It is never the crowd or the masses that bring water to the desert but the twos and threes who truly gather in His name. I am sure that He will meet you in the midst of your wilderness, loved one, and I can only testify that I have always found Him faithful.

I have only shared a morsel of my wilderness experience. There are so many other stories to tell and lessons learned. I do know that we all need circumstances and troubles that assist in stripping away the old life and nature. When we get into the tough place, the elemental place, where we are helpless and have to call on God, we find Him. We learn that we really cannot do anything without Him. Some of you cannot imagine going through my puny little troubles and others could say, "That's nothin'!" God knows what we can bear. The rigors of our wilderness experience will expose us to ourselves so that we may find our shelter, water, fire, and food in Him. When we do, we then reflect the glory of Paul's reality, "Christ in you, the hope of glory" (Col. 1:27). Until next time: Good trekking and God bless you,

Your Friend in the Wilderness,

Henry

# CHAPTER 4

# *Shelter: Who's Your Daddy?*

Dear Fellow Traveler,

*I* have a vivid memory from my childhood. My friends and I built all kinds of forts down in the wooded areas adjoining the railway yards in Winnipeg. We would dig a deep hole and use whatever we could to cover it. We would then camouflage them so that other competitors wouldn't come and steal our fort from us. Later, in the wilderness of Ontario, I would build structures near our summer home. I never really thought about what was motivating me to build these shelters. In retrospect, I think that my desire to build forts may have reflected some basic instinct of self-preservation in me.

As a teenager I learned the art of taking my shelter along with me. Hiking the West Coast Trail in Pacific Rim National Park in British Columbia taught me some of the pitfalls of insufficient shelter and the necessity of using proper shelter. Since we were taking many days to make the trip we were simply using individual tarps to keep our pack weight down. One night near Tsusiat Falls it was such a beautiful night that I didn't use my tarp, opting to slept under the stars. At about three in the morning I awoke, freezing. Although I was several hundred yards from the falls, I could see mist rising in the moonlight that reached the ground far beyond me. I probably suffered hypothermia that night. Consequently I learned a valuable lesson—shelter must be sufficient for the type of conditions you might find yourself in.

As I grew into a man and was raising a family, I stopped trekking into the wilderness. I was content to live near the forest while keeping the comfort of my home. It was not until a few years ago that I felt the need to reconnect. I took a wilderness survival course after reading several books on the subject. During the course we built a shelter out of material that was available, using no tools. Attention had to be given to where the shelter was built. If it was in a water course or a low spot we could wake up soaked, or worse. We built a frame and then put large sticks on top; followed by smaller sticks, dirt, and vegetation. It was remarkable how much material was necessary. It was also remarkable how much sweat was produced in building that shelter that would meet just our most basic needs.

When we were finished we had a shelter that would hardly be discernable to the untrained eye. It was tight, made to fit only one person. This would keep any of us warm without any blankets or clothes. Each person crawled inside to try it out. There were sticks jabbing all over the place. The smell of the earth felt like a presence but the shelter would keep us alive under very extreme emergency conditions. What pride we felt in our pile of dirt and sticks. How empowered we felt to face a wilderness emergency. Humans need shelter. We are actually pretty fragile and we live in many varying climates. We need to keep the rain off, the sun off, the bugs and animals out, and the heat or the cool in.

You may cringe at the idea of my little dirt house. It is clear to me that it would seem like a terribly shabby dwelling to most of us in America who have so much. Most of us can not imagine struggling with sticks and dirt just to insure our survival. This may well be true of our attitude towards spiritual shelter as well. Some people have become very sophisticated builders. They seek to lead the church to more complex and better looking structures than those that the Lord Jesus Christ has already erected. Some of the simplicity of the spiritual house that Jesus built, as it is reflected in the New Testament record, may look like a pile of sticks and dirt to much of the American church.

Of course true shelter is built on the only foundation that there could be—Jesus Christ the Chief Cornerstone. By using the picture of a building the apostles Paul and Peter illustrate, through the construction trade, something that really cannot be seen. Paul cautions the Corinthians that they should use appropriate building materials in the construction of their shelter (1 Cor. 3:10-16). Peter goes a step further and says that the building is made up of 'lively stones" (1 Peter 2:5). If you put the two metaphors together the Church is constructed of people who are made alive in Jesus with spiritual materials as a framework and mortar. The building metaphor uses people as the construct rather than a physical or theological construct. To be part of God's building you must have Jesus living in your heart.

One very common and deceptive phrase masks what God wants to do in the realm of shelter. The term is, 'going to church'. The word translated as church is from the Greek word *ekklesia*[1] which refers to a group called out of another group. In the case of God's people it refers to those called out from the world and participating in Christ's body as members of His Kingdom. Although the writers of the New Testament referred to the Church at Ephesus or Corinth, it was always in the context of the greater whole. This still applies to those of us who are part of the **called out ones** today. Therefore, in Biblical terms, the Church does not refer to a building. It certainly was not used to differentiate the believers in one city from believers in another city. None of the distinctions that we make by denomination, culture, or location were important in the name **Church.** What was important is who was being spoken to and what they were called out to be: a specific people representing God.

A wonderful illustration of how God views the Church is used by Stephen in illustrating how God viewed Israel as, "the church in the wilderness" (Acts 7:38). God has always sought a people for Himself. His general terms have always been the same: repentance, separation, and faith. Before Moses, those who came to God found His favor through these means. Adam & Eve, Abel, Shem, Job, Abraham and the Patriarchs all displayed these characteristics in relation to God. Through Moses we see God establishing a Church of people who were chosen by God, separated to God, and required to live by faith in God.

Before Jesus came there were certain requirements that had to be met to appropriately participate in the life of God. An individual had to repent and convert to Judaism, separate themselves to the nation of Israel, and live by faith in the covenant that God gave Moses. This was the only way to appropriately participate in the life of God. Israel's mission was far more than they ever accomplished. They were to be a light to the Gentiles bringing the way of salvation to all men (Isaiah 49:6). Israel's mission was to invite people to join the nation of Israel and participate in the covenant of God. This was a centripetal or ingathering mission. The mission of the New Testament Church is a centrifugal or a 'sent out' kind of mission. We are sent out to invite all men home to their heavenly Father through Jesus Christ.

Thus we see that there is little justification to present the Church in relation to any building. We do not go to church, we **are** the Church. We gather together for strengthening and instruction in the Bible to prepare us for our 'outwardly propelled' (centrifugal) mission to a dying world. Again we are not speaking about the things that we do but rather the people we are. It is preposterous for us to present Church as gathering once or twice on Sunday for a 'Service' and maybe a weeknight or two for 'Family Night', 'Bible Study', and so on. Although I generally like to assemble for worship on Sunday as well as to gather for prayer with others, we see no such demarcations in the day by day fellowship of the saints, as presented in the Bible.

Words are powerful. So are generally accepted concepts. Something has become clear to me and many of the people of the remnant. Substituting buildings, furniture, ritual, leadership, or denomination as the defining characteristics of a group can be very destructive; no matter how well-meaning people are. Such minor concerns will diminish the continuity and value of the nature of people gathering in Jesus' name. Things that can be useful in their places can become substitute shelters and objects of devotion. When this happens, man's ways and machinations will move to the forefront. Consequently, God's objectives and the fellowship of His Spirit will be moved to a subordinate role. To diminish the meaning of the gathering of believers to certain familiar characteristics or interests that compete with the fellowship of Christ will destroy the benefits that God has for His *ekklesia* (called out people).

It is necessary to fully arm ourselves with a Biblical understanding of what Church is. Barring a spiritual revolution, things will not change. The simple knowledge that what is being presented as 'church' is not normal to God will be a great protection. The remnant will not just settle for less. Most people will continue to gather at a building but this is not the Church. The service or programs are not the Church either. The living family relationships and fellowship that find their roots in God as our Father through Jesus his Son by the power of the Holy Spirit are the mortar of the Church. Many of the Christians in this world have no building or formal leader but they are still the Church. The remnant will seek much more than just Sunday-go-to-meeting Christianity. They will seek the living fellowship of Christ.

That's why I ask you, "Who's your daddy?" Everyone who believes on the Lord Jesus Christ is adopted into the family of God. The Bible calls believers the children of God with the common spiritual outcry, "Abba, Father." (Romans 8:15; Galatians 4:6). In Ephesians 2:17-22 believers are referred to as His household, His citizens, His house, His temple, and His habitation:

> *"And came and preached peace to you which were afar off, and to them that were nigh. For through him we both have access by one Spirit unto the Father. Now therefore ye are no more strangers and foreigners, but **fellowcitizens** with the saints, and of the **household** of God; And are built upon the foundation of the apostles and prophets, Jesus Christ himself being the chief corner stone; In whom all the **building** fitly framed together groweth unto an holy **temple** in the Lord: In whom ye also are builded together for an **habitation** of God through the Spirit."*

God Himself becomes our shelter when we join His family. We all move into a new relationship with a family that is hallowed above our earthly family (Matt. 12:48-50). There is nothing that makes a home more of a shelter than the care and concern of a father. This simplicity is the genius of God. He calls it 'Church' where two or more are gathered in Jesus' name (Matt. 18:19-20). There is no location, building, denomination, or human sanction required; just two or three. Is that too simple for you?

King David did a lot of camping in the wilderness. There is no doubt that his early life as a shepherd was filled with camping out. The skills that David learned prepared him for the years on the run from King Saul and later from his own son, Absalom. David knew the value of setting up on high ground. He referred to God as his rock many times in the Psalms. David experienced more trouble than most of us and lived a very austere life in the wilderness for many years. He must have had many makeshift shelters that ranged from boulders and caves to just a leather tarp or portable tent. In all of those years he always regarded God as his real shelter. Just as rocks would shelter him from the desert sun, David referred to the protection of God's shadow (Psalm 91:1). He spoke of God in an agricultural sense: as a mother bird who sheltered him with her wings (Psalm 57:1). In the same way that David dreamt of a place to call home he saw God as his real home, *"For in the time of trouble he shall hide me in his pavilion: in the secret of his tabernacle shall he hide me; he shall set me up upon a rock."* (Psalm 27:5). David knew that God was his home and his habitation.

The family of God is described as a camping and wayfaring people. They were called "strangers and sojourners" (Lev. 25:23; 1 Chron. 29: 13-15; 1 Peter 2:11). We are pilgrims walking through the spiritual wilderness of this world. Our only permanent dwelling is a city in another part of the universe, built and made by God. All of us fellow-travelers have the commonality of family, direction, purpose, and final destination. With these major similarities we still may walk profoundly different pathways in this present wilderness. We must never accept as a substitute some of the shelter that either well-meaning or more insidious individuals offer to us along the way. Some of these have very pleasant or even Biblical names. Such names trouble me because they often do not reflect Biblical practice. It is really important to know where **not** to camp or take shelter.

The Bible teaches that Christianity is not defined by the individual alone but also by the gathered saints or Church. It is absolutely clear that both in practice and by commandment the New Covenant believers gathered often. The main purposes of this gathering were corporate prayer, Biblical instruction, fellowship, and worship (Acts 2:42). Because the saints realized that they were part of God's family they met daily, joyfully, and with zeal. They were all brought together by the unity of the indwelling Christ as manifested by the Holy Spirit.

Little is said of the locations for worship in relation to the gathering. It is clear that the believers were rather practical and utilitarian. In the New Testament people gathered in homes, at the Temple (while it existed), in public places, by rivers, at synagogues, at rented buildings, and no doubt at any other location that would serve the needs of the particular group. Any reference to the idea of the Church as a building is profoundly absent. They would not likely understand the term 'my church'. They saw all Christians as part of God's family so that the term 'my church' would seem like an oxymoron to them.

By contrast, in today's America much attention has been given to the building called the church. In our culture, church is clearly understood to mean a building where people gather for worship. There is no reason to argue with this basic definition because people will not even understand why you would; it is culturally ingrained. Besides, it is the misapplied allegiance and devotion that many give to a building, leader, group, or denomination that should cause us concern. We must constantly be aware of the power of such foreign interests. These wrongfully placed allegiances can be expressed in many ways.

Firstly, the **building itself** can somehow be thought to be holy because it is dedicated to God. This is a very common theme which is promoted by many in the ministry and is partly true. Dedication of things for God's service was common in the Old Testament as it pertained to the Tabernacle, the Temple, and the Priesthood. Dedication of objects and places was completely foreign to the New Testament Church. Both in practice and belief the Church was directed by a dynamic unseen force; the Holy Spirit of God. He was and should be the Director of each event, with no direct reference to the old idea of buildings and sacred places. If a group of first century believers possessed a building, it would have been used as a simple tool for God's work and nothing more.

The beauty of salvation through Jesus is that God moved his dwelling place out of a building and placed it into the hearts of men (2 Cor. 3:3; Eze. 11:19-20; Eze. 36:26-29). What makes the gathering of believers sacred is that Jesus is in attendance (Matt. 18:20). Wherever we gather then becomes a holy place because Jesus declares that He walks in the midst of any believing group. The reverence that some give to the place of worship has become a substitute for a day by day meeting with God. The glory of each individual believer is that they are mobile houses of worship, a habitation of God through the Spirit (Eph. 2:19-22). When individuals gather in one place it then becomes 'Christ in session' as each person is able to edify the whole by the reality of what Christ is doing and giving to everyone. The gathering of a group of redeemed individuals becomes another habitation of God through the Spirit. This is the 'temple' that Paul refers to in 1 Corinthians 3. The believers in any given place constitute a Temple of the Holy Spirit.

A second disturbing trend is the **pride of possession** of 'our church'. This possession does not refer to the harmless identification that people feel when they are part of an identifiable group. It is also clear that people should enjoy the place and the people that they gather together to fellowship with. Nevertheless, it is at the very center of the human heart to do the visual thing and find physical representations of God that will suit human taste. God said that we need to avoid anything that would 'conjure up' an image of God (Ex. 20:4). Such attachments can become subtle forms of idolatry. I believe such attachments are manifested in as many ways as things that people can own or desire, even in the context of the church building (Col. 3:5).

Some folk grow attached to the architecture, design, and decoration of the building. "After all," they say, "This is the house of God and we have to have the best of everything for the house of God." Since we have established that the individual believer and corporate gathering of God's people is now God's house, the preceding statement is false. The church building and its contents are tools and no more. People can become sentimentally attached to furniture, plaques commemorating giving for things in the church, and signs of all kinds that represent the history of the church. These things and the building itself can become hindrances because there is an inordinate affection symbolically attached to them (Col. 3:5).

For example, in one church that I attended there was a pretzel church that had dimensions of twelve by twelve by eighteen inches. It sat on top of the organ for the first three years that I was there. I finally asked about it and somebody told me that it had come from a place hundreds of miles away. It had been left around because someone, who no longer attended the church, had brought it. It fell off the organ the next week. I find the old joke about how you move an organ in church a troubling reflection of this insidious wickedness. The answer is, "One inch per week." Many ministers can attest to the truth of this so-called joke.

When people take unhealthy ownership of a church building, much time, effort, and money may be spent on the building that should be spent on people and communities. The deception comes with the activity involved. People may spend much time and money on a building so they have something to show for their work. They have enjoyed the activity in doing the job. In this case the problem can be that in striving to look for something visible to come from our work, God will be left out of the equation. Generally, God would be much more likely to be concerned about 'His Building' (the people) than a building (1 Cor. 3:9-11).

Does this mean buildings are evil, as some assert? I believe that the present attitudes towards buildings and their contents are symptomatic of a **greater problem**. God will lead His people to use all kinds of resources for His Kingdom. Again, the remnant must arm themselves with the knowledge that things are used for their utility and nothing more. Paul cautiously advises us to use the things of the world without abusing them (1 Cor. 7:31). I have had little success in changing people's attitudes in these areas. I believe trying to do so is a waste of time. What I do know is that where such affections rule, it is best for a remnant person to move on. You can consume years of your life fussing over such things with little success or satisfaction.

One final note on our buildings—many believe that the building is the main place where people will be led to Christ. In other words they view the church building as the focal point **for evangelism**. This view is not in keeping with the centrifugal nature of our mission. It is clear that the New Testament saints gathered for fellowship and saw themselves as **sent out** into their society (John 20:21; Matt. 28:19-20). Each individual's realm of influence became their ministry focus. Only after people were led to Jesus did they introduce them into the Body, since being regenerated was a prerequisite for actually understanding what was going on. There is no doubt that people will come to Christ in Gospel-preaching churches. God's method is for each of us to practice 'every believer evangelism'. Only when we use God's methods will we see the New Testament results we desire.

Another unhealthy manifestation of false shelter today is the **marketing and warehousing** of Jesus. I have a close friend who recently explained to me that we should definitely use proper business practices and approaches in running the church—that the church should, in fact, be run like a business. Over the years I have heard many people argue the same point many times. Their belief is that American business developed its methodology from the historic Christian principles and traditions of America itself. I heartily disagree with this view and find myself largely in disagreement with every practice of a business methodology in relation to every priority in the church. Nevertheless, my friend articulated very succinctly what the philosophy and practices are in a great many churches today.

In my lifetime I have seen the consolidation of the process of shopping into the mega-store phenomenon. The multitudes of supplies that are needed to build houses have been consolidated into warehouses containing every kind of product that you need to finish the job. I now can shop for my food in sizes that I may never be able to finish while they are fresh. The variety available to me is very extensive. If I go to a movie, I may be able to see any of sixteen pictures. Appliances, technology items, medical treatments, toys, books, and just about anything else you want to buy, can be found somewhere in giant volume outlets. The sales hooks are convenience, variety, and lower prices. The incentive for the companies is profit and survival.

As well, we are a profoundly manipulated society. Rather than resist this trend, it appears that we **expect** to hear a 'pitch' for anything that is worthwhile. Most people allow themselves to be marketed to from morning to night. We pay for cable TV where we are bombarded with profound visual enticements to purchase things. It is the same on the radio and surfing the World Wide Web. People in America are increasingly stimulated to have more and more. This is evidenced by an unprecedented debt to income ratio which has often been reported in the media at the time of this writing.

Today, many small and large churches are using enticements that rival the secular business world. Many leaders who promote the marketing of individual churches use the same techniques as the mega-stores. They then point to the crowds they attract as evidence of their success. There is little doubt that a service and needs-oriented approach to a meeting will attract unconverted people. More often this approach will also attract other churchgoers to change churches. In such cases the growth of the mega-church does not come from evangelism but from the dynamics of marketing—to appeal to existing Christians.

As churches move towards this kind of growth they often drain people from other viable and useful fellowships. It is clear in this day that the average professing Christian will choose a church largely on the basis of what the church can do for them or the draw of a successful looking group. In just the way that less sophisticated or diversified businesses fail in competition with mega-stores, many small churches are sent into death throes by mega-churches. This phenomenon is driven largely by demographics and market share. The competition for 'customers' is so intense that many of the courtesies taken in the past relating to Pastoral phone calls and inquiry into where people have come from are dispensed with.

Some time ago I had a conversation with a very nice Christian man. He is a very talented musician and a gifted worship leader. He also has enjoyed great success in his chosen profession and is moving towards becoming very wealthy. He asked me if I would be interested in joining the staff at his church. They were looking for an associate and he thought my direct style might blend well with his Pastor's relational style. I asked him how many people attended and was informed that they had grown from a few families to over four hundred people in the space of just a few years. I was told that there were a lot of upscale professionals attending and that the people really loved their church and their Pastor.

I asked how many people he knew who had been directly converted through the ministry of the church. I asked him because I knew he was in a position to know. He said, "None." Almost the entire growth of that church was based on presenting what Christians wanted in both music and message in a neat and tidy package. If I had gone there I imagine it would have been a disaster. I suppose, few if any would have understood what I was talking about in relation to the cost of discipleship. Worse yet, they might have understood completely. It is my opinion that the person who presented God's claims on the believer at that place would soon be asked to leave.

Please understand that I love outreach-based giant churches and outreach-based little churches. I think we could use about ten thousand more big ones in America. Nevertheless, if we market Jesus in a business manner, as so many churches now do, we will grow to depend more and more on methodology and less and less on the presence and power of God. Many who started out well have supplanted the original purposes of their individual church founders by becoming slick and sophisticated instead of simple and powerful. The simplicity of the functions of spiritual gifting in the church is always present in a healthy fellowship. The remnant person will not be impressed with the 'bells and whistles' but with the simplicity of fellowship and purpose. They will seek the Holy Spirit's witness. Otherwise, why be there?

Another pair of troubling words that have been much abused in the brick and steel church is 'covering' and 'submission'. The word **covering** is often used to refer to Christ's relationship with us, to a man's relationship with a woman, and to a minister's relationship with his congregation. Although this terminology may sound like it illustrates Biblical relationships, the Bible never uses the term 'covering' in relation to leaders and followers. I suppose the term sounds nice but is it a 'God' term or a 'man' term? Do any of the apostles call themselves 'coverings' or demand submission? This terminology either infers or demands that a person must submit to their 'covering' to please God. I cannot find that terminology or tone anywhere in the New Testament.

My main concern with the term covering is the way it relates to the minister. The Bible states only twice that we are to submit to God's ordained authority for our own good and once that leaders should be submissive to the flock (1 Cor. 16:16; Heb. 13:17; 1 Peter 5:5). This covering is not imposed as a condition of relationship or membership in the church. It is up to a congregate or a minister to recognize and choose to submit to authentic God-ordained authority. In our day, the problem facing the remnant and religious alike is finding obedient, mature, godly, called leaders. If they have no fruit in their lives we are to discern them as false. Jesus said that the fruit of the leader's lives was their measure (Matt. 7:15-20). Paul and Peter give long lists of qualifications for leadership (1 Peter 5:1-4; 1 Tim. 3:1-14; Titus 1:5-9). How often do we ignore these qualifications and at what cost?

As a husband I am to give godly leadership to my wife and she is to obey me. What people don't understand is that although I may try to impose my leadership upon my wife I will never succeed in 'making' her submit to me. It is really up to my wife to give me the **gift** of submission. In the same way, God does not impose His Kingdom, right now, but gives us a lifetime (longer or shorter) to either choose to continually submit to His will or not.

What I have often seen is unhealthy leadership imposed rather than submission given. This is called a 'covering' by some but often reflects the spirit and attitude of control. This explains a lot of the guff and utter nonsense that both congregates and ministers put up with in the name of Jesus. Imposed leadership clearly violates the Spirit of Christ. During His ministry Jesus invited people into a relationship with Himself where they would become learners and He would be the teacher. This was an intimate honor that many departed from when the going got tough. At one point Jesus was down to the twelve and gave them the opportunity to leave as well (John 6:66-68). Jesus always left it up to His followers without any of the clever control manipulations that the world uses. He never reverted to control, guilt, fear of rejection, or religious manipulations. Neither does His leadership in this day. If you are being controlled or manipulated in the name of 'covering' you are being used and deceived. It is unhealthy to submit to such leadership. A person, who has been so used, should leave.

I have submitted to many leaders that I recognized had the call of God in their lives. I instinctively knew that I was in a spiritual wilderness and I needed help to find my way through. God provided many mentors, several pastors, spiritual parents, and later in ministry, experienced ministers. My most powerful relationships for discipleship were with lay people who had powerful walks with God and made time for me. I saw them as often as they would let me. I received what they would impart to me. I listened and gave weight to what they told me. I came and went at their convenience. None of them had to demand my love or devotion. They earned my devotion by caring for me and loving me as Christ loved the church. Detached power-based relationships will not produce disciples. This kind of covering will never give shelter in the wilderness.

Finally, there is great danger in taking shelter in **sectarianism**. I use that word rather than denomination because it is more inclusive. Listen to Paul's comments on the problems in Corinth (1 Cor. 1:10-17; 3:1-16). They had favorite teachers and divided under the banner of their leader's names: Paul, Apollos, Peter and Jesus. This was based on their overwhelming pride. Their problem was that they were dividing what God refused to have divided, based upon the opinions and preferences of men. Paul's logic was simple, "how can family say they are not family?" Denominations are not the only ones who are proud or who divide over doctrine or practice. Non-denominations do the same thing. By their very names, Independents show the same attitude. Behind all of this is people's desire to be identified with a contemporary living name as well as participating in the salvation of Jesus Christ. Paul is clear that Jesus will have none of it. The other motivator is simply the pride of being 'right' and we all know how important that is.

It has been my contention that we will find God's remnant everywhere, both inside and outside of the institutional church world. Anyone who dwells within the institution church will become aware of the insidious pride and deception that can be expressed when people lend allegiance to sectarian interests—our church, our great fellowship, our presbytery. It can be very easy to find acceptance with like-minded people who share our world-view but this should never be our shelter. Likewise there are those who define themselves by saying they are not of this group or that group. They know what they are against but are doubtful of what they are for. We must only define ourselves by a humble relationship with Jesus, not by saying, "Me and mine are the real Jesus crowd." The essence of cultic behavior is to believe that your group offers the only 'truth'.

It would be useful to use your imagination here for a minute. Think of God looking down on this puny little earth He has made. He sees over six billion people that are tinier than ants and knows each person in their entirety. He knows exactly who is in His Church and who isn't. Imagine how appalling it is for Him to look down on the very rich professing Christians in America, Canada, and so on. Small groups spend their time and substance dividing from other professing Christians in tens of thousand of little groups. They all have their little, puny, prideful arms folded while insisting that they are right. In the mean time the greater portion of the world has not heard the message of the Gospel once. All of the little groups that are 'right' are busy proving they are 'right' or just so happy that they are 'right'. In the mean time those who are lost have not seen His message of love lived out. They will only know that we are Christians by the love that we have one for another (John 13:34-35). Could this be a problem for Father?

Paul had some good advice for us in the light of this present distress. In 1 Cor. 7:26-31, Paul was speaking to fathers who didn't want their betrothed daughters to marry. As he advises them, Paul expands on the thought. Those who get married should not allow marriage to hinder their walk with the Lord. He explains that those who are married should act as if they are not married in relation to their walk with God. He then speaks of legitimate emotions and advises that we should not allow them to dominate our lives in a way that will hinder our walk with God. He then recommends possessing, without possessions possessing us. Finally Paul states that the present world is passing away. For this reason, in whatever way we use things we had better not let things use us. This is all another way of saying deny your self-life, take up your cross, and follow Jesus (Mark 8:34).

I am always worried for people who are possessive. They say, "My car, my house, my children, my life, my career, my church, my denomination," and so on. People who talk like this have a basic misunderstanding of the calling of God. We give up our rights the minute we receive Jesus. The follower of Jesus lays claim to nothing. We give up our pitiful little toys, receiving in exchange, life eternal and a shelter in the time of storm. That is why, if we find ourselves in any kind of sectarian or denominational setting, we need to be sure that the individual group has not become our shelter—that we participate in it without it controlling us. It is important that we do not yield up the best of our lives to the false 'covering' of our particular denomination or church. It is imperative that we do not attach ourselves to any sacred stuff, whether it is a building, the things in it, or the human pride associated with any status attached to belonging to a church.

A substitute shelter is kind of nice. It is already built. I do not have to do any work; just obey the rules of the landlord. I just move in and let everyone know that this is where I live. I may live here safely for years and never experience the superior accommodations that my Father provides. Sooner or later my shelter will be tested (Luke 6:47-49). The problem with the substitute is that when storms come it may not keep out the rain or the wind. It may let the odd rat in. When I have difficulties the landlord may not care. I may find my fellow tenants do not share my values and over-rule me. The shelter may not adhere to the building code. In fact Jesus states that any shelter that we may find, other than Him, is built on sand and will be completely ruined.

I realize that I have not offered a lot of practical solutions beyond recognizing the problem. I have no solutions. Most proponents of false shelter believe in what they are offering. I don't think that there will be a large-scale return to Biblical fellowship in America unless God allows us to have a lot of trouble. In the meantime we will have to live with the brick and steel or leave it. More and more of the remnant are leaving. Many people have just started to fellowship in homes (Acts 2:46; 20:20). There is a remnant of good leaders out there. It is time that remnant people found the good leaders and worked with them. There are remnant people everywhere. God is our shelter. If we listen to Him, He will place us just where He wants us.

As I mentioned before, we are told in the Scripture that we are strangers and sojourners here on earth. We're just passing through. Once we have passed through this present spiritual wilderness we will have a home "who's builder and maker is God" (Heb. 11:10). Do not let the shining monuments of this life distract you from your course to the place being prepared for you. Although the storms and heat beat upon you, your Shelter will never fail.

Just Passin' Through,

Henry

# CHAPTER 5

# *Washed With Pure Water*

Dear Fellow Traveler,

Water is one of my favorite things. It has been prominent in the history of my life and I see it as a gift from God. As a child I grew up on the Canadian prairie. My father worked as a mechanic and my mother was a teacher. Both of my parents worked when I was young which was a little unusual in the early sixties. The extra income helped my parents to get ahead and buy a summer place when I was the age of seven. The summer place was a one acre island, five miles from Kenora, Ontario. It was on the Lake of the Woods, a very large lake in Northern Ontario and Minnesota. Every year we would travel from Winnipeg to Kenora every weekend from May until October. My mother often spent several weeks at the island with us during the summer and we spent most of our vacation time there.

There were no amenities there except for an old propane stove and refrigerator, circa 1940. We used kerosene lanterns for light. We used a coal stove for heat. We threw biodegradable waste off the back dock and got our water in a bucket from the front of the island. The water was pure and delicious to drink. So much of my youth was spent on and in the water. My sister and I swam by the hour. As well, we fished by the hour, at a time when the walleye still had no mercury in them. Pure water cleansed me both inside and out.

There were few things more comforting to me than the taste, sensation, smell, and sound of water.

At twelve I left all that behind as my father moved to the warmer climes of Vancouver and then Victoria, British Columbia. My dad loved the wild and soon bought a fixer-up cabin cruiser. Although my teen years were difficult, there was always weekends on the boat. I received my ocean education in the Gulf Islands and the Inside Passage near Vancouver Island. The ocean was and is vast, pure, and cleansing there. Salt water disinfects and is good for the skin. The ocean waters were teeming with marine life. I learned new sounds, caught different fish, and felt the wild danger of the ocean's power to move and destroy.

As an adult I contracted my own house at Shawnigan Lake on Vancouver Island. My main motive was the shared use of one hundred and forty-seven feet of waterfront with a swimming and boating area. I wanted my children to enjoy some of the benefits that I had as a child. We stayed there until God's call took us away.

Our first Pastorate was at the small town of Lake Cowichan. We rented a beautiful home on the river there for about five years. One of the most beautiful things in my life at that time was swimming in that swift cold river. As I swam upstream I had such a sense of peaceful smallness. I really loved how I felt incredibly close to God when I was in that river. There was such purity, such a clean smell, that I am driven to have a swim whenever I return for a visit.

I love to drink really pure water. I love the flavor of clean water. There is nothing my body craves more than hydration. Every system in my body uses water. I am sure that you know that the majority of the body is made up of water. The blood, tissue, and all individual cells depend on water exchange. The importance of water circulation through the lymphatic system is now clearly understood. As we move, our bodily motion circulates water throughout our lymphatic system. Water is life.

In the wilderness I need water badly. If I do any physical activity water replacement is required. I need to find pure water because if it is contaminated with viruses and bacteria my body will get sick. I need to clean myself and my clothes. Water is absolutely important and central to my physical survival. If a person lives without water for more than a week it is thought quite unusual. In any survival situation finding water is of the utmost importance.

Water is important in the spiritual wilderness. Water is used as a positive picture of the New Birth, spiritual cleansing, the indwelling Holy Spirit, and many aspects of the Christian life. Actual water is used in baptism as a symbol of the transformation of the believer. Baptism is a public profession of faith. In our spiritual wilderness we must continually allow the Father to supply us with His water. Jesus uses water as a metaphor for the real life our Father supplies. Jesus continually invites "whosoever" to drink freely (Rev. 21:6; 22:17). The beauty of His spiritual water is that it is in vast supply, is always pure, and is easy to get. We need to keep filling our bottles so that we will never be caught short in the journey of life.

The apostle John records the many references that Jesus made to this Living Water in his Gospel. At the beginning of His ministry, Jesus made it clear that His ministry would be one of transformation. He changed the water in large clay pots, dirtied by hand washing, into wine of the best quality (John 2:1-11). With God it is all about what is going on in the hearts of men. He wants to take the stale, dirty waters of our lives and transform them into celebration. What Jesus brings, He first brings to the heart of a person. He makes it clear from the outset that the old wineskins of our religious effort will be insufficient for the life that He will bring (Matt. 9:17). Just as the Father supplies for our physical life day by day, so He supplies the power for our new spiritual life, day by day.

In the third chapter of the Gospel of John we see the famous conversation with the religious expert, Nicodemus. Here Jesus uses the terminology of the New Birth which has become so common today. Jesus refers to being born of water and the Spirit (v. 5). Immersion in water was the sacrament Jesus gave to represent what happens at the New Birth. Paul used this same terminology when speaking to Titus of salvation: "the washing of regeneration, and renewing of the Holy Ghost" (Titus 3:5). Although the Blood of Jesus atones for our sin, it is the power of the Holy Spirit that makes us alive to God. Just as water purifies, rejuvenates, and empowers the human body, the water of the Holy Spirit continually brings to life and rejuvenates our spirit. This continues from the moment we receive Jesus into our hearts.

We are baptized as a symbol of this new life and a testimony of Christ's presence. Paul used water baptism as an illustration for the Romans of the source and purpose of the Christian life (Romans 6:1-13). The purpose was not just to forgive our sins but give us the power to overcome sin. The waters of the Holy Spirit purify our spirit-man. The waters of baptism were a perfect identification for Paul. He identified the immersion with Christ's death and coming up out of the water with Christ's resurrection. This was not just a mental exercise or a mental assent for Paul. This was where he drew his **identity** from.

The cleansing water was identified with the cleansing work of the indwelling power of the Christian life, the third Person of the Trinity, the Holy Spirit. Paul's appeal was not primarily to a theological position. He was speaking of an **indwelling reality** that grew in its scope, both consciously and unconsciously, day after day and year after year. Paul had reckoned himself dead. He had died daily for so long that he could pronounce, *"For to me to live [is] Christ, and to die [is] gain"* (Romans 6:11; 1 Cor. 15:31: Philippians 1:21). What a glorious yieldedness he had attained as he allowed the water of the Holy Spirit to flow through him.

We have the story of Jesus' conversation with the woman at the well (John 4:1-42). Jesus made reference to the similarities and differences between physical water and the water of life that He would provide. Many people live to sustain basic needs. Others live to satisfy many different superfluous desires. Sooner or later such pursuits will leave a person thirsting for more. You have to give the woman at the well credit—as a woman of great unquenched desire she really had sought satisfaction. In this world we may have many years of fanciful happiness, if we are fortunate enough. Sooner or later fulfilling the desires of the flesh will leave our God-space aching. This woman was a deceived religionist, like so many today in the professing church. In spite of her religious beliefs she kept right on fulfilling the desires of her flesh.

Notice how she jumped at the chance to receive **living water**. She had worn herself out trying every way she could to get some satisfaction but to no avail. Immediately she asked, "How?" She was still in the earthly realm, thinking she could save herself a trip to the well but Jesus had set the hook. It is His presence and power that gives life. As soon as the woman received the water of life she could not contain her good news. Life begets life and her living water overflowed even to her skeptical neighbors who, understandably, doubted her credibility.

I remember clearly when I was first saved. At an intellectual level I really didn't 'get' a lot of the Christian life but I knew that I had moved into the realm of life. Suddenly everything was fraught with new meaning and power. It just made sense to share what had happened to me. What was compelling about my witness at that time was the knowledge that my friends and associates had of my degenerate life. It stood in contrast to what I suddenly put forth as my regenerate life. I was not smart enough about the Bible to win many arguments. Nevertheless, everyone knew that something of a different order had taken place, even with my poor representation of the pertinent facts. Like the woman at the well I had suddenly moved from death unto life. This life from God is of the most astonishing sort. It proceeds from the infinite abundance of God.

My dear friend, I have to admit much amazement about those who talk about being 'happy' in the Christian life. The record shows that Jesus used the word happy once. He said that if we embraced the slave-leader model that He showed us and did what He said, that we would be happy (John 13:17). Happy is a human feeling. Joy is a God-imparted emotion. Like its giver, the Holy Spirit, joy comes from outside of us to dwell within. Joy is the bi-product of letting the Spirit of God have His way. My happiness usually depends on circumstances. God's joy has sustained me through all manner of difficulties like water replenished in a well as quickly as it is drawn out. Isaiah was a prophet of future joy and saw God's salvation in just these terms in Isaiah 12:3: *"Therefore with joy shall ye draw water out of the wells of salvation."* There is nothing like finding a well of pure water in the desert. Jesus is our well of salvation in this present spiritual wilderness.

The waters of Bethesda were famous. The story was that an angel occasionally dropped by to stir up the water. When he did, the first person into the water was healed (John 5:3-4). The very name,

Bethesda, is associated with healing. Many such associations exist to this day. From hot springs to salt springs, waters are associated with healing. Jesus became the true healing waters for a man by Bethesda with just His word (John 5). Rather than have him wait for the stirring of those waters Jesus simply told the man to get up and walk. I love this. In contrast to the chance arbitrary visitation upon a fortunate person associated with Bethesda, Jesus healed a man who did not stand a chance.

The comment of the Scripture is that Jesus often healed all who came to Him. The only recorded exception was in His own home town where they were used to Him (Matt. 8:16; Matt. 13:58). There is healing in the atonement. Healing has been part and parcel of the ministry of Jesus and His followers. Oh, the simplicity of it all, if we will believe! Our poor modern minds have been trained in the facilitation of illness since childhood. We often have to get backed into a corner before we will call upon Jesus for His healing. Jesus' well of healing is still available, since He is the same yesterday, today, and forever.

Most of what we see today is hucksterism rather than giving freely. I wonder whether Jesus would bother renting a stadium and taking up an offering? Jesus said we have freely received and that we are to freely give. When we manifest the genuine gift of healing, people will chase after it in the way people thronged Jesus. Such astonishing healing advertises itself. We must allow ourselves to receive His faith and gifting. When we do this, Jesus will freely work through us and then we will see what we truly have believed for. Jesus is quietly walking through the Church in our day healing His children. I have noticed that some of the most profound healings are done quietly and simply. After all, God needs no ego gratification because He is so completely humble. He does all things to the perfection of His will and time.

Jesus described the continual flow of God's Spirit in the believer's life as "rivers of living water" that flow out of their bellies (John 7:38-39). Some Charismatics and Pentecostals use this description as proof of a baptism of the Holy Spirit. I think, instead, that this is an acid test. Every believer needs to ask himself, "How's my river flowing?" Just a cursory observation of the daily lives of professing believers leaves one with another question: "Where's the river?"

If we were to look at the downright miserable professors of faith, all those folk who are trying to talk themselves into believing with positive thinking, and the gang of 'right people', there is one common denominator. None of them have a **river** flowing out of their **belly**. Water is the great identifier of the 'current-event' Christian—a Christian who has God in him **today**. This river has an unstoppable source which is our infinite God. There is no reason for it to flow weakly or dry up.

It is my contention that a great deal of negligence must occur for the river of God to quit flowing. There are a lot of songs about jumping into God's river nowadays but that is not Jesus' terminology. Jesus tells us that if we receive Him that the river is in us. We do not have to go any further than faith in Him to receive all that He has. That is the choice irony of faith. Men are not necessary to impart a blessing. God has removed intermediaries to His presence. God is present within each individual who comes to Him by faith. It should really be obvious where God is by the rivers of water. These rivers will bring joy, testimony, salvation, and healing to whoever we meet. Through us, God wants to take salvation on the road!

As a general principle, Jesus rejected the ceremonial washings of the Jews. He did do a symbolic washing to teach us something about the direction our hearts will take once they have been cleansed by His blood and the indwelling Holy Spirit. In washing the disciple's feet Jesus put Himself in the place of the **lowly servant** (John 13:5-7). Jesus holds forth servant leadership to His disciples as the evidence of His cleansing. Show me a leader who has a servant's heart and I will show you a person who understands, at its very core, the message of Jesus.

This ceremonial cleansing also points to the disciple's spiritual cleansing. Peter became extreme and wanted more than the other disciples but Jesus said that the washing of the feet was sufficient. The cleansing that Jesus gives us is sufficient. We do not need to add our own emulsifiers and emollients in any human effort to assist in the cleanup. The outward washing represented the inward cleansing of His forgiveness.

John gives an account of an event that amazed him (John

19:34-35). The soldier who put a spear in the side of Jesus caused **water** and **blood** to flow from the wound. Some physicians would say that this was either because Jesus died of a broken heart or that the pericardium was pierced which allowed both water and blood to flow out separately. What is obvious is that this event made an indelible impression on John, to the point where he reassures us that his testimony is true. He brings it up again in his first Epistle General (1 John 5:6-8). The water, the blood, and the Spirit bare witness on earth. Jesus' blood atoned for our sin.

Faith in Christ's atonement cleanses us by the regenerative power of the Holy Spirit. Faith in His resurrection means we can live by the life-giving power of His Holy Spirit. The power of His death to cleanse us stands in juxtaposition to the power of the Holy Spirit who raised Him from the dead so that we can live for Him. The water speaks of the perfect cleansing and power of our salvation. When we feel weak, overwhelmed, and unable, we have the facts to encourage us. Jesus' perfect salvation means that His strength will be made perfect in our weakness (2 Cor. 12:9).

Paul speaks to the Ephesians about marriage. He presents the redemptive work of Christ as a model of sacrifice for husbands in relation to loving their wives. Paul states that this redemptive process is the washing of water (baptism and sanctification) and the Word. The stated purpose of this washing is to present the whole body of Christ to Himself, *"not having spot, or wrinkle, or any such thing; but that it should be holy and without blemish."* (Eph. 5:27). The very desire of Jesus in His redemptive work was that our hearts would be **clean**. Our cleansed lives will show His glory more clearly than any sermon or church program. This is the purpose of the process of sanctification. God's plan is not just to save us from sin's consequences but from sin's power (Romans 6:14). It is our work to cooperate with the Holy Spirit and God's work to build us into the individuals that He wants us to be in order to represent His Kingdom (Eph. 2:8-10). Because we are forgiven our sins, we are privileged to allow God's Spirit to enable us to unlearn lifelong patterns of evil behavior.

God's water will **change** the tone of our **language**. An unfortunate reality in our day is dirty words from allegedly cleansed mouths (James 3:11). James argues from the same place as Jesus on this matter (Matt. 12:34-37). Jesus rejected outward pretension without God's water. He said that what comes out of a man defiles him. It is not surprising that many professors of religion speak with such foul language today considering the general atmosphere we are living in. We might do well to mourn with Isaiah who said, *"I am a man of unclean lips, and I dwell in the midst of a people of unclean lips"* (Isaiah 6:5). If the great prophet Isaiah could admit that his language was corrupt maybe those who speak corruptly today ought to just admit it, too.

When we were children we used to chant, "What you say is what you are!" What truth we spoke. James was telling us to let God's river flow with pure words. Peter cautions us that if we speak we ought to speak as the oracles of God (1 Peter 4:11). Peter is saying that our mouths should speak as if they were God's mouth. This is why we need to let the sweet water of God flow so that we may represent the King and His Kingdom.

Jude and Peter use one negative reference concerning God's water. They both say that teachers who do not allow Christ's river to flow in their lives are like clouds that promise rain and deliver none (2 Peter 2:17; Jude 12). There are few things worse than having the hope of quenching your thirst dashed by a 'fluffy cloud person'. A lot of folk who minister God's Word speak big and deliver little. The river of God is not flowing from their belly. The letter is killing instead of His Spirit giving life (2 Cor. 3:6). A lot of preachers and teachers may provide ministry a mile wide but the trouble is that it is often only an inch deep. They have not allowed God to water and empower the Good News of His Word. Remember, life always begets life.

In the book of Revelation, Jesus renews His invitation to anyone who is thirsty to *"drink of the water of life freely"* (21:6; 22:17). In the wilderness we may have to search high and low for water. There are clear demarcations in this present spiritual wilderness. There is a remnant in our day who will take Jesus up on His gracious invitation. In heaven there will be no imperfection where mankind is concerned. Instead of an unseen river flowing out of our bellies we will see the river of life flowing directly from the throne of the living God (Rev. 22:1). What a time and place of fulfillment there will be by the River of God! At that time, our God will be all in all and we will be perfect through the resurrection power of Jesus.

Water is a metaphor that God uses repeatedly to illustrate the life-giving power of His salvation and His Spirit. Volumes of commentary have been written about the passages I have used. There are a few interesting arguments over word usage. Sometimes I wonder whether Bible scholars aren't prone to the ego-gratification of finding something new. Maybe we should be looking at bigger pictures that will help us live more fulfilled lives. For instance, do we need to argue and prove that the blood and the water mentioned in the Gospel have a concrete parallel with what John is writing about in his first Epistle General? Ultimately, I don't think it needs proving. Arguing such small points seems to be like the biologist who will study an interesting tree without reference to the greater forest. Each one of the word pictures that John and the other New Testament writers paint for us look to me like photos in a mini-album. The question is, "What common theme or themes emerge that will help me to live now in this present spiritual wilderness?"

Foremost, when we take all of these references together we get the idea through word pictures and repetition that there is a **vast abundance** of life to be had and lived. The Source of this life is making it clear that all we need do is ask Him for it. Isaiah prophesied about this outpouring long before Jesus came upon the scene (Is. 44:3; 55:1-7). I love his reference about floods on the dry ground. In the arid Middle East, floods in the desert are not a common occurrence. When it rains in the desert there is fantastic beauty and growth. The lavish language of the Scripture should inspire us to expect lavish and abundant life, here and now. If we are lacking this abundance it may be because we have been spiritually thick and slow to believe. Jesus repeats Himself over and over again for the purpose of turning our spiritual lights on. He simply wants us to believe that He will abundantly water us.

In the times of the Patriarchs, digging and maintaining wells was imperative for having adequate water for your family and flocks. This is why we see the records of special watering places. It was vitally important for Isaac to establish the wells that his father had dug (Gen. 26). It is clear that we need to give extensive attention to the borders of our lives. We need to establish the wells of true fellowship with other believers and honest meditation on God's Word. We need to let God's river flow from our belly, edifying ourselves by praying in the Holy Spirit.

Spiritual prosperity will bring as much jealousy against us as temporal prosperity brought against Isaac. There will always be the Philistines who wish to block up the wells. It is likely that the Philistines of old represent men or spiritual beings who wish to stop up the rivers of life that flow out of us. We must then allow the Holy Spirit that the Father has placed in every believer to carry us along like a leaf riding along on top of the stream during the fall.

I am fascinated by the complexities of irrigation in our modern world. In the Lower Mainland, east of Vancouver, as well as in northern Washington State, it is common to see the canals and irrigation ditches which crisscross the landscape. What is more interesting are the vast sprinkling systems that propel water over acres of vegetable fields. It is now big business to supply and maintain mobile watering systems over vast acreages for the purposes of irrigating areas that could never have been reached by irrigation one hundred years ago. What a vast difference from the little wells the Patriarchs used for their family flocks.

Maybe Jesus wants us to understand that we can have more water than we need. The whole underlying idea of a seeming over-abundant supply of the water of life would be **sharing it**. Instead of just taking care of our own, as the Patriarchs did, we can be like modern sprinklers in this most harsh spiritual desert. What a lovely picture I have in my mind right now of 'Portable Sprinkler Christians' taking the water of His salvation, power, healing, and hope wherever they go. Isn't this the reason that the testimony of the first century Church was so effectual? They had received freely so they spent their time and substance to allow everyone around them to taste of the water of life.

The revelation of our Source will continually allow the remnant to live abundantly in the midst of a spiritual wilderness. The remnant will be wells, some hidden and some well known, where others will come for refreshing. It seems that our Father is not very discriminating about who He will give His water to. He will not use the arbitrary measure of the religious person or group in finding one deserving of mercy but calls to all the undeserving to receive freely (Rev. 21:6). It is clear that His mobile temples (or mobile sprinklers if you like) will share His water with whoever is willing to receive it. Be one of God's mobile sprinklers where you are, my friend. Have water that you may give water,

Your Fellow Well,

Henry

# CHAPTER 6

# *Fire: Are You A Burning Flame?*

Dear Fellow Traveler,

*I* remember a November day over a dozen years ago as if it were yesterday. The morning was quite cold for Victoria in November, perhaps thirty-eight degrees Fahrenheit. I dropped by a friend's house in the morning to visit and have coffee. I found him in his vacant lot with a very large bonfire, as big as any I had ever seen. He had huge pieces of wood, ruined furniture, two sofas, and many other combustible items that would have filled a large living room from floor to ceiling. The fire itself had sustained flames of about ten to twelve feet in height and was about ten feet in diameter.

My friend quickly enlisted my help to carry other items to the fire. After a while we sat on the sofas adding items from time to time and just watching the flames. A little later I went and picked up coffee and snacks. We spent all morning sitting by this giant fire visiting, laughing, and relaxing. Finally, the flames started to slow down so we got up and threw a ruined sofa in the fire. A little later we threw in the other one. The pleasantness of that morning still makes me smile.

I have been close to fire all of my life. Our cabin had a wood and coal stove. From the time I was seven it was my job to take some paper and sticks and kindle fires on cold mornings. I would hunt for little stray logs lost from log-booms on the lake and tow them home. The next job was to cut and split multiple cords of wood. I did this every year, stacking them in our boathouse and under the back stairs. This provided the wood that was needed each year to keep the fire going. I often tended the fire at different times during the day.

As an adult, most of the homes I have lived in have had wood-burning stoves. I have had a life-long association with fire. I have camped often and sat by the fires I made. I have many happy memories of bonfires and burn piles. To this day I can remember the burnt smell of my grandfather's brick incinerator at the edge of his retirement house in rural Manitoba.

We take heating and cooking so much for granted. In a way, we have removed ourselves from the imminence and necessity of fire. We contain the fire neatly in an insulated burner. We can carefully control the flame and temperature of our cooking. I would venture to say that fire is a little **wild** for the average person today. Perhaps the average person would feel uncomfortable using and handling fire. Our closest encounter might be the pre-packaged pressed logs that we use for aesthetic pleasure in our fireplace which are easily lit with a match.

In stark contrast to our domestication of fire, it is still necessary in its raw form in the wilderness. There are few skills as important as being able to quickly make a fire. Any light or heat you will obtain in a survival situation will come from fire. It takes care, skill, and energy to build and maintain a fire. It is necessary to nurse it at the beginning and control it at all times. Fire purifies what goes inside the body and warms the outside of the body. Even under optimum conditions you will not fare very well without fire. Your whole wilderness camp will revolve around your fire. You will thrive only so far as you are able to skillfully use fire day by day.

In our present spiritual wilderness it is essential to have fire as well. In his annunciation of the Messiah, John the Baptist placed the immersion of the Holy Spirit and of fire as the apex result for whoever would believe (Matt. 3:11; Luke 3:16). John could have said that Jesus would make His followers nice people, wonderful witnesses, great singers, or eloquent preachers. John did not speak of these abilities because that was not primarily what Jesus came to do. Jesus came to provide salvation for humanity so that they could become a fireplace for the Spirit of God.

It astonishes me how easily His servants are swerved from His central purpose for their lives. How few have **FIRE**! If John the Baptist and Jesus said this immersion in the Holy Spirit was central, then why do few leaders point to the fire Jesus and John had? Why don't they even listen to them, for that matter? If the fire of God is central to our spiritual survival and foremost on the mind of Christ's forerunner, as well as Jesus Himself, then where's the fire?

You cannot do much in this present spiritual wilderness without fire. Jesus said it is the Spirit that makes us alive and human flesh will not help at all (John 6:63). The apostle Paul said that the letter kills but the Spirit makes us alive (2 Cor. 3:6). Paul explained that when God gave the Law to Israel it was wonderful. He goes on to say that it is much more wonderful that all who believe can receive God's own Holy Spirit. The fire of God's Spirit in us fulfills the righteousness of God's law in us (Romans 11:15ff; 2:25-29; 8:1-5).

John the Baptist named the Holy Spirit as the One who would immerse Christ's followers. He used fire as a physical example of what this essential immersion would be like. This baptism is not simply something that happens as a pronouncement from God's throne. John is describing an experience for the children of God to continually participate in. We all know what fire feels like. If we get too close, it singes us. If we are too far away, we get cold. When there is fire, there is light cast within sight of it.

Let me assure you, fellow traveler—you will know when you have God's fire and you will know when you do not. This is all about relationship. I knew when I fell in love with my wife because it burned inside me. I had to have her, to know her. So it is in the spiritual realm—I have to have Him, I have to know Him, because it is set on fire in my heart. Our heart is set on fire and our mind is thus illuminated.

I want to clarify what I am not speaking about for a moment. Although my relationship with Jesus has an emotional dynamic, God's fire is not an emotional binge. It is not speaking with other tongues as the Spirit gives me utterance although I highly recommend we seek this infilling. It is not some sort of worship experience, singing, laughing, dancing, or any other outward expression. These may occur. In fact, when God's fire falls something has to happen. Nevertheless, mere outward expressions or any carnal emotional outbursts in His name are not God's fire. I am speaking of an inward reality that makes a person aware of God's fire.

The Person of the Holy Spirit taking up residence in the human soul is the powerful privilege that is the apex experience of our salvation. After all, what is greater than God living inside a person? What a parallel we see of this great presence of God in the story of the inauguration of Solomon's temple. Solomon does all of his stuff. He is very careful in his dedication of the Temple. There are lavish sacrifices made and nothing was held back from the Lord. Nevertheless, the party really gets started and the excitement really mounts when God Himself comes to dwell in the Temple by His Holy Spirit (2 Chron. 5, 7:1ff). The evidence that God was dwelling there was the fire and the smoke that came from God's own presence. He did what no other God had done. He made it clear that He accepted the sacrifices. He evidenced His presence in such a manner that no one could deny that He was at home.

So it is with the individual set ablaze by God's Holy Spirit. I remember what happened right after Jesus came into my heart. It was like the purest love I have ever experienced. It burned in my heart. I had been brought from death to life and I was full of wonder that He could ever have chosen me. It was His fire in me that was the excellence. From the first days, Christ in me was perfect. I sure wasn't perfect but everything Jesus' Spirit led me to do was perfect. That is the great misunderstanding within the religious establishment of our day. God does not fix us up like some sort of spiritual renovation project. God burns us up with the refining fire of the Holy Spirit. We don't work, He works. He does it all and we cooperate with Him (1 Cor. 3:18). Our work is to let go and let Jesus' Holy Spirit do the work—that's it.

So we come to the question posed in the title of this letter: "Are you a burning flame?" Every believer becomes both God's messenger and God's message (2 Cor. 3:2). This is why He immerses, saturates, baptizes with the Holy Spirit and fire. God makes His ministers a flame of fire (Heb. 1:7; Ps. 104:4). This does not just refer to angels but to the Priests in the Temple. In the New Testament model we all are kings and priests unto God, heirs of God, and joint-heirs with Jesus (Rev. 1:6; 5:10; Romans 8:17). Every believer is a minister, called of God, and gifted by the Holy Spirit for the Kingdom. We all are powerfully sent, propelled outward with the fire of God burning in our hearts. The fire of God will always get the appropriate attention better than any 'strange fire' that we might offer (Lev. 10:1-2).

Jesus manifested the fire of the Holy Spirit throughout His life. Strange to us in this day of pallid emotionalism and pretentious passion for God would be the white-hot zeal that Jesus displayed in His day. Silently He made a cat-of-nine-tails out of leather, as he watched the normal daily business at the court of the Gentiles. The Gentile's court was the place where the heathen was supposed to come to draw near to God and be converted. After hours of crafting, Jesus wielded His whip with wild power and frenetic action. He beat and drove out those who would denigrate the purposes of God (John 2:17). In our culture Jesus would be arrested for assault and jailed. Yet how much of church fellowship is involved with the same foreign interests of crass commerce and opportunism?

Jesus' zeal cost Him. The emotional fires of zeal will often make those who don't possess it uncomfortable and resentful. Jesus was single-minded. His approach was militantly over the top and Jesus desired only His Father's glory. This fire of zeal not only alienated Him from the religious elitists but even from His own family (John 7:1-5). They looked at Him strangely (Ps. 69:8-13). He just went too far! He was always fasting and praying! He made all kinds of grand pronouncements about who He was and what was required to serve Him! Who did He think He was? They were as good as Him! Many fine, upstanding people reproached Him. Jesus said that there will always be reproach for those who follow Him (Matt. 10:25). Isn't that why so many people 'cool it' with the zeal thing? After all we don't want to go too far, do we?

The plus side of the fires of zeal is the credibility it gives to our message. The remnant instinctively knows this. They have figured out that the fear of man brings a snare (Prov. 29:25). When God's fire is in our heart and on our lips, we care about representing our God. Those who see us may not wish to participate in this New Life but they can be sure that they have encountered it. Even the salesman knows the power of believing in the product they are selling. We have a Friend who can fix all of our ills, forgive all of our sins, and heal all of our diseases. White-hot zeal that accompanies the telling of the Good News will make the message much more compelling to the hearer.

In the wilderness fire is the great purifier. As I stated in an earlier letter, you simply must boil water and cook food or risk life-threatening consequences. In the lakes and rivers of British Columbia there is a virus that causes an intestinal woe called Beaver Fever. The cleanest looking lakes and rivers can have viruses from the fecal matter of beavers and other animals. If you drink the water you will soon be disabled by the resulting diarrhea and cramps. The best looking meat can have parasites. You must apply strong heat for an adequate amount of time. Then the water and food is useful. Until it is cooked, it is of no use.

Human nature is the same. God's Spirit must refine us with fire so that the corruption of our human nature is destroyed. Then God has something He can work with. We must constantly be cooked and boiled so that our fleshly nature does not contaminate the message and presence of the living Christ. Our efforts must be to allow our spiritual fire to be lit every day by the Holy Spirit. If we don't, we should not be surprised if we start to smell spiritually rotten and stagnant.

God's fire purifies us. Any honest look at mankind will confirm any doubts you may have about our need to be purified. Some years ago I was irritated when a Bible teacher told our class that the closer you got to God the more you became aware of your own sin. Time and experience have taught me it is true. I know I need continual purification and I have never met anyone who didn't. That is because in my flesh (humanity) dwells no good thing (Romans 7:18). The flesh has to be put to death. Just as physical fire purifies flesh so spiritual fire purifies flesh.

The Bible talks about the children of God being manifested

(1 John 3:1-3). John says that if we hope to be part of God's resurrection manifestation that we must be focused on purifying ourselves as He is pure. Then we will be manifested **now** as well as later. In the same way that the Blood of Jesus cleanses us from sin, so the fire of God renews us so that we are able to put off all the superfluous deeds of our carnal nature. Like taking off our dirty clothes and putting on clean ones we are cleansed by Jesus. His Holy Spirit clothes us in robes of pure white (Col 3:7-17; Eph. 4:21-24; Rev. 3:4-5).

In the wilderness, fire repels pests. In Northern Ontario they compose songs about the insects that can bite and torment you. Fire and smoke help to repel these pests as well as other unwanted visitors in your camp. The smell of smoke is a powerful insect repellant. Have you ever taken a hot needle and put in on the behind of a tick? He leaves immediately without leaving his head behind to get infected and cause harm to your body. If you do not have fire in the forest you may literally be eaten alive by insects and bothered by animals.

In the spiritual wilderness the fire of God in your soul will **repel** the infernal forces of **Satan**. It is much harder for the devil to deceive someone who is on fire for God than it is for him to deceive someone who is very cool towards God. The devil's full-time job is to get us to enter into temptation. We are a lot less likely to even be tempted when we are empowered by prayer in the Holy Spirit. All Jesus had to do was show up and the forces which held men against their will screamed for mercy (Mark 1:23; Luke 4:34). The Spirit of God in Jesus was the same Spirit depicted in Revelation 4:5: the seven lamps of fire burning before the throne of God. The heat and light of the Spirit of God powerfully repels the forces of darkness from our lives.

One of the important aspects of the Gospel that we hear little of today is the need to embrace **trials** and **tribulation**. Trials and tribulations are compared to fire because they are part of God's purifying toolbox. In contrast to the touchiness and sensitivity we hear today, Peter's Epistles rage against evil in the church. They are a wakeup call for those who want an easy Christian walk. Peter states plainly that we should not be astonished by all the troubles we get as if it were strange. He believed and taught that fiery trials were part and parcel of following Jesus (1 Peter 4:12-15). Nobody who wants to follow Jesus will get a pass. Peter compares these trials to the sufferings of Jesus and the reproach of Jesus. His footnote (v. 15) confirms that these trials are a result of persecution and misunderstanding. They are a result of faithfulness to Jesus not the consequences of our sin or crimes against the state. Peter debunks the notion that self-inflicted trouble should be regarded as God's fiery trial.

As well as Jesus, Peter may have had Job in mind when he spoke of tribulation. Job was assured in the midst of his trouble that the trials he was suffering would bring him forth "as gold" (Job 23:10). As you heat gold the impurities float to the top and the gold is purified. The Scripture speaks of the work of sanctification with the same kind of terminology. Peter had come to understand that fiery trials are revealing. They show us where we are both strong and weak. As God applies the heat of troubles we discover our sinfulness and weakness. We then call on Him for purification and strength. I have never really enjoyed this kind of fire. Its application is difficult and humbling. It usually looks a lot better after a set of trials is over and we see the results. Peter called this burning process the "trying of our faith" and states that it is more precious than money (1 Peter 1:7). Why? It has eternal consequences that give glory to God.

We will be **judged by fire**. Paul speaks about our life activities in the context of hot fire (1 Cor. 3:13). Only what is non-flammable makes it through a fire. Paul was frustrated at the worldly attitude that he had found in the leadership at Corinth. He sternly warned them that they had better build 'the called out ones' with supernatural power and materials. This goes beyond a personal application and refers to the church as well. We need to understand that just as a fire vigorously consumes whatever is flammable, so the holy flame of His perfection will burn away anything that did not originate with Him in the first place. Self-examination and self-purification are to be a central part of our walk with God. We need to participate in the life of the Holy Spirit in such a way that we can say with Paul, *"And herein do I exercise myself, to have always a conscience* *void of offence toward God, and [toward] men"* (Acts 24:16).

I have experienced the fire of the Holy Spirit at many times during my Christian life. As I mentioned earlier, I received an immersion in the Holy Spirit within a few days of committing my life to Christ. When the Holy Spirit indwelt me, it was like fire came up through the floor and warmed my soul white-hot. I spoke with other tongues but was more aware of God's power. I also experienced a sense of Mind and purpose that has influenced my life ever since. It has taken years of listening and study of God's Word to discern the difference between my own emotions (flesh) and His Holy Spirit speaking but I have grown to hear Him quite clearly. The process has been very hard and painful. Jesus always keeps His promise that the Comforter would lead us into all truth and cause us to understand His Word (John 14:26; 16:13).

I came to Jesus a desperately flawed and evil individual. When I was first saved I had little concept of how far my sinfulness went. If I had known, there is no way I would have even started the journey. Heart and motives are the most important things. Without a clean heart, pure motives, and God's fire, I may pray and work for Jesus all day long with little result. Yet the Bible teaches that my heart is deceitful and desperately wicked and asks the ironic question, *"Who can know it?"* (Jer. 17:9-10). Of course the answer is the same for all of us; only the Lord can know our hearts. His Holy Spirit deals with our motives and intents so that we are able to walk right and get answers to prayer. It is only His fire that can burn away the soiled intentions of our fleshly souls.

What a **dirty job** the Holy Spirit has as He dwells within us. I marvel that the third Person of the Trinity would take such a dirty job. Yet there He is day after day working in us. Immediately, I found out that His presence was like a big flashlight that He shone around inside of me. He took the Word of God and convicted me of sin. He made me aware that God was always watching me. Before I was born again I had lived a soulish and selfish life. As well, I had some real personal upbringing issues. There were all kinds of habits and thinking strongholds to overcome. The fire of His conviction and purpose set me free from bondage after bondage. He would take the words from the pages of the Bible and build them into realities.

The Holy Spirit would take the words of the Bible and burn me with conviction. If I sinned against knowledge I would burn with shame and guilt. I thank God that He has been able to make me sick of myself. The deeds and practices I loved became repulsive to me. His fire enabled me to embrace His Way.

An old minister once told me, "It's not the mistakes you make when you are young that you live to regret but the ones you make when you are old." It is disappointing to find out when you are older that even though you know truth, you don't always end up doing truth. The fiery trials of life showed me I was much less of a man than I thought I was. The disclosure of my utter weakness by circumstance and failure brought the dross of my life to the surface. This allowed the Holy Spirit to burn it out of my life.

This burning away of the self-life seems to happen in **cycles** (Romans 5:1-9). I believe God's goal is to bring each of us to total dependence. He showed me time and again that, aside from Him, I was a complete bankrupt. I have found that the only way to please God is to **completely** depend on Him for everything. Let's all listen to the cry of Saint Paul in his old age when he says of his ministry that its excellence came from the Holy Spirit and not from himself (2 Cor. 4:7). Paul continually stated that although he was doing God's things that it was really God working in him. That is where all of my learning and understanding have taken me so far—utter dependence.

Simple abiding and prayer in the Holy Spirit in my day to day life have released the fruit of the Holy Spirit. I look back and realize that I was raised a bit tough. I am actually glad my parents pressed responsibility and toughness on me but it has been a hindrance to the fruit of the Spirit. I learned the wrong lessons from some of my difficulties and hardened myself further. Over the years the fire of God has **burned away hardness** and put His fruit inside of me. Because I am more secure in God's love I don't need to protect myself from pain. God wants us to be transparent so that people can really see Him. He does this by imparting His fruit to our souls (Gal. 5:22-25). As our soulish nature is burned away, the nature of Jesus is seen in more and more situations.

I am amazed at some of the entertainments I enjoyed ten years ago. Now I find it hard to look at most of it and impossible to enjoy it. I really do not enjoy a lot of the legitimate pleasures I used to. Many activities, hobbies, sports, as well as personal ownership, have all lost their luster. I have to say that this has little to do with any effort I have made to live a 'more godly' life. In fact, I fail often when I resolve to be 'good'. God has outsmarted me. He just takes away my evil and fleshly desires along with so many human ones. I have lost much of my inclination for even those things which the church crowd deems legitimate. If I just yield to the fire of God's presence, day by day, He changes my inclinations and desires.

At other times, if I sin, Father has given me a whippin'. When this happens I become convicted. There are times that I have reproached and loathed myself. In my case, there have been times when it has been really necessary to get sick of myself. Besides, I can't stand the sensation of not feeling His pleasure for long. When you have God's fire in your life it is a misery to be deprived of His presence. God's work in me will continue. It's just whether I want to do it the easy way or the hard way because He will have His way.

God's fire has taught me to pray while working, traveling, and walking. I often used to feel really bad about not praying. I learned to pray a bit each time I felt bad. Soon I prayed a lot but not in a way that people could see. I found myself using private moments to hear and listen for God's mind for situations rather than trying to 'tell' God what He already knew, over and over again. I found that I often could not express what I felt to God. This is where my heavenly language has been of the utmost importance. As well, there are groanings that cannot be uttered (Romans 8:26). I believe these groanings are spiritual burdens for prayer, directed by the Holy Spirit. These breathings of the Holy Spirit have brought me around to what the real needs and issues are that need to be prayed about. These groanings have also quickened my faith so that I can move from supplication to thanksgiving. Once you know you are going to receive something, do you keep asking for it or do you start thanking God for it?

My friend Al and I learned the most important lesson about prayer. We learned that if two people pray in the Spirit that God will renew them. We started to just get together and 'let her rip'. That was our term for praying in the Holy Spirit with all of our heart and strength. We would pray in tongues until we knew God's presence was upon us. Then we could effectually pray in known tongues for circumstances and people. What has been amazing is that wherever I find people who will 'go for it' in prayer, I find true fellowship and edification. I have since come to understand that the tongues aspect is not necessary for God's power to fall but the 'going for it' is absolutely necessary. Tongues make it easier though, because God's prayers that He prays through us are always perfect.

This is how to **build a fire** in the spiritual realm. We found that three vital times of this kind of prayer per week, with two or more people present, was enough. Often this would only consist of ten to twenty minutes but the power and strength it gave us was tremendous. I have taught others the value of this practice. It seems that people either get it or they don't; period. You have to be willing to completely let go of yourself and **CRY** out to God (Jer. 29:13). When you bring this dynamic into a group of praying people it revolutionizes the meeting. Suddenly, there are profound answers to prayer and profound growth for those who participate.

Be aware that those who will not participate will usually react violently with objections like, "I don't see the use of this, God is not deaf," "I don't believe that you need to speak with other tongues," or "that's not my way of doing things." I really do not blame people for feeling that way because they have never been taught about or seen the fire of God in human souls. They think prayer is about them and their desires and needs. They come with their lists and desires and never find out what the Father wants. What they don't understand is that prayer is an encounter with the Living God and He is a consuming fire (Deut. 4:24; Heb. 12:29). Although many people are blind to the value and power of this kind of prayer, I can't live without it. I need all the help that I can get.

It is easy to start a fire with a blowtorch! I had a friend who used to use a tiger torch to light his fireplace. He needed no kindling and only a couple of minutes with such a large and intense flame. We have the 'Tiger Torch' of the Holy Spirit available. Revival fire is not a 'someday' thing. If I have God's Holy Spirit living in me today with the fire burning bright, I am revived. If we can get together without the resistance and hindrance of unbelief and personal agenda and pray in the Holy Ghost, we will have revival (Jude 20). Today many people put revival way out of reach but revival can be lit by the tiger torch of the Holy Spirit right now.

I know you are out there, you beautiful remnant you! You are like the five wise virgins who purchased oil. You have trimmed your lamps and you shine (Matt. 25:1). The unquenchable presence of the Holy Spirit makes you iridescent to those around you. At your homes and in your businesses you are overflowing. You are the light set on a hill so that everyone can still see Jesus. I love you!

Wishing You Much Fire,

Henry

# CHAPTER 7

# *Is Your Food Really Food?*

Dear Fellow Traveler,

*A*nyone who knows me will tell you that I really love good food, especially when I am really hungry. I live in a part of the world where food is abundant and inexpensive. My choice of and access to food is pretty much uninhibited. Still, I will usually opt for simply prepared meat and vegetables with certain fruits. You see, over the years I have eaten much as the rest of America has eaten and found that it causes me to swell up in front and behind. I learned that a lot of the snacks and meals that I can eat when I am out do not contain any food value at all. In fact, certain fats and most sugar can really disable my metabolism and make me gain weight. So like most guys pushing fifty I have to learn new lessons in self-control—but I sure do enjoy eating.

In the wilderness, living off the land requires a lot more energy than it requires to open the fridge and choose your meal. When I was being schooled in emergency survival techniques I was given a two foot stick, rounded at the ends. All along the pathway to and from our camp there were empty plastic containers tied to stakes. As we walked we practiced hitting the containers. The idea was that if a person was caught in an emergency situation they could throw a stick at a potential meal. This would be about the only way a person would be able to subdue an animal to kill and eat it. My instructor told me that there were no vegetarians in an emergency situation. Even the idea of killing an animal ourselves is abhorrent to the average American because we have been so far removed from the killing of animals. We now call it food 'production'. The fact remains—to survive in the wilderness your ability to get food is central.

Many of the skills involved in finding food are only academic to me since I have only read about them in books and never really practiced them much. I would be hard pressed to find the appropriate plants to feed myself in the forest or the desert. It really becomes important to know what is and is not really food. The art of tracking and stalking animals, not with guns or trucks, but on foot and with the most primitive tools, is something that takes a great deal of skill and practice. How do I prepare an animal once I have caught it? What parts of a cattail can I eat and which do I discard? Which plants and fruits are edible and which are noxious and poison? In the wilderness I need to know the answers to these and many other questions. Suddenly my survival depends on a whole different set of rules and principles.

At salvation we were plunged into a spiritual wilderness here in America. We did not really know that it was a wilderness. Many have not figured it out to this day. Jesus said, *"Man shall not live by bread alone but by every word of God,"* (Luke 4:4). But who will help us to learn to eat? There is no shortage of volunteers to teach us. There are ministers of all denominations and non-denominations. There are all kinds of cults and schisms who will diligently school us. There are on-line Bible gurus grinding their favorite little axes. There are 'Christian' chat rooms, book stores, home study groups, TV ministries, and Para-church organizations. There are Bible Schools and correspondence schools teaching every angle that man has come up with. There are dozens of translations and transliterations that purport to make the Bible more 'understandable'. In the midst of this confusing din we must here the voice of the Lord saying to us "take and eat" (Eze. 2:8-10; Isa. 55:1-3; Rev. 10:9).

In my case I had a fascinating array of people stepping up to teach me. I worked with a Lutheran minister forty hours per week, pumping gas. He was very willing to instruct me from his perspective. I had a Brethren teacher trying to get me to believe the way he did. I was led to the Lord by an ex-convict. He and his friend baptized me and taught me my first Bible lessons as well as many Pastors would have done. I had three street preachers from Pentecostal, Salvation Army, and Brethren backgrounds who taught me how to witness and share my faith on the street. I had Charismatic Christians at a street church giving me instruction. I had a lot of instructors and I was really teachable. What a lot of arguing many of them did to get me to believe the way they believed.

Fortunately, I had the Holy Spirit living in me. Even then, I could sense Him turning on the lights as I read the Bible. I remember distinctly expounding on Romans to a person in a coffee house about the third week I was saved. I had no background in the Bible and no idea what all the circumcision and uncircumcision was all about. I was still able to communicate some of the basic truths of the Bible to that person. I learned early that if a person was going to experience anything that the Bible is talking about that it would be imparted by the quickening power of the Holy Spirit. Reading the Bible is not primarily an exercise in cleverness or intellectual prowess. It is an exercise in imparted life and spiritual experience. Feeding on God's Word from the Bible is not just knowing about truth but experiencing the truth that is recorded there for us.

Over the years I have seen many who have had more opportune beginnings than I did fall by the wayside. They were taught correctly and brought along correctly but failed of the grace of God (Gal. 5:4). I have seen some people emerge from terrible teaching and backgrounds to become very fruitful. The key that I have seen for successfully following the teachings of the Bible is an honest heart. I call this honesty being a 'Student of the Word'.

I will tell you what I mean when I use the term '**Student of the Word**'. The Student of the Word is humble. They know that God has exalted His Word above all of His names and that the Bible is not like any other book (Ps. 138:2). The words within the Bible are living and when received, become life to the disciple. The learner understands that the Bible does not **contain** the Word of God but **IS** the very Word of God. They do not come to prove their point but to be instructed on the mind of God. The Student of the Word never regards the study of the Bible as primarily an academic exercise.

Reading the Bible is a life-changing encounter with the Living God.

Such a student will handle the Word of God as a workman handles precious materials (2 Tim. 2:15). They will ask the Holy Spirit for light since He is the only One who can open God's Word to us. The Student of the Word will grow more and more sweetly reasonable. In the presence of God they are receiving with meekness into their very being the Word of God in the same way a tree provides sap for a grafted branch (James 1:21). The true Student of the Word has received from God real love for His truth. Because of this they will not be damned with the world (2 Thess. 2:10-12).

Once you are committed to being a Student of the Word there are some utensils to help you ingest God's Word. Jesus said that we 'live by' God's Word. I think this is a direct parallel with natural eating. You only 'live by' food when you take it in and digest it. The very molecules, fats, amino acids and sugars from the food become part of our body. Knowing all about the food is insufficient to produce digestion. The food must be **internalized**. It is the same with the Word of God. There is so much more to ingesting God's Word than just reading and understanding it. There are many important factors that will allow us to truly assimilate the Word of God into our being and thus to partake of its life-giving and transforming power.

The Holy Spirit of God is very important in the digestive process. He is the One the Father sent forth, in Jesus' name, to teach us all about the Living Word, Jesus (John 14:26). He is our Bible teacher who will lead us into all truth (John 16:13). Most of the Bible is easy to understand, intellectually. It is clear what God likes and hates because His commandments are very clear. But how do I put it all together? How do I learn the relationship between Law and Grace? How do I incorporate what I have learned into my daily life? Where does my power and ability come from to obey God's Word?

The unction or anointing of the Holy Spirit is what takes the words off the pages and builds them into our lives (1 John 2:20). We are His workmanship created in Jesus Christ to do good works (Eph. 2:10). Most of our trouble comes from reluctance, at certain points, to follow His holy leadings. Our trouble is not so much with understanding but doing, because to read the Bible is to constantly be convicted for change. We should always be encouraged that the third Person of the Trinity will enable us to obey by quickening the Word of God to our hearts.

It is important to have certain truths of the Bible pressed upon our hearts. The best way to do this is by **memorizing** Scripture. This has fallen out of vogue in many quarters. I was impressed recently to hear of a discipleship program that required its students to memorize a list of four hundred Scriptures over the first year. Most of us would be quite daunted by such a task. Not long ago it was very common for evangelical Christians to memorize both single verses and longer portions of Scripture. It is good to compare this practice with feeding information into a computer. If you do not program the computer it is hard to expect it to do anything. Memorizing Scripture allows the Holy Spirit to bring it to our memory and thus feed our souls day by day. It also gives us ammunition to stand against the temptation of the devil.

I have found meditation on the Bible at least as important as reading or studying it. You may read the Bible through like a novel, over and over again, and not ingest its message. Meditating on God's Word is like chewing your food. It is really important to thoroughly chew your food to get maximum digestion. As a person quietly and thoughtfully reflects on the truth of God's Word they will constantly see new light shed upon it. David spoke of meditating on God's Word both day and night because he was delighted with all of God's words and ways (Psalms 1:2; 63:6; 77:12; 119:15, 48, 148; 143:5). Our spirit is a lot like our minds or our bodies. If you put garbage in you get garbage out. If you put good things in you get good things out. If you meditate on God's Word you will dispel so many of the ugly things of this life and find that you have ever increasing peace.

The process of memorizing Scripture **produces faith** in our hearts because the Word is no longer something we know about but has become something that we know (Romans 10:17). As we digest God's Word it becomes part of our being and we find that our soulish chains fall off. We are thus freed to do the things that God has told us. Since Jesus is the Word, He comes alive in us. He quickens us by His words which are spirit and life (John 6:63). Do you see the unity of the Holy Spirit and Jesus' words? The Holy Spirit will never do anything unless it is in alignment with God's Word and God's Word is always quickened by the Holy Spirit. This is why, as God's Word is planted in a humble, receptive student that it will always produce faith. This faith expresses itself by a greater and greater conformity to God's Word and will.

When we place God's Word as the only arbiter of life's affairs we then start to discover what God promises and what God does. This will lead us into **praying God's Word**. We will pray about the things we know He wants to do. As we do, we will be sure that He will do the things that we ask (1 John 5:13-15). We will ask for the things He wants us to have because we will be sure that He will give them to us. So many of the best prayers that we learn to pray are the ones that pertain to our understanding of His will, our conformity to His will, and our abilities in His will. These are all aspects of total submission to God's known will, not vague prayers to fulfill some unknown purpose. We are told that as we knock, seek, and ask that we will have open doors, we will find truths, and we will receive answers (Matt. 7:7-11). What could be better to rehearse before God than prayers that originate from His own Word?

One of the greatest eye openers for me was to start to look at the **big pictures** that the Bible presents. For close to fifteen years I had studied and taught the Bible from a devotional point of view. That was very much in keeping with the teaching and lives of my mentors. I was most interested in finding ways to practically apply the Bible for personal obedience. This tended to produce in me a small picture approach to the Bible. That is, I was really mostly concerned with what the Bible might say to me, personally. I would reach my moral conclusions from God's Word concerning the things that were big issues in my personal life. This produced a tendency to give more weight to truths that were opened to me in more profound ways. Some of these 'revelations' were not big picture, life-changing stuff for people around me. They just were not very important. At times I became unbalanced because I was not putting what I learned into an over-arching larger picture.

The most fortunate part of my Bible College education was my choice of colleges. The teachers there were of the first quality and very true to conservative textual criticism. What happened at school was that I received a beautiful thumb-nail sketch of the 'big picture'. I learned a lot less than I thought I would. However, I was able to organize what I had learned over the years and place it into perspective. Since that time I have really not changed my views on any major doctrines very much. Since the Holy Spirit has brought balance to my life I do not agonize that everyone does not believe like I do.

I have found that there are few things that I would really battle over. I would probably only spend time reasoning with people who were sincerely committed to being Students of the Word. I have found that it is nearly impossible to convince somebody, who has great esteem for their own point of view about the Bible, that they might be incorrect anyway. Such discussions may be what the Bible describes as vain babbling (1 Tim. 1:6, 6:20; 2 Tim. 2:16; Titus 1:10, 3:9).

The first big picture items that will cure imbalances and untruths are the **Gospel accounts** themselves. Matthew, Mark, Luke and John tell me what Jesus taught, said, and did. Jesus is our interpreter. When I am not sure about something, I go back to the Gospels again and again. Jesus draws perspective and clarification in relation to the Older Testament, the Acts of the Apostles, the Epistles and the Revelation of Jesus Christ. The whole Bible relates to what Jesus did and said as the Living Word. I have read the Gospels more than any part of the Bible by far. I teach them to people more than any other part of the Bible. I preach about the ministry of Jesus more than any other part of the Bible. I am astonished and amazed at what Jesus taught and what He said that His followers would be able to do. I have found that there was not much subtlety in Jesus' message. The Gospels are an account of His direct and clear instructions for those who would follow Him in faith and obedience. I believe that a great deal of error occurs when we look away from Jesus, the Living Word.

The second big picture item is the **Book of Acts**. Although the account of the early Church is not all about doctrine, it gives invaluable instruction about how they dealt with the most difficult problems of their time. We see the immersion with the Holy Spirit, the 'power-encounter' presentation of the Gospel, the beginnings of Church order and government, and the early instructions for Gentile believers as it related to Law-keeping. Luke gives us a great historical record and we see repeated themes occurring throughout the book. All through the Acts we see the direct involvement of the Holy Spirit in directing the corporate Church as well as the lives of individuals. We can be very confident that He still desires to lead and direct in the same way today (Heb. 13:8). The whole book is an extension of the Gospel of Luke and shows what Christ did through His Church by the Holy Spirit.

The third big picture item is the major themes of the **Epistles** (letters). Jesus' death on the cross and resurrection from the dead are the basis for the themes of atonement, redemption, justification, sanctification, and glorification. Salvation by grace through faith is done with God's foreknowledge, election, and predestination. God's direct involvement in our lives becomes the basis for the themes of adoption, sonship, and assurance of salvation. We find Paul's vision of the church, the realms of leadership, and the gifting of the believer throughout. There are exhortations to a holy life in just about every Epistle written. There are also stern warnings to the believer about the judgment that will happen if they neglect to obey the Bible. All of these themes flow from the head of the Church, Jesus Christ. They are extensions of His teaching and plan for us.

The final big picture is the account of the **Older Testament** as it relates to creation, the fall of man, original sin and God's dealings with man in the record of Salvation History. We now see the Older Testament as fulfilled by Christ's perfect life, His atonement on the Cross, and His resurrection from the dead. We are to use the Old Testament stories as examples of how God deals with men (1 Cor. 10:11). Jesus affirmed that believers would experience a greater righteousness than the Law ever produced. He summed this up by saying that the least in the Kingdom of God would be greater than John the Baptist (Matt. 11:11). In other words, anyone in the Kingdom of God will have the righteousness of the Law fulfilled in their life through Christ's imputed righteousness (Romans 4:22-25) and the Holy Spirit's power (Romans 2:26; 8:24). We see Jesus reflected in animal sacrifice, the construction of the Tabernacle, the order of the Priesthood, the construction of the Temple and the promised coming Messiah. All of the prophets were looking for Shiloh (Messiah, Christ) to come (Genesis 49:10). Thus Jesus doesn't annul the Older Testament, He fulfills it (Matt. 5:17-19).

So we come to the point of asking, "Is your food, really food?" The Bible is pure food value but for many, a huge mental block remains. Like the customers at a drive-thru many people are impatient. They do not want to wait too long for their sustenance. They complain, "I find the Bible hard to read or understand." The same people will not turn off the TV and spend an hour really getting into it. They are too lazy to do their own food preparation so they both do not eat and die spiritually or they eat that which is not spiritual food. As I mentioned earlier, there are some dangerous non-food items that many substitute for the meat of God's Word. People who continually consume these spiritual non-food items banish themselves to baby-land for years to come.

Some people are '**Lost in Preparation**', using ministers and the TV evangelists as substitutes for feeding themselves. If TV preachers have become your main food source you may easily end up with warped theology that will overthrow your faith. You can do more for yourself by reading the Bible for twenty minutes a day and it's free! There are some very good ministers at different churches but they are not able to teach you what you need to know in forty-five minutes on a Sunday morning. Even if you make it to the mid-week service every week (the Pastor's wild dream) it will take you years to learn the basics. Poor Pastor! You expect him to be deep, interesting, powerful, and have a word that is just for you every week. How in the world can that happen?

There is a word just for you every day my friend. The Bible is the instruction manual and if you study it day by day you will grow. We eat food day by day and we must partake of God's Word, day by day. The most brilliant preacher in the world cannot do as much for you as you can do for yourself by becoming a diligent Student of the Word. Further, no true minister of the Word is ever 'bothered' by being disturbed during the week by a sincere inquiring congregant. As a Pastor, I always loved it when people phoned me during the week with questions about God's Word.

There is a famous and popular TV preacher I have watched who often only uses one Scripture to reinforce the half hour talk he gives each week. This is an acid test for preachers and teachers of all kinds. How many Scriptures do they bring to bear and how do they handle them? In many churches there is really quite a shallow presentation being made that will not grow Christians or convert the ungodly. Many TV evangelists speak much about prosperity and ministry support. They bring a twisted sowing and reaping message—warped to entice you to give their 'ministry' more money. They are short on the cost of discipleship and long on what will cause people to follow them.

What a benefit ministers and TV evangelists can be when they preach a lot of balanced Bible. I can think of one TV teacher that is doing so many so much good. This is because they bring a lot of balanced Bible truth to bear on the need to live the sanctified life. I love ministers who have come from an audience with the living God with words of truth burning in their hearts. They have done the appropriate amount of Bible study and preparation. As true work-men, they will cause their people to be enlightened and grow. Unfortunately such people are becoming more and more rare. There is no substitute for a home-cooked meal, is there?

Those who are part of God's remnant know that they will have to answer to God one day so they are diligent studiers and ardent learners. They will not be judged by a Word that they are ignorant of but by one that has already dealt with them in this life. They are careful who teaches them because they already have the Teacher inside of them. Deep calls to deep and remnant people seek others of like precious faith. They want to compare notes and stimulate one and other to good works (1 Cor. 2:13; Heb. 10:24).

Some other people get '**Lost in Translation**'. There are an increasing number of translations that have appeared in the last thirty years. When I was first saved there was the KJV, ASV, NIV, and NASV. Many conservative believers were troubled about the NIV at that time. There had been little need to retranslate the Bible into English for a few hundred years but in my lifetime we have seen an exponential growth in translations and transliterations. Transliterations are not translations at all. They are filled with extra figures of speech or words that the writer believes will make it easier to understand the Bible. In other words it is the writer's **opinion** about what the Bible means. This practice constitutes adding and subtracting from God's original Word which is very dangerous and forbidden by Scripture (2 Peter 3:16; 2 Tim. 2:15; Rev. 22:18-19).

I have an unpleasant suspicion that some of the growth in translations has to do with money. There is no copyright when a publisher sells the King James Bible. Copyrights make the Bible translation a piece of intellectual property. They are owned by publishing companies. There is more profit to the publishers. More and more versions mean more and more sales which mean more and more money. The writers of these 'bibles' make a profit as well. Christian publishing and music have changed from a ministry to the church into a growth industry. In fact, Christian publishing and music are among the fastest growing sectors in their respective fields. Is it possible that such increasing markets can push profitability concerns ahead of doctrinal purity?

This may be good business but I believe it is causing more and more confusion about what the Bible says. Many of the new versions are perversions of what the original Greek and Hebrew parchments actually say. The whole practice of multiple translations promotes the idea that the Bible is hard to understand and needs to be interpreted. Few in our day realize that men gave their lives to accurately translate the Bible into the languages of the people. During the Dark Ages the lay person could not read or even see a Bible because it was thought the laity was 'unlearned' and would not be able to understand its Truth. Most of the Bible is simple and easy to understand until men come along with their beliefs and interpose them onto translation. Eventually, the alleged translation looks nothing like what the original parchments were saying.

I am afraid that ministers have not protested enough. It is not uncommon to hear all kinds of translations and non-translations quoted by pulpit men today. Often they are doing it to prove a point that doesn't matter. They should stand and protest the fiddling and diddling with God's Holy Word. I am sure that this is what Jesus was referring to in Revelation 22:18-19:

*"For I testify unto every man that heareth the words of the prophecy of this book, If any man shall add unto these things, God shall add unto him the plagues that are written in this book: And if any man shall take away from the words of the book of this prophecy, God shall take away his part out of the book of life, and out of the holy city, and [from] the things which are written in this book."*

Those ministers who use translations that add and subtract from what the original Greek and Hebrew copies say are in grave danger.

Thus we have Babel confusion in the church with all of our 'versions'. It is a time like the time during the Judges when every man is doing what is right in his own eyes (Judges 17:6). In contrast the Bible speaks of the Way we walk in, clearly: *"And an highway shall be there, and a way, and it shall be called The way of holiness; the unclean shall not pass over it; but it shall be for those:* ***the wayfaring men, though fools, shall not err therein."*** (Isa 35:8). God's promise is that even a fool who follows Jesus will not fall into error. What does this tell us about those who want to make the Bible difficult when it is simple?

I remember giving a New Testament to a fellow I worked with a number of years ago. He had never looked at the Bible and was happy to read the New Testament. I had shared quite a bit of my experience with him night after night. He came back a week later and shared his impressions over lunch. He said, "It is clear that Jesus was the greatest man who ever lived but I do not want to serve him. Jesus said not to divorce my wife and marry another and I have done that. Jesus really seems to discourage accumulating money and I love money. I want to get as much money as I can." Further conversation revealed he understood very well what the message of the Bible was. I was astonished. He had read the Bible once and was very clear what Jesus required: a total commitment. He did not want to make a total commitment. If an unregenerate man can understand the Bible that clearly after one reading I am sure that the children of God will understand the Bible if they would only care to.

Other folk find themselves '**Lost in Explanation**'. Some people are unduly affected by books and commentaries. I am sure that this has been a problem for me over the years. I would tend to pick books about topics I was interested in and then go overboard with the topic for a season. More than once I came up with some pretty haywire ideas. After reading one of these goofy books I realized the power I was giving the author. I took most of my books and gave them away to a minister. I have given away the equivalent of another library since that time and it has been very helpful and therapeutic for me.

Don't get the impression that I don't read books or use reference material. It is just that so many people give such credence to everything some authors say. Some writers have a huge following based on their personalities. They are people's heroes. Some writers publish with a theological ax to grind or certain underlying slants that many people are unable to pick up. Books written by men can give us insights into the Bible but must never become a **substitute** for the Bible. The Bible is such a unique book because it is God's Word and no other book can help us nearly as much.

There is still another important aspect of eating in the spiritual wilderness. It has to do with our ability to really accept what Jesus has said at face value. It is amazing how many believers will think you are mad if you actually get literal about some of the things that Jesus has clearly said. We'll talk about that in my next letter. In the mean time, love and embrace God's Word. As Paul the Apostle said when he was departing from Ephesus for the last time: *"And now, brethren, I commend you to God, and to the word of his grace, which is able to build you up, and to give you an inheritance among all them which are sanctified"* (Acts 20:32). As we feed on the words of Jesus we will be built up and we will overcome. Remember, you are a champion. Receiving with meekness the engrafted word,

Your Fellow Student,

Henry

# CHAPTER 8

# *Crazy Talk*

Dear Fellow Traveler,

*I*t is one thing for a person to say they believe the Bible from cover to cover. Upon examination one may wonder how many people are really able to swallow all of the truths that Jesus has presented to us. There seem to be major aspects of God's Word that cause people consternation today, even if all we do is talk about doing them. In effect, to obey Jesus in some of the ways He has laid out for us seems like 'crazy talk' to people. These nice church-going folk will become so agitated over some truths that they will tell you that it just isn't sensible. They may tell you that you need to be more balanced. Others will tell you that you are going off your rocker. Jesus ran into this reaction more than once so it should not surprise us if there will be times when we will seem crazy in seeking to obey God's will.

Many people argue for a balanced presentation of the Word of God. The word balance is the key here. **Whose balance** are we talking about? Are we trying to negotiate a reasonable lifestyle in this world that will please both us and the Lord? It has been my experience that the word balance comes up when people feel we are going too far with an idea. I want to be clear that I do not advocate cut and paste Christianity. This is the practice of taking a few teachings of Jesus and being extreme for extreme's sake.

Nevertheless, an honest look at what Jesus said will make some of our lifestyles look a little weak and pallid in comparison. There are certain themes that come up again and again in different places in Jesus' ministry where His answer is pretty much uniform. I believe in a balance that compares spiritual with spiritual to come up with convictions to live this life (1 Cor. 2:13). This may make us look unbalanced in this crazy end-time world. It may also make us appear crazy to the present American end-time 'church'. It will not seem unbalanced in the sight of our heavenly Father, whom we are commanded to obey.

My intention is to express a few simple things that Jesus said. Check your reaction and see if you agree or disagree. My goal is that we might think about what Jesus said without the mitigation we have learned from others or created for ourselves. Some of these subjects are not even seriously discussed or taught in our day. Obviously my small list of examples is not meant to be in any way exhaustive. I know that the remnant would agree that the point of God's Word is to live it out in this world, by His grace. The heart of the true believer is to obey, but do we? Jesus said some pretty troubling things. There have been many times where I have been challenged by His Word to go far beyond current conventional wisdom.

Jesus started out His ministry talking like a man without much business sense. In the context of doing good to evil people during the Sermon on the Mount, Jesus tells us to give to anyone who asks us for money and to lend to whoever asks us for a loan (Matt. 5:24). During the Sermon on the Plain, in the context of loving our neighbors, Jesus goes even further and tells us to lend without expecting to be repaid (Luke 6:30-36). Do you know anybody who handles their finances like that? I know one person who has been close to that standard. She says that she could take a cruise around the world (about a one hundred thousand dollar value) for what she hasn't been paid back.

Let's face it, very few people take Jesus seriously about what He says concerning giving and lending. Most people are looking to be smarter and more sophisticated than this. We may reason thusly, "Why lend to somebody who can't pay me back?" Jesus tells us that if we don't live this way there is nothing special about us. Even most of the commentators that I have read qualify giving and lending according to using good sense. I believe Jesus was infinitely intelligent and could have qualified His statements about giving. Instead, it seems clear to me that He goes out of His way to make a blanket statement. Could it be that Christ's design is to expose our greed to us?

Jesus goes further than this. Jesus associates faith in God as our Father with action. He tells His followers to sell their goods and give alms (Luke 12:25-34). It is clear that this would not be the kind of stewardship that would be popular today. This smacks much more of Socialism or even Communism, than Capitalism. In fact, this quote has been the bill of sale to the Christian for these political philosophies in times past. In reality, giving away legitimately earned possession never works unless people do so willingly with a conscience toward God. It is interesting that Jesus lays the truth out and lets us deal with it, and the truth with us. Do we believe Him? Then we will sell what we have and give it away. Let's face it; this is too extreme, so we seek to mitigate the extent to which we take such Scriptures. Each person has to decide to what extent he will respond to what Jesus is saying. The way Jesus frames His commandment leaves that between the individual and God.

Jesus was speaking to profoundly oppressed and poor people in Israel at that time. None of the social safety nets we take for granted existed in any form and loans were extremely hard to get. In His dealings with the rich young ruler we may have some insight to how Jesus would handle us in America. The rich young ruler was the exception, not the rule in Israel. He was rich. America is like the rich young ruler amongst the nations in our day. Even our poor have much more than most people in the rest of the world.

Jesus loved the rich young ruler (Mark 10:21). The young man was really trying hard to please God but he was in bondage to his money. Jesus has the cure for all things that bind us—being loosed from them. Jesus had the cure for the sickness in the soul of this fine young man. The cure was to get rid of the 'stuff' and learn the power of generosity. I believe that Jesus' cure of divestment would do many wealthy church-going professors of religion in America a great deal of good, too. I am sure that this cure is indicated for many. When we reject Jesus' teaching about deceitful riches, the Word is choked out and we go away sad like the rich young ruler (Mark 4:19; 10:22). We may practice a form of godliness but we will be stalled because we said no to His call.

In contrast, it is clear that these considerations do not apply to many professing Christians. That is because they are already up to their eyeballs in **debt**. They cannot really give because they owe so much! Jesus taught a simple and frugal lifestyle was central to a godly walk. He said we should not even worry about food, drink, clothes, or shelter (Matt. 6: 24-33). I do not think that birds or lilies worry at all, do you? At the time of this writing it is often in the news that Americans owe more and save less than at any time in history.

Are we 'lily' Christians today? Are we content with food and clothing or do we want more (1 Tim. 6:7-9)? It is pretty clear that many Christians pay no attention to Paul's statement that we should owe no man anything except our debt of love (Romans 13:8). This attitude was Paul's response to Jesus' many commands to live a simple life. In God's eyes, indebtedness is a grave responsibility, comparable to slavery (Prov. 22:7). I cannot tell you the people I have seen go shipwreck over the years because of financial obligation or dissonance.

I have given the equivalent of at least a tithe for most of my Christian walk but in all honesty I can find no Biblical evidence that it is a New Testament practice. I have weighed every argument in favor of tithing and believe that they are all gross misuses of Scripture. I am sure that the New Testament teaches something much more **powerful** and **pervasive**. The New Testament teaches the complete **ownership of God**. Paul called himself a Hebrew of the Hebrews (Phil 3:4-6). If anyone was going to teach tithing it should have been Paul. Paul did teach the principles of sowing and reaping (2 Cor. 9:6), faith promises (2 Cor. 8 & 9), complete giving of our being to God before giving a gift (2 Cor. 8:1-5), and weekly giving (1 Cor. 16:2).

Paul was careful never to call Christian giving a tithe. The point is that to call Christ Lord is to **possess nothing** of your own. Therefore we must check with the **Boss** about how much we may

**keep** and what things we may possess. I'm not kidding! Everyone has to decide before God what he or she will give and who they will give it to. Paul taught that it was a matter of individual conscience and Paul called it **giving** (2 Cor. 9:7). A person cannot call tithing giving or giving tithing.

Many teach that it is a sin not to tithe but they have a problem. The tithe in Israel never related to money but to the agricultural return of the land (Lev. 27:30-32; Num 18:26-28; Deut. 14:22-23). This return was animals and produce. It was to be eaten by those offering sacrifices and given to the Levites in lieu of having no inheritance (Deut. 14:27-29). The rest of the people who had no producing land would give no tithe, just offerings. Are there any Levites at your church? It was to be brought for those who served in the Temple. You cannot call the church the storehouse because it is not the Temple.

Hopefully, most people who have a very narrow interpretation about tithing would not have us be circumcised or keep a Saturday Sabbath! Jesus did not bring that for us! There is no evidence in the Bible that any Gentile believer ever tithed or was expected to. Isn't it amazing how this topic can push people's buttons? Is it pushing yours? Are you able to consider the truth of what I have said? Remember, tithing is a less demanding principle than the ownership of God. It is likely God would have us do much more than a tithe. Most professing Christians do not practice tithing anyway. Only seven percent of all Protestants tithed in 2004.[1] Many other believers do so under duress or without an understanding of the New Covenant practice of giving.

It is clear to me that if we taught the principle of **generosity**, which is characteristic of the New Testament model, that we would have unprecedented financial support for any work of God. Even the world gets behind a worthy cause. People need to know that they should provide for their leaders in a better way than the average person (1 Tim. 5:17). Many affluent people need to get delivered from their ten percent religion (if they even have it). They need to support many ministries, poor people, and helpless with a large percentage of their income. Again, the question should be, "What can I keep?" There is such a beauty in giving because we have the opportunity to reflect the image of God. Rather than a rule of law we see the heart of grace. Tithing is the Law and giving is grace. I would take a church full of givers over a church full of tithing people any day of the week. The most generous people in God's Kingdom are the givers because they know no boundaries where generosity is concerned.

The whole concept of the **ownership** of God is expanded upon throughout the ministry of Jesus, culminating in the Cross. The sermons that Jesus preached set forth a standard of holiness and obedience that would quickly undo the religious dilettante. Lust is like the sin of adultery, hate is like the sin of murder, and pretending to be religious is the hateful offense of hypocrisy before God. Jesus systematically tore down men's phony self-recommendation to God. In the middle of the Sermon on the Mount Jesus recommended that His listeners 'settle out of court' (Matt. 5:25; Luke 12:58-59). In other words, just beg for mercy from a kind Father. Jesus' teaching does not just help to clarify God's will for men. Jesus shows the thoughtful soul that there is no way a man can do God's will on their own! All men are **undone** by the perfections of God's plan. We are exposed as frauds and failures by our inability to obey God; by our downright unwillingness to do His will. Jesus forces every man to make a decision. We either admit our complete need or proudly reject His salvation.

Then Jesus moved on to what love really is. You have to love God first. How do we do this? Jesus gives us the answer: *"Thou shalt love the Lord thy God with all thy heart, and with all thy soul, and with all thy strength, and with all thy mind; and thy neighbor as thyself."* (Luke 10:27). It is the practical applications that we struggle with. Jesus stated that we need to take up our cross and follow Him (Matt. 16:24). At the center of this command is a life of self-denial. We do not just yield up to God our own selfish ways but our legitimate human rights. We must give Him our American right to live our lives as we please. We are called to follow, not only in a symbolic death to ourselves, but a very real daily death to our selves (Luke 9:23).

Jesus cuts to the core issues—**join His family** or put your own family first. In this present spiritual wilderness you will meet many people who have died spiritually because of their preference for their family over God. Jesus wanted us to be clear that He would disrupt family harmony along the Cross line (Matt. 10:34-39). Many people do not take this part of the Bible seriously. Some cater to wicked children who become more set in their ways as their parents seek to 'rescue' them. Many people spend a lifetime of God's time and money running after their children. These parents are often God's main hindrance to their children's salvation.

Many adult children knuckle under to their carnal parents. They feel that it is too much of a hassle if their parents don't understand them. Many children compromise because of their desire for their parent's money. Sometimes people just love their parents more than God. I have lost count of the spouses who gave up on God because their husband 'wouldn't let them go to church' or their wife 'just didn't enjoy going'. In the wilderness the test will come. Is it going to be family or is it going to be God? Jesus promises one hundred-fold eternal rewards for those who will forsake family for His sake and the Gospel's (Matt. 19:29).

The family of Jesus must have been annoyed when they wanted to see Him and He said that the crowd was His family (Matt 12:46-49). Could it be that they thought He was a bit crazy just like some of the leaders and crowd were saying (John 10:20)? Had they come to take Him home? Perhaps they thought that Jesus was just going too far. It was a very serious business to scold and reprove the religious leaders the way He did. When Jesus went to His hometown did the people know His whole sordid history? Did they know He had been born out of wedlock? Was Jesus brought up with reproach and misunderstanding? It is clear that He was just too familiar to the people in His hometown (Matt. 13:55-58). Because of their preconceptions, they could receive nothing from Him. Jesus' own brothers didn't believe on Him but rather goaded Him to come out and declare publicly that He was Messiah (John 7:37). Jesus suffered misunderstanding with silence and grace. He was fully God and He knew it.

Do we really take Jesus seriously? If we do then it should not astonish or hurt us when people say we are mentally deficient or of the devil. Jesus said that such accusations would simply be part of the cost of following Him (Matt. 10:22-26). That is why the Lord told us to sit down and count the cost (Luke 14:28-29).

Many do not want to take self-denial to its logical conclusion, but Jesus does. He said that we must **hate** our lives and give them up to gain eternal life (Luke 14:26; John 12:25). To most professing believers that is just crazy talk. If the truth were to be told very few Christians in America take Jesus seriously at this point. They love their lives and families very much. They want to stay away from 'extreme' things and just have a happy and secure life. After all, isn't that our right? What a stark contrast to the hundreds of millions of suffering Christians around the world who have forsaken all. Jesus compares both His death and our death to self, to a seed that must 'die' and be planted to bring forth life (John 12:24). Out of the grave Jesus rose incorruptible. Out of our death to self, the new life of Christ lives through us, incorruptible (1 Pet. 1:4, 23). The Word of God that regenerates us is incorruptible and what it produces is incorruptible.

Where are the crowds of leaders teaching this truth as the forefront of their message? Where are the calls to self-denial and death? Where is the cost of discipleship? Where are the crowds lining up to sit at the feet of Jesus and learn of these things? The oppressed Jewish nation left Jesus after hearing the preaching of the Cross. Is it surprising that a self-involved, self-indulged, lazy, blind, Laodecian, North American church finds other aspects of the Bible to talk about (Matt. 16:24; Mark 8:34, 10:21)? I think not! Jesus' Cross is my cross. I am not just to 'identify' with the Cross, I am to embrace and carry the Cross. The Cross is our only hope, beloved!

Listen as Jesus 'ramps up' His claim on His followers. He told them that they must eat His flesh and drink His blood. Today, we are clear on Christ's meaning but His listeners probably had no idea what He meant. We might not join a cannibalism club, even with Jesus in charge. What a stumbling block! So they left and followed Jesus no more (John 6:66-68). As soon as Jesus revealed the Cross as His method of salvation He was rebuked by Peter (Mark 8:31-34). Many want salvation but Jesus' invitation isn't to 'come and dine' but to 'come and die'. In the spiritual wilderness the only way to survive is to die to your whole world of plans and learn to listen to His plans. It is the only way to live.

Early in my walk it became clear that Jesus advocated a walk of non-violence. It is clear that Jesus was non-violent and did not advocate the use of force to extend His Kingdom. Jesus said not to seek revenge for injury (Matt. 5:38-41) and that citizens of heaven are not to take up arms to further His Kingdom (John 18:36). Over the years I have heard powerful stories of the suffering of believers and their families. I understood that they did the right thing in not resisting but I doubted in my heart that I would have such grace. My spiritual dad told me about refusing to fight in the Second World War as a conscientious objector because of His faith. He spent three years away from his wife and family in a work camp. Many professing Christians would despise such behavior.

I have been impressed at the lavish extents that Jesus goes to tell me that I shouldn't fight back. As a young man I could stand the idea of suffering violence upon my own person but I knew that if anyone ever tried to hurt my wife and kids that I could react violently. As I thought and prayed about it I realized that the violence I was concerned about was lying dormant in me. I had to deal with it. The remnant will have to deal with this latent violence too. Then, when our persecution comes, we will take it like Jesus. Most of the Christian world has had to work these problems out while being persecuted and killed.

Why is it that so many professing believers enjoy violent entertainment and video games, sometimes as a family activity? It astonishes me greatly that people cannot make this connection. If the Lamb of God is living in our heart, what pleasure is there in feeding violence? Does this not set us up for possible failure in the future as well as grieving the Holy Spirit? It is clear that many of us need to understand the consequences of violence. Jesus knew that if violence in the heart of a person was fed that it would grow like a monster. The "Sons of Thunder" wanted Jesus to call fire down upon those who rejected Him. Jesus told them that they had the wrong spirit (Luke 9:54-56).

I believe I understand the mindset of people who shoot at abortion doctors in the name of God. In fact, if we look inside ourselves, we can probably understand a lot of what we call senseless violence.

These shooters use the same deductive logic that Christians did when they joined the war against Nazism. Both decisions are made on the basis of a greater good and protecting innocence. It is hard to think of anything more innocent than an unborn child. Yet, Christ knew how well we can convince ourselves that we are right. He said, "No," to the use of physical violence in His Kingdom because he knew how twisted we can become. As God said to Cain: *"But if you do not do what is right, sin is crouching at your door; it desires to have you, but you must master it."* (Gen. 4:7 NIV).[2]

There will always be wars and believers will have to decide whether they will participate or not. That is why I am so worried for those who profess Christ and **rejoice** in war. It is so human to think we are right and implore our God to fight on our behalf. Such emotions and thoughts are natural and would be legitimate, except, to be a Christian is to change citizenship (Heb. 11:14-16; Phil 3:20: 2 Cor. 5:20). Citizens of heaven are ambassadors for peace and yet so many professors of religion argue for wars and political expediency. There is no doubt in my mind that they really think these worldly tools will produce God's results. We do not have to do much study of history to find that this nationalization of the Christian religion has been practiced by countries and empires. I am not a pacifist but I wonder at the Jingoism I encounter in the American church. Maybe we just aren't taking Jesus seriously about being non-violent. After all is our citizenship in heaven or here on earth?

There are many more examples that I could give of important aspects of Christ's teaching that we choose to modify or ignore. Whether I am even right about these subjects is not the point. The point is how fervently we adhere to the teachings of Jesus. True students of His words have to give the same weight and context to His teachings as Jesus did. In this present wilderness it is imperative that we do not fall in with current prejudices about the application of His Word or the practice of the **real faith** that Jesus came to impart to us. I want to give one more example that is central to fellowship in the Church and yet is rarely practiced.

Jesus taught us how to deal with sins and hurts between each other in His Body. His motive for keeping relations right between believers is also clearly expressed. Christ states that Christians in fellowship have His authority to bind and loose heavenly things on earth (Matt. 18:18). That is, when Christians gather they change the very direction of earthly events. Secondly, Jesus said that two or three Christians who agree in prayer on any matter will receive the answer to their prayer (Matt. 18:19). A third time, Jesus reinforces these promises with another similar promise. Jesus states that where two or three Christians are gathered, He is spiritually present with them (Matt. 18:20). These three statements combined together form one of the most potent and staggering promises of the Bible. Christians gathered together are unified under the Blood of His Cross. They have the power of His Spirit and are called to shape the direction of human history in their day. I often muse at the number of people needed. I find myself grateful that fifty unified people are not the minimum requirement; only two or three.

This is an awesome responsibility and potentiality; if we could but believe the promise. Jesus knew how difficult even those who believed could be to one another, so he chose to vest His power in the two's and three's. This principle is given to us in the context of individual human relations and greater Church discipline. Inexplicably, God requires human cooperation and partnership to extend His Kingdom on the earth. The hindrance to His power and will in the midst of His 'called out ones' is human disobedience— sin. Since we are all prone to sin we must deal with it as some dread disease. We cannot succeed as a group with sin dwelling in our midst. Only a little reflection upon this matter will bring the realization that this answers the great question of why the professing church is so generally powerless and anemic.

As with most of the precepts of God, the guidelines are simple. If a believer sins against you or you know that they have sinned against God, you are to go to them, one on one (Matt. 18:15). This is where a lot of the failure begins. If a brother or sister sins against us we often talk to others before we go to them. This is a breech of obedience that affects our prayer life. The whole idea of speaking one on one is that nobody else needs to know. If you and I can solve the sin problem in front of God, publicity is legitimately cut off, and the name of Christ is glorified.

I don't know how much people obey this commandment since I will never hear about it. I do know that many people choose not to obey this commandment. They do so with alarming frequency. They then wonder why their lives are not powerful for God. Since it only takes two or three believers to move heaven and earth, individual restoration becomes of primary importance. I cannot afford a grudge, unforgiveness, or anger against you or you against me because we have such a great work to do together in God.

If a person is in a bad place they may reject your council or they may reject you as a person. Jesus says that you should then gather a couple of witnesses and rehearse the matter again (Matt. 18:16). This kills frivolity. People do not tend to frivolously accuse others of something if the matter is to go public. It is really important to involve the spiritually mature in this process (Gal. 6:1). Their maturity will bring perspective, experience, and confidentiality to the circumstances. Sometimes reconciliation will come with a different point of view represented. Notice that this gives the individual more time to think about their actions and it keeps the matter quiet longer. What great respect Jesus wants us to use in handling the wayward soul. Our motive is always towards restoration and not vindication. He calls it, "gaining our brother" (Matt. 18:15).

The final solution is the Church. This is the last resort and Jesus refers us to the Church as His representative in the world. A person who is so obstinate to go against the counsel of an entire fellowship needs to be moved into the realm of the unbeliever (Matt. 18:17). The unity of the Church and its great ministry of being history-changers for God is too important for selfish and unruly individuals to spoil. The whole history of Israel and the Church is replete with tales of individuals who hindered or spoiled what God would have done. Jesus was very clear that those who have come to Him rid themselves of sin. Sin is very dangerous because it has a yeast-like ability to spread. This will inevitably go beyond my own life to corrupt others around me (Luke 12:1; 1 Cor. 5:6). Therefore, those who refuse the program of profound change, which includes departing from evil, are not to be included in Christian fellowship.

What a startling contrast this is to the cavalcade of humanistic dealings we bring to some situations and the sometimes unfair or cruel treatment we give to others in the name of correction. I have seen many cases where individuals who were clearly living in sin were either ignored or tolerated by the leadership and congregation of a church in the name of kindness and love. Of course such a reaction was neither kind nor loving since it effectively killed the prayer life and vibrancy of the church. There is no doubt that such toleration led others to believe that they could sin with impunity. At the same time, I have seen many situations where a person has fallen into a sin and sought help from the church. Their reward was public humiliation as their personal business was blabbed all over the place and they were ostracized by individuals in the church. These are the two extremes and you find many other cases that fall in between.

The instructions Jesus gave to maintain our human relations are simple enough. Why don't we just follow them? I am sure one of the reasons is that although Jesus has not created a complex system for dealing with individual sin, sometimes it can be hard. Most of us hate confrontation and misunderstanding. We only want to follow these guidelines if it suits us. It is also clear that much of the institutional church leadership regard such an approach as disastrous for church growth and harmony. It is easier to ignore sin than to deal with it. Many have learned that church discipline is often not worth the problems it engenders. As a result, we see a patchwork quilt approach to sin. We deal with what bugs us and leave what does not. We speak people's business when we should go to them privately. Conversely, we are private about sin when the church should be publicly warned. Again, we largely ignore important simple instructions that will bring harmony in the church.

So it is that the Student of the Word is committed to doing truth in a current spiritual atmosphere that treats eating the Word of God like going to a giant buffet. At this buffet the feasters choose what they wish and leave what is distasteful to them. Not so for the Students of God's Word, for they are interested in obeying the whole counsel of God. The remnant has to pick through the mounds of opinion and false practice and find ways to do what Jesus said. The only way for us to survive is to examine what others would say is madness or crazy talk. We must do those things that Jesus has commanded. Then our souls will be satisfied and our hearts will bear witness that we are the obedient children of God. I pray for you my friend that you will live with a conscience that is devoid of offense toward God and man. I pray that you will find abundant food in this present spiritual wilderness.

Your Fellow Student of the Word,

Henry

# CHAPTER 9

# *The School Of Silence*

Dear Fellow Traveler,

*M*y previous letters have covered spiritual wilderness basics. Now we will spend some time dwelling upon the art of hearing God. I use the word art because this is not a scientific endeavor where we pour ingredients into a beaker, mix them together, and heat at a certain temperature—making note of specific results. There is a process involved with learning to hear God. We need to find His specific will for our lives and live bravely enough to launch out in new directions. This process brings into play the basics we have discussed along with the use of intuitive skills, prayer, sensible applications of truth, and true bravery. Nevertheless, as with art, there are tools to use and processes to be followed to produce the desired result. As well, even the most gifted artists must practice. We begin by finding ourselves alone with Christ out in the School of Silence.

The thing that you will notice almost immediately in the wilderness is the absence of familiar noise. Most of us who live in cities have unknowingly suffered a shortage of quietness. Many noises confront us daily. We are surrounded by the sounds of automobiles and transportation. There are the sounds of appliances in our homes along with machinery to modify the atmosphere and temperature. When we are out and about there are people noises, construction noises, and activity noises of all kinds. We take for granted the sounds of planes, trains, and other methods of transportation. In the public domain there are recorded voices, music, announcements, and video and television presentations. Even those who live in rural settings often impose the noise of television, radio, and music upon their surroundings.

The first thing we experience when we go into the wilderness is the deafening roar of silence. This is the ring and roar in our ears that is caused by the absence of noise. This can be very unsettling. As our hearing gets adjusted we notice a different kind of noise in the wilderness. If we are near water we hear its movement. There is the music of rain, whether intense pounding or gentle pattering. The wind has telltale sounds that reveal its intensity and direction. We hear the natural motions of plants in the wind as well as the motion of living things. Birds move in the trees and sing their little tunes. Animals are often unseen and yet we know that they are there by the sounds of their movement. We hear sound more clearly as the ringing goes out of our ears. We begin to hear things that are far in the distance or sounds that are very soft.

All alone in the silence there is another sound that we start to hear—the voice in our head and then the voice in our heart. With no one else around we start to hear our internal voice. Our mind wanders or we start to reflect clearly on whatever comes to mind. In the School of Silence the toughest challenge we will face is facing ourselves. When we are alone, and unengaged by the distractions that modern life brings, we are confronted with our internal life. There is no external act to convey and no distraction from who we really are. Whether we are satisfied with ourselves or not we have to face ourselves in the silence of the wilderness. Accompanying this silence comes a sense of being alone; all alone. We will start to understand our level of contentment and maturity according to our loneliness and sense of anxiety. Silence is like a mirror that reflects our soul back to us in a way that nothing else can.

Although a person may never leave the physical city the spiritual wilderness will lead them to the silent place of reflection. Our faithful Father will arrange circumstances that are conducive to silence. We may become alienated from friends, lose a job, or have a health problem. We may simply follow the inner urgency to get alone. God will compel us to shut off and shut out the noise that surrounds us. His purpose is to bring us to the place of a new kind of hearing. He will do it within the realm of the School of Silence. As all the maddening stimuli are quieted, our soul will become quiet. The place in our soul for spiritual discourse will be aroused. Jesus and the prophets of old practiced seasons of quiet prayer and reflection. Christ's followers will also have seasons of quiet separation and reflection with their heavenly Father.

For the soulish person this will be very difficult since they are almost completely taken up with their own satisfaction and their carnal desires. Many carnal professors of religion are constantly bombarded by noise. They have turned it on for the subliminal reason of quieting the inner conversation. Their flesh will obstinately resist the quiet place of reflection. They intuitively know that their conscience will be convicted and their self-centered life will be revealed. Since many Christians behave as if they are babies or carnal this 'noisy crowd' includes a lot of professing Christendom. Make no mistake here; I am not talking about having a little quiet time every day. I am speaking of protracted seasons of aloneness with the silence that will accompany it.

As a very young Christian I was expelled from my household. I found myself living with a man of God and his family in the back of their bakery. I lived in a room with his two little boys. I worked in the bakery for my board and a bit of pocket money. I was essentially cut off from my old life, friends, and family. A lot of the work we did was at night and it was very quiet. I had to face myself, my fears, and my failures during that time. This family had no television and cared little for worldly entertainment. The only outings were on Sundays for ministry. My friend and I lifted weights and worked. That was about it.

In those austere conditions I had a lot of time to read and reflect. I was an energetic eighteen year-old. As I look back I see how badly damaged I was as a person. I had to face my sinful habits and leanings. There was no way to escape how worldly and undisciplined I was. The long hours of working alone were a tremendous ministry to me. My mentor spent a lot of time teaching me. He often took me along with him when he went out. I still had a lot of time alone and the silence was deafening as I learned with baby steps to hear the voice of God over the inner voice of Henry.

I have had many such seasons since my conversion. Usually they were pretty unexpected and often unwanted. I had several seasons of injury where God was able to help me realize that He was the Great Provider, not me. I heard my specific call to ministry in the cauldron of frustrating silence and pain. The sorrow of death has stripped me clean of aspirations to acquire possessions. There is nothing like looking in the closet of a newly departed loved one to teach the fleeting nature of our things. In the Valley of the Shadow of Death I have seen my need to be divorced from the concerns of this old world.

One of the great misunderstandings of our day is what the nature of prayer truly is. Many speak of prayer as petition and intercession. Many grand pronouncements are made concerning 'having a positive confession' with the goal of receiving what you desire from God. The Bible clearly teaches that those who believe already have everything that pertains to life and godliness (2 Pet. 1:3). The madness for things has made us blind to a greater benefit of knowing God. Rather than spending our time telling God everything He already knows about what **we** think is wrong and what **we** think should happen; we can learn to listen. In the School of Silence we learn to hear Him tell us things we do not know. God will share needs that we may have never even imagined. The Bible tells us that human eyes have not seen, human ears have not heard, and human hearts have not understood what God has prepared for those who love Him. It goes on to say that **God has revealed it** to those of us who believe by His Spirit (1 Cor. 2:9-12). Paul is not just speaking of our heavenly home but our heavenly relationship that we have with our Father right now.

Over the years the School of Silence has taught me a great deal. It has been of immeasurable value to me because it is the place where I learned to hear the voice of God. I am persuaded that God wants to speak to us much more than He wants to hear from us. Can you imagine how silly it would be for us to interrupt a famous instructor, on any subject, with the paltry comments of our meager experience? Yet, is this not what we so often do in prayer? I believe God wants us to shut our mouths and listen or at the very least to pray in His Holy Spirit. As we settle our souls in the place of silence and give God the same respect that we might give some great Teacher or Ruler, we will find that Father is ready and willing to speak to us.

In fact, I believe that God may be shouting at us. In Proverbs 1 wisdom is personified to be calling in the streets but is ignored by the foolish and unlearned. Wisdom's reaction is to laugh at the well deserved consequences that follow (Prov. 1:24-30). The written Word of God and the inspiring Holy Spirit are the sources God uses to enlighten us to all of the Father's wisdom. I have this picture in my mind of a person praying away, telling God all of their woes, and leaving without ever giving an exasperated Father an opening to reassure them or to answer them. Many pray without any expectation of ever hearing an inner answer from God. In contrast, we can see that God is most assuredly crying out by His Spirit and His Word to a lost and wayward church and society. He would like them to stop everything and learn to listen to Him.

Jesus said that His sheep knew His voice and they followed Him (John 10:26-28). It is thought by many too difficult a thing for God to speak personally to His followers and yet this is clearly what Jesus means. He promises to speak to and guide the 'other sheep'. This must refer to all who were yet to believe (John 10:6). Obviously this guidance comes primarily from His Word but it is reasonable for all 'sheep' to learn to discern their Master's voice. We aren't very bright compared to God and like sheep we are easily led astray (Isaiah 53:6). In the way that it was essential for the individual sheep to listen intently for the voice of the shepherd so it is essential for those who are Christ's sheep to learn to hear His voice. What a privilege and blessing to be led and taught by the Living God and to learn the sound of His voice. This is not for 'special' people but for all those who call upon the name of the Lord (John 6:45).

It is an interesting fact that we lack confidence in this area of listening for God's voice. In fact, it might be fair to say that most people will exhaust every human avenue before listening for God. I believe people struggle like this because of both the legitimate and illegitimate fear of failure. It is both sensible and reasonable not to want to go haywire. Many have seen the kind of lunacy that represents itself as a warning against 'going too far'. As a young Christian I met all sorts of flaky people who said that God had told them to do all sorts of things that were not Biblical or even reasonable. It is legitimate to be skeptical about such assertions.

It is illegitimate to let fear rob you of God's promise to lead you to pasture (John 10:9). God has specific plans and pathways for each individual. It is preposterous to think that God wants a majority of His people to just sit while the few do all the work and ministry. The Bible clearly teaches that every person is a member of His body and each of them has a specific function (1 Cor. 12:27). Only the Shepherd can lead the sheep to where they ought to be. Jesus wants to teach us to hear His voice and ignore every competing voice.

The first competing voice that God will silence is that of **the crowd**. In society the voice of the crowd is represented by both form and fashion. This is the voice of expectation of what we should do and be. It is not hard to see the vanity of such voices but there is a crowd that is much closer to us. This is the voice of the **religious crowd**. These are the people who aspire to teach us, lead us, and direct us in the things of God. As I mentioned before, many will assert their authority over us in the name of their position or revelation. What we have seen happening on the American Christian landscape is a faddism unparalleled in history.

Since we are able to communicate in so many ways we now see mass-marketing to Christians. One expression of mass marketing is by movements such as the Shepherding Movement, the Faith Movement, the Laughing Revival, and so on. There always seems to be a large group of people who ardently adhere to the latest movement or fad. Another expression of this mass-marketing is programmatic approaches to be superimposed as cure-alls for church's specific needs. These schemes run the gamut from purpose to finance to education to marketing the actual church itself. Many popular authors start fads and followings all by themselves.

Paul said something substantial when he stated that he was "free from all men" (1 Cor. 9:19). As we wait in the silent place the Lord will deliver us from the powerful influence of men, their opinions, and control. We will see how often we have been propelled forward by the 'mob mentality' that often influences individual churches and movements. When in the quiet of his own company Isaiah saw the Lord, he had to confess that he had been carried away by the mob backsliding of Israel. He admitted that he had gone along with the crowd in the uncleanness of his lips (Isa. 6:5). Notice the contrast between Moses and Joshua on top of Mount Sinai (Ex. 24:13-18) and the crowd at the bottom (Ex. 32:17ff). As Moses waited over a protracted period of time in the quiet to hear the voice of God the carnal mob at the foot of the mountain started a new religion.

Men are no different today. In the absence of a visitation of God they will just **make one up**. This is one of the reasons for our present spiritual wilderness. There is huge resistance in the natural heart of men to the rigors of the School of Silence. God cannot be coerced into a 'quickie' blessing. Before He uses us, He has to make us fit for service. The beginning of service is to present ourselves to God as living sacrifices (Romans 12:1-2). Many who present themselves as living sacrifices quickly jump on the altar and then right off again. They then quickly hurry off to the business and noise of the world. There is agony in the minutes and hours when we have run out of anything to say and finally exclaim, "Speak Lord, for thy servant heareth" (1 Sam. 3:9). Once we find out how little we really have possessed God and how little He has really possessed us, then we have begun.

I am persuaded that silence, listening, and waiting must be practiced day by day and year by year. There is a far greater challenge for us than the religious mob. That challenge is the person we look at in the mirror every day. The soul of every person is relentless in its day by day battle for ascendancy and control of that person's will. My 'self' will pull all sorts of tricks out of its bag to distract me from seeking the silent place. My 'self' will further try to substitute its own voice and will for the voice and will of God. This is where God's Word is so important. We have to try our own spirit as well as the spirits of others. All hope of selfish control must be abandoned in the pursuit of the voice of God. His plain Word has to be applied to the human soul. Every soulish feeling must be told to go. Whatever thoughts and intents are not of God must be rejected for those that are of the Father.

**Praying with the Spirit** can put me in the right place to discern. As I pray in my heavenly language my self-life is both revealed and brought into subjection to God's Holy Spirit. When I become quiet and wait, it becomes much easier to recognize the thoughts that are of God and those that are not. I am sure that as we pray in other tongues that a lot of what is being dealt with are the bondages of our souls. As well, afflicting spirits from our enemy the devil are revealed and defeated. As we are infused with God's presence we find it easier and easier to discern what He is saying to us. This Presence is translated into power in the public place where God's Kingdom dwelling in us is released. This occurs because we understand His plans and directions for our lives.

Men do not give spiritual gifts and ministries: God does. It is not the laying on of hands or the ordination of man that reveal life direction and gifts. These are first discovered in the quiet place with God. As the noise of the world is filtered out and the presence of God fills us, the Father starts to enlighten our puny minds either little by little or with bold strokes of spiritual lightening. Vision is imparted to the hearts of men in the silent place in the wilderness, not the loud and crowded market-place type church meetings, often organized for such impartations. A person should have an inkling of God's direction or a vision of God's will before somebody else tells them what their life's direction ought to be. Then the leader or prophetic person will just be confirming what the individual has already heard, rather than directing their life. Many people are seeking to fulfill callings that are not theirs or visions that others had for them. This happened because they never learned the value of waiting and listening for their own vision from the Father.

**Waiting** is part and parcel of the School of Silence. We do not go to class at our own will but as scheduled by the School or Teacher. I go to hear. I listen intently. The Teacher may not be there but I must wait. We have little idea of the workings of men's spirits and souls but our Teacher does. Waiting can often be an emptying event. David said that his soul was poured out like water before the

Lord (Psalm 22:14). I think I know something of what he meant. In the quiet place we are sometimes poured out before God like water and lose all of our strength. We see ourselves for what we really are, full of weakness. Sometimes the heavens will seem as brass and we will have no sense that God is listening at all.

David knew that God's presence never forsook him but some of this waiting in silence was a bit tedious to his soul. That is why David spoke to himself and told himself to wait on the Lord (Psalm 27:14). In fact David spoke to his soul over and over, telling it what to do. He told himself how to behave in God's presence and for His glory. The word soul refers to self. Maybe when we tell our soul what to do we are exercising **self** control. I wonder if David's reverent waiting for God is where his desire and design to build God a Temple came from? If so, his vision went beyond his own lifespan.

To choose to wait and to listen to God will **separate us from people**. This process can cause us to have seasons of loneliness. As I mentioned before, the amount of loneliness and the angst that we feel are measures of our maturity. Part of the cost of hearing the voice of God is loneliness in the quiet place. It is a place we ultimately have to choose because, even if God seemingly puts our lives on the shelf for a season, we can choose to fill our surroundings with the artificial noise of modern media and entertainment. Like no other generation the choice for silence is squarely upon the individual. The life of silent waiting is very rigorous. That is why so many of God's remnant have shied away from the silent place.

Look at Jesus. While others slept Jesus went forth to a quiet place to pray. Jesus said that the Father who had sent Him gave Him the words to say. What an outstanding kind of waiting this was! Jesus had perfected the art of hearing so that although He was the Word, as a man He still had to receive His words and works from His Father (John 5:17-19; 8:28 & 38; 10:18 & 32; 15:15). Jesus had an immeasurable indwelling of the Holy Spirit (John 3:34). He had all the power and manifestation possible for a man without any human inhibition. Yet, Jesus spent long nights and early mornings waiting to hear what His Father had to say. Many who point to the fact that Jesus prayed 'a lot' miss the point. His fellowship with the Father was perfect. He still found it **greatly desirable** to protract

Himself from the company of man to seek the company of His Father. It was not the volume but attitude and focus that made Jesus' praying so fruitful and effective. Christ waits for us in the quiet place to teach us the holy art of prayer, supplication, waiting, and (wonderfully) hearing.

So the remnant is faced with a choice. Are they going to be 'down' with the new fads for prayer? Will they 'soak' in rooms filled with the new generation of Christian tunes and recorded prayers from other meetings, setting the alleged spiritual tone? Will they 'get down' with the prayer concert which is often much more concert than prayer; where music is exalted above intercession and silent travail? Will they participate in 'harp and bowl' worship and intercession where the Presence that inspired the name is often ignored or neglected? Will they go to some 'revival' where they can 'get the blessing' in some church or gathering and bring 'it' back home? Or will they seek out the old pathways? Will they learn the way that revivals and renewals occurred in the past? Will they follow the example of the few venerable old saints who still remain as the products of past moves of God?

How cool we are today. Our forefathers waited by the half and the full night in bygone days. They were not hard to rally for a 'week of prayer'. There used to be such a thing as a 'tarrying service'. Those who knew the power of God didn't go forth on their own with some new program or initiative. They waited in the quiet place after all their prayers were spent while the Spirit of the Living God hovered over them. Then Jesus spoke or moved or healed and changed lives, powerfully and permanently. Our forefathers knew the angst of the dark night of the soul. They knew the desperation of those individuals who understood that if God did not speak, nothing would happen. I have had a taste of such meetings and times alone. Still, I have heard stories of much greater power and manifestation of the Holy Spirit.

One brother shared a story with me about His silent waiting time. During the Prairie Revivals of the Forties in Saskatchewan, this man was meeting with other believers night after night to be endued with power from heaven. He and some neighbors would wait in a woodshed late into the night after a full day of farm work.

He told me his story, "And one night it was my night! I saw the roof of the shed open up and a ball of fire six inches in diameter come out of heaven and hit me in the head. The Holy Spirit filled me and I have never been the same again!" I will attest that this particular man had such power and grace when he prayed that I knew that he had received something permanent in the silent place of waiting.

My own spiritual father left an indelible mark on me. He and Mom prayed out loud and they waited in silence by the hour. Just entering their house was like going to the best church meeting. The Presence of the Lord was always there in power. Few things have made the impression on me the way staying at their house did. Sometimes I would wake several times in the night. There would be long seasons of quiet followed by groans, prayers, and petitions and then further seasons of quiet. Dad knew and loved the quiet place. What great insight just hearing him pray gave me into the deeper ways of God! Because they loved the quiet place, Mom and Dad's lives were full of a deep and satisfying presence of God. What went unseen by others were the countless hours of waiting in silence for their Lord to come, visit, and refresh.

This would be no more than sentimental drivel if it were not so Scriptural. Moses spent his forty years in the School of Silence as a solitary shepherd. The brash young man whose first move as the advocate for his people was to murder an Egyptian was transformed into the meekest man in the world during his silent wilderness wanderings (Numbers 12:3). He spent those years unlearning the attitudes of Egyptian royalty and learning the humility of God's royalty. Were it not for the silence of the wilderness Moses would not have been in the right place at the right time to have his encounter with God in the burning bush.

By all records John the Baptist, the greatest prophet in history (according to Jesus), spent most of his adult life in the wilderness (Luke 1:80; 7:28). That was his nickname: *"The voice of one **crying in the wilderness**, Prepare ye the way of the Lord, make his paths straight."* (Matt. 3:3). John was filled with the Holy Spirit from his mother's womb (Luke 1:15). Either he had removed himself from the religious mainstream or, more likely, had never joined. He went to the silent wilderness to receive his lessons from the Lord. John had received no religious advice and there is no record of 'advanced education'. He was educated on the backside of the desert 'camping out' with God. He knew who had called him, what his message was, and how to deliver it. Did he ever deliver the message! It is amazing what God will teach you when you get away from the noise of popular religious thought.

Jesus had his forty day fast alone in the wilderness. It is clear that Jesus continued separations and fasts throughout His ministry. During His time in the quiet of the desert, He fulfilled God's plan, defeated the devil, and received the strength and direction He needed to start His public ministry (Luke 4:1-14). It is also clear that throughout His ministry Jesus was both tempted and afflicted in such a way that He cried out to God (Heb. 5:7). We see this temptation culminate in the Garden of Gethsemane.

The quiet place not only revealed the voice of His Father. It also revealed the voice of the one whose work Jesus came to destroy. The devil attacked Jesus in His humanity. This fellowship with the sufferings of mankind was a silent and heartbreaking battle that no one but the Father could help Jesus with. This battle had to be endured to perfect and prove Christ's total obedience as a qualification to be a spotless sacrifice (Heb. 5:7-9).

The remnant must also enter the School of Silence so that they may speak a fresh and fiery message born of the Spirit of God. We must go and be stripped that we might be clothed. We must go reverently that we might approach the throne of the Great King. We must quiet our spirits and sprinkle our consciences with the blood of Christ that we might hear the Master's voice (Heb. 10:22). How sweet the peace and assurance He gives. What comfort the unction and witness of His Holy Spirit will bring—what mental health! How clear and powerful the vision we will receive because we have received it from God. As we dedicate ourselves to the School of Silence what rewards we will find! We will be able to go forth with the confidence of those who have been sent by God! It is an empowering thing indeed when we have been sent forth by God rather than by the action of man.

The message that God will renew to us in the quiet place will be no new revelation. What will occur will be a return to the simplicity of the old message. God wants to ingrain and renew the **fire** and **desire into** those who wait upon God for renewed strength. Isaiah states: *"But they that wait upon the LORD shall renew [their] strength; they shall mount up with wings as eagles; they shall run, and not be weary; [and] they shall walk, and not faint."* (Isaiah 40:31). True waiting upon God is far superior to the chants, breaths, and vain repetitions of so-called 'reflective prayer' becoming so popular today. God's true silence will re-acquaint us with the personal presence of God and His power.

Dear friend, you do not have to run into the forest or the desert to seek silence. You can turn off the radio and the telephone in the car. You can sanctify a quiet time in your household. You may start to rise early and find a secret place or stay up late and wait for Him in the night watches. You can go for a daily walk and pray and listen for His voice. The first step is to see the absolute need to seek the place of silence and the second is to follow through in finding it.

From the School of Silence,

Henry

# CHAPTER 10

# *Tracking The Will Of God*

Dear Fellow Traveler,

*T*he art of tracking in the wilderness has been turned into a science in our day. Men like Tom Brown Jr. have taken the ancient art and chronicled the nuances of tracking. A tracker can tell you all about the animal or person they are tracking. The finest detail about their quarry will not be overlooked. A good tracker can tell whether the animal or person being tracked is small, large, strong, or injured. They can even gain insights into the individual personality of what they are tracking. The tracker can tell you how long ago the tracks were made, what the animal was doing, and often, why it was doing it. They can find trails used by animals and how frequently the trails have been used. Good trackers read trails like you or I might read the newspaper.

Since the goal of true trackers is to be in complete harmony with their environment, their interest goes far beyond the basic needs of finding food and materials for survival. Their desire is to understand as much as is possible about what the living things in their realm of influence are doing and why. Trackers see themselves as custodians of the wilderness. They learn the art of enhancing the environment as well as helping both plant and animal to thrive. Their involvement in their hinterland has nothing to do with sport but with mutual respect for the natural realm as the Creator has made it. There is great reverence in their approach to the wilderness. They do not intrude as outsiders in their natural world but participate in it, as their home.

Tracking is essential for the survival of the true wilderness wayfarer. They do not need to bring many supplies with them. They use what is already supplied to both live and thrive. Nothing is wasted. Everything that a tracker takes from the natural environment is taken for its particular use. As you move about in the wilderness it is essential to know what wildlife is there with you and to understand what each species contributes to the greater whole. There are tracks that will tell you where your dinner is and there are tracks that will tell you that something is near that may regard you as dinner. A good tracker will know the workings and movements of any creature from the ant to the grizzly bear.

It takes many years to become a competent tracker. To meet someone on the street you might never know they possess such skill. The tracker has submitted themselves to careful training and instruction. There has been much to learn, courses to be taken, books to be read, and most of all, persistent practice. Like any other complex skill you just can't learn tracking overnight. The truly great tracker is very rare indeed. Just to be able to learn from them takes a great deal of planning and money. Their time is not cheaply and readily available.

So it is with those who would learn to track in the spiritual wilderness. Of course the Object of our attention is God. Every person who has truly received the Lord Jesus as their own personal Savior wants to know how they are to spend their particular lives. This is what God's people spend their time tracking. They seek to learn every skill and nuance of following God's particular personal path for their lives. I believe there are all kinds of signs along the way but we have to learn what the signs are and how to read them. Very often God's guidance is staring us in the face but we have not developed the skill in identifying certain events as 'God things'. In this letter we will discuss some of the basic 'tracks' that God leaves for us to find our way in the spiritual wilderness. Our discussion will by no means be exhaustive. Many complete how-to books have been written over many generations relating to the personal leading of God. This letter will be just a thumb-nail sketch of some obvious signposts along the way.

**Vision** is the starting point of any journey. It is essential to know where you are going before you set out. It is true that if you aim for nothing you will no doubt hit your target. Much has been written and said in our day, both in the secular realm and Christian world, about having a life that is purpose-driven or vision oriented. The idea of 'true north' fits our little metaphor because true wilderness wayfaring includes being able to find our direction and to reach our destination with maps and compasses. The Bible, the Holy Spirit, and good teachers can be compared to our map and compass. Learning the art of tracking can be compared to our particular path to our heavenly home and God's particular plan for each person along the way.

I welcome the large amount of writing about finding purpose in the sphere of Christian life. I view a lot of the material that is available at the time of this writing as a wonderful tool to assist in revisiting the practice of Christianity as individual disciples and as church fellowships. It is evident from a cursory reading of the New Testament that one must repent and receive the rule of the Kingdom of God in their life. Once Jesus is enthroned upon an individual's heart there are four basic activities that are essential to grow in the Kingdom. These activities are simply outlined for us in Acts 2:42. It is imperative to learn God's word, consistently fellowship with other Christians, live the life of a worshiper, and pray to the Father in Jesus' name (Acts 2:42).

Accompanying these essential activities is the call of God to share the Good News with everyone possible (Mark 15:15-16; Matt. 28:19:20). This presentation is to be given under the anointing of the Holy Spirit (Mark 16:20; Acts 1:8). God promises that signs and wonders will follow the preaching of God's Word (Mark 16:17-18; Acts 4: 30-32; 5:12; 15:18-20; 2 Cor. 12:12). It is clear that our mission to 'go' was central in the mind of Christ and central in the practice of the first century Church. Although this description is short, it is easy to see that the writers of the New Testament were focused on these basic purposes in representing the Kingdom of God.

In contrast to such simplicity I find it interesting that we have become so **complex** about finding purpose as Christians in our society. I think we follow after more and more complexity because the average person in America has more opportunities than they can ever imagine fulfilling. Too many choices can cause confusion. Adding to the confusion, many churchgoers are not well versed in the basics of Christianity. This makes it very difficult for then to know what is really important to God. The result is that many church people find themselves both busy and yet feeling aimlessly confused. The mad pace of society has people doing what seems right without much reflection on where they will eventually end up. Somehow, vision has been bypassed by necessity, duty, or just the frenetic pace of life. Often people find themselves in their thirties or forties before they start to ask themselves, "What in the world am I doing here?"

It is hard to imagine a shoe maker in Tibet, a street cleaner in Calcutta, a migrant worker in the Philippines, or a nomad in the Saharan desert needing a complex program to figure out where their new-found Christianity might lead them. They know who they are and what they are doing. They have limited prospects on what else they might do. Their conversion to Christianity would definitely have profound disruptive effects on their daily lives because of persecution and cultural misunderstanding. Yet the simple directives of the Christian life that I listed above would be enough to sustain them, along with recognition of the Lordship of the indwelling Christ. Any alteration of their basic life's work would be perpetrated by a profound revelation from Jesus with powerful direction from His Holy Spirit. They would need continual miraculous intervention on their behalf. Usually, an individual's ministry begins within the sphere that they are called until God moves them to another sphere (1 Cor. 7:17-24).

In many cases we have made Christian purpose more complex than God has. It is our passion and vision for the common elements of the Christian faith and our faithfulness to fulfill them that will define our walk with God. All Christians have uniformly simple and common commandments to obey and fulfill. Vision grows as the Father is sought. Then specific personal fulfillment of the Great Commission and Christian fellowship grows from what develops in an individual's faithful walk with God. It is my impression that many are developing purposes before they have had a vision from God about where to go and what to do. To fit our analogy, they have not learned how to track the specific will of God for their life. When a person receives a vision from God they will be sustained by His imparted perseverance during all kinds of difficulties and challenges. It is clear that there must be a vision to sustain an individual in this present spiritual wilderness (Prov. 29:18).

**False humility** tells many that God would not have a specific vision for 'little old them'. In reality, the humblest and weakest of us have still been bought with the infinitely expensive blood of Jesus Christ. It seems reasonable that we can move forward with the knowledge that He has a perfect and knowable plan for all of His children. The whole volume of the Bible bears witness to this truth. As God's children and joint-heirs with Jesus, it then behooves us to seek the plan He has. We have to start on the premise that there is a general plan for us all and a specific plan for each individual. As the Hebrews 11:6 clearly states, *"But without faith [it is] impossible to please [him]: for he that cometh to God must believe that he is, and [that] he is a rewarder of them that diligently seek him."* Faith demands the understanding that God is Personal enough to reward us for responding to His promise, in His way, in our life.

I am a great believer in personal vision and family vision. Each person needs to find their own personal vision. Each family needs to understand God's family vision for them. A sensible response for any person who has no such directional knowledge from God would be to stop their religious activity and seek the mind and face of Him who holds their life in His hands. Many people make good plans, lay out direction, and then ask God to bless them. Often, their planned activities do not align with His plan and vision for their lives. In other words, what seems like a good idea to people is often not God's plan for them. The same goes for churches and leadership. A person must first be 'sent' by God to experience God's blessing in their activity for Him (Luke 10:1; John 20:21). That which does not proceed from a God-given vision and commissioning may seem to be good; but it will never be His good. He may use the plan or program but it will never equal the results of something

God has commissioned.

Once God does give us a vision our lives are **set in motion**. As we fulfill what God has prepared for us as individuals we should expect that He will expand our vision and give us more responsibility. It seems to me that God is not a Communist, handing down five year plans. Instead, he sets us in motion towards our vision, often on a 'need-to-know' basis. He'll leave 'tracks' for us along the way. Although there are always seasons for retooling and redirection, fulfilling one aspect of His plan will often lead us to new and greater vision than we ever had before. It is characteristic of vision from God that it can never be fulfilled by human means alone. It must be large enough that it can only be fulfilled by His grace.

So we see that the Christian with vision is a person in motion. God's leading will come as an individual moves ahead. Paul traveled on his missionary journeys. There were seasons when Paul did not even know where he was going (Acts 16:6-9). Paul did know that he was sent to the Gentiles, so he kept moving out to where the Gentiles were. His vision was to preach the Gospel to the Gentile world and minister to Gentile believers (Romans 11:13). Paul had a vision, was sent, and had a design. Later, while Paul was writing from prison, I wonder if he knew we would be reading his mail as Scripture. What kept Paul obedient was the power of his encounter with "the heavenly vision" (Acts 26:19-20). Once we are given vision, commissioned by God, and are moving forward; there are some principles that are inviolate in tracking the will of God. These principles are quite simple. It never ceases to amaze me that they are so often violated by people who seem sincere in seeking God's will. Let's take a look at these principles.

Any vision or leading we receive in the spiritual wilderness will be consistent with God's Word. The Bible is our **manual** for spiritual 'tracks'. All subjective evidence must be subjugated to Bible truth, whether this evidence is from human, emotional, or spiritual sources. If a career path causes an individual or those around them to commit sin, that path can never be the will of God (Romans 6:1-2). God does not want any of His children to be bartenders, escorts, bookmakers, or criminals. He just does not lead people to do that for Him. Yet, many seek careers that are not wrong in themselves;

they are only wrong for the life God has called them to. They are using their abilities and talents for what they want rather than for what God wants. Christians are never just working to earn money. Yet, in compliance with God's laws, it is clear that Christians are to work, support their family, ministry, the poor, and the weak (1 Thess. 4:11; 2 Thess. 3:10-12).

Sometimes a ministry will **compromise** the qualifications for spiritual leadership given in Scripture. This may happen because there is no one to fill the position. Those making the decision may have a personal affection for the person being promoted. Sometimes promoting an unqualified person may just be the easiest thing to do. These rationales for promoting a person into leadership cannot be pleasing to God. If a novice fills a spiritual position, it is always a disservice to the novice and the people under their influence (1 Tim. 3:6). If a ministry does evil while doing good, it violates the spirit of the Gospel and displeases God (Romans 3:8). When people who are in spiritual authority sin and continue their ministries without correction and corresponding repentance they will not prosper (Gal. 6:1; 1 Tim. 5:19-20).

I have both seen and heard of ministries where the people involved will use foul language, even when preaching Bible messages. Some ministries that are doing great work have allowed fornication and even homosexuality to go on quietly behind the scenes. This can never be pleasing to God. Any vision or ministry that will please God must love His truth enough to defend its credibility through the godly lives of its workers. It is astonishing how many people trudge along in a ministry that is willfully violating God's Word. Then they wonder why they are miserable and unfulfilled. If the ministry will not deal with the sin in their midst it will not prosper. If you are involved in such a ministry it is time to get out.

There are also those who go for a more emotional kind of leading. They **feel** 'led' to do things that are not necessarily wrong but are more consistent with humanistic desires than with Spirit-breathed ministry. There are all kinds of clubs, activities, and programs that churches do to provide service to the community or to raise the church's profile in their community. This may seem to make sense. God will certainly lead churches to serve their communities, often in unusual ways. Nevertheless, many churches will do community service for altruistic but humanistic reasons.

This kind of ministry is often motivated by what a few people or leaders in the church think ministry is. This is often the reason why programs that were truly useful in years past are continued far beyond their useful lifespan. The acid test is spiritual temperature. Is the church vibrantly alive with the power and manifestation of the Holy Spirit? Are people being transformed? You will generally find that clubs and programs become substitutes for spiritual vitality. It is surely impossible to justify community service in an atmosphere of spiritual laxity.

The Bible presents the oft-gathering of the saints as a single-minded pursuit of the vision and mind of the Holy One of Israel. However they may appear, God's tracks will **never lead us into sin** or compromise because our personal holiness is always at the top of God's agenda (Lev. 20:7; 1 Peter 1:14-17; 2 Cor. 7:1). The exhortation to follow after the nature of God is the central part of our representation of His Kingdom, so all vision and leading will reflect a growth in all the fruit of the Holy Spirit. Each individual becomes a "living sacrifice" that is transformed into the likeness of Jesus (Rom. 12:1-2).

Somehow, all vision leads to **edification of the saints** and the **salvation of souls**. I attended a church at one time that had a vision statement with seven emphases. It was very nice. The only problem was nobody could verbalize it. A lot of work had gone into formulating the vision. Money was spent in putting up beautiful posters with the vision statement on them. I am sure that a lot of what we are doing here in America is culturally driven rather than proceeding from a vision given by God. Following a vision arrived at by human intellect is a sure way to assist worldliness to pervade a fellowship. We are to gather to edify the saints and go out to win the world to Christ. The simplicity of this mission is very offensive to many. This is why so many people add complexity to make church fellowship more palatable to their own spiritual taste.

I'm not sure if the Pastor of the church with the seven-fold mission statement did the best thing. He told the people that they were going to simplify their vision. From that day forward they were to be all about 'souls'. Everything that they would plan and do would be about leading new people to Jesus Christ. That seems to have been the mission of the first century Church and was central to the way the Church was organized. We see the body of believers gathered together to learn. They were then propelled forth by the Holy Spirit to teach others about Jesus (Mark 16:20).

I know that many people will feel that such an approach is simplistic. I agree, but what is the matter with that? Maybe we need to run some of our complex plans through a simple 'reality check'. It is clear that our mission is to lead people to Christ and make them disciples (Matt. 28:19-20). Therefore everything that does not contribute to these goals should be regarded as suspect. If you think about it, there is vast latitude in the things you can do for 'souls'. The variety of approaches may be as vast as the diversity of humanity.

Let's use a familiar example; the Christmas cantata or play at a large church. A great deal of time, effort, and money is spent in selecting the play or musical. Planning, building props, preparing workers, rehearsals, advertising, lighting, and many other details must be dealt with to bring the production off successfully. Of course, such an event is ostensibly for 'souls'. I have heard of many people that made decisions for Christ at these events. Imagine that such an event took seven thousand man-hours to produce with one hundred workers in total.

Now further imagine what kind of results may have been accomplished if one hundred workers spent seven thousand hours visiting and helping the people in their own neighborhood with the intent of giving them the Gospel. Which would do people more good? Which would be more effective in reaching souls? What would be more fiscally responsible? Which is less appealing to people's flesh? I know that some churches do both but unfortunately these churches are in the vast minority. The fact is that God will lead us to do uncomfortable but effective things to bless His people and win others to Christ. Even though it sounds simplistic, tracking God's will really is all about 'souls'.

Tracking God's will should **not be confusing**. In fact, the Bible states that God is not the author of confusion (1 Cor. 14:33). There are usually two major causes for confusion about God's will. The first cause is **spiritual superiority and pride**. Did you ever meet somebody who made every question of life complex and unanswerable? It is easy to miss the simplicity of what God wants. I think this is something that held me back for years. I would read books about the Bible to learn about topics I was interested in. It would have been wiser to have just obeyed the simple truth that I was already reading. I really thought I was too smart for such simple answers from the Bible but I was really just proud. I believe that this prideful attitude is the cause of much confusion in the American Church concerning what God will lead us to do.

Most of the great truths of Scripture are simple to understand. To love God and my neighbor as myself is easy to understand but how many of us get like the lawyer did with Jesus and say, "Who is my neighbor?" (Luke 18:19ff). Usually, when God reveals His will to us it is easy enough to understand. Are we the ones who think it might be beneath us because the task may require sacrifice, humility, or love? These attributes are not complex but sometimes they are hard. I have seen many believers who got a word from the Lord they didn't like so they just passed it over. They felt it could not be of God because it put them in a humble place. The Bible teaches us that love builds people up but knowledge makes people proud (1 Cor. 8:1). The simple law of loving God first and your neighbor as yourself will often clear up any confusion concerning which direction you need to go. I also found out that God's love is not a feeling but a right decision towards Him first, and then towards other people (Mark 12:28-32; Romans 13:8-10).

The second cause I found for confusion was **selfishness**. People want their own way so much that when they are confronted with God's plan for their life they cannot or will not hear it. Natural human resistance to spiritual things gains ascendancy and they become double-minded. They may want to please God but they also want to please themselves at the same time. The double-minded person becomes unstable in every area of their life (James 1:8). When you talk to such people they will tell you that they just don't know what God wants. Others will tell you that they feel God wants them to do something but they are afraid of the consequences. When you seek to know the will of God for your life you have to be careful not to despise its humble nature or simplicity. God may not call us to a great public work but He will call us to a **good** work.

In seeking to track God's specific will for my life I must make a **distinction** between my own natural gifts and the spiritual gifts that God has imparted to me as a consequence of my salvation. I remember before my ordination that I went through a series of interviews and tests. One of the tests was designed to help me identify my spiritual gifts. The test was a standard personality test that was 'religified'. After I took the test, it revealed which great person in the Bible I was like (I have often wondered if such comparisons did not cater to our pride). It also helped me to identify which person in the Bible I was aspiring to be like. I was supposed to be able to figure out what I would stress in my ministry from this test. The amazing thing was how accurate it was as a personality test. The mistake the individual made who gave the test was that they confused natural traits and abilities with God's imparted spiritual gifts.

Spiritual gifts are imparted as a consequence of salvation and God's calling for each particular individual. They are given according to the thinking and plan of the Holy Spirit (1 Cor. 12:11). Spiritual gifts have nothing to do with our natural abilities and inclinations. Some people make the mistake of thinking that God will use their natural talent. It's only natural and that is the problem, the natural man just doesn't get spiritual things (1 Cor. 2:14). Part of tracking God's will is discovering the spiritual gifts and ministry that He has imparted to us. Natural means are of no use. His Word, His Spirit, and His insight are the only means to discover His plan for us.

Last but certainly not least is the development of a '**good gut**' for tracking God. As we grow in God we start to know the difference between our urges and God's leadings. When all of the above factors are taken into account we should look for the unction or witness of the Holy Spirit. As we apply God's known truth to our lives and shed the sinful and fleshly impulses of our earthly nature we grow more and more aware of His purposes. We develop spiritual feelings that were previously not a part of our lives. This is what I mean by developing a good gut. Just as worldly people develop instincts for dealing with worldly situations so spiritually regenerated people develop spiritual instincts for dealing with spiritual situations (1 John 2:20).

My mother always said, "Familiarity breeds contempt." She usually used this saying with reference to some unsavory individual that she didn't want me to keep company with. I suppose the saying means that if we hang out with people too much it ruins the quality of our friendship. Just the opposite happens in the spiritual wilderness. The more familiar we become with God's Spirit, thinking, and leading, the more we live in reverential awe of His workings and plans. Our behavior becomes increasingly conformed to His will. With God familiarity breeds **respect**. We grow in the grace and in the knowledge of His will (2 Peter 3:18).

In the last letter we talked a bit about praying in the Holy Spirit. This is an essential practice in developing unction. As we pray in our heavenly language and pray the will of God through His Word, we develop an inner conviction, an inner knowledge of God's particular purpose for our lives. Even the mature traveler who ignores this essential practice will find themselves spiritually dulled. Their ability to track God's direction will be hampered. God is a God of current events, a God of the living not the dead (Mark 12:27). He is a 'right now' kind of God. Yesterday's manna is insufficient for today. The fasteners for the armor of God are the different aspects of prayer that hold the equipment together. We are "one spirit" with God and as we cultivate that connection, our sense of leading will become more intense and detailed (1 Cor. 6:17).

A godly 'gut feeling" about major life direction usually will occur consistently over a **period of time**. Such major direction is not the product of an emotional moment or day. We are emotional beings. It is very natural for us to be moved negatively in relation to that which we naturally dislike and positively in relation to that which we naturally do like. Often God's greater vision for our lives will bring about profound changes in our personality. When we start to have an idea of what God wants, we may not like it. Nevertheless, there will be an underlying and abiding conviction that the direction and plan are of God. Our gut must tell us that we are doing the right thing. It will harmonize with all of the other factors for tracking God's will. At times everything can seem to say 'go' while our godly instincts will still say 'no'. That is why a 'good gut' is so important in finding the will of God for our individual life. Ultimately, I am responsible to hear from God. No one can consistently do it for me.

I have to say that I look carefully at the person who publicly and often proclaims 'God told me'. I think that such terminology is often used to add weight to what the person is saying. This practice tends to ignore the **hallowed nature** of the privilege of God speaking to an individual. I am even more suspicious if a person tells me that God told them something for me. I believe that each one of us needs to ardently seek God so that we might know His specific will and plan for our lives (Heb. 11:6). God may tell you something about my life to encourage me or correct me. Generally I will already have understood it myself because I will have heard from Father already.

I am not the kind of person who has received visions and my dreams lack a picture quality. I am moved by understanding concepts. I do not have great three dimensional thinking abilities. Nevertheless, God has spoken to me and continues to do so day by day. Most of what God gives is enlightenment concerning His Word and truth. Sometimes I will have something for others to be given in due time. Occasionally, I will receive something spectacularly impressed upon my soul that is unmistakably life-changing. I still go through all the processes I have listed to 'try the spirits' and prove the will of God (1 John 4:1).

I am persuaded that God wants to speak to you. The enemy of your soul will tell you that this cannot happen and ask you, "Who do you think you are?" If you have received Jesus personally, you are a child of God. He is profoundly interested in speaking to you, giving you vision, and causing you to succeed. He may use profound events such as visions, exhortations, and dreams. He may unfold His will quietly in your soul. God will speak to you in the best way for you, so always be assured that God will speak to you when you seek Him with all of your heart. I trust that He will impart new strength and vision to you this very day.

Keep on Tracking His Will,

Henry

# CHAPTER 11

# *Self-Correcting Behavior*

Dear Fellow Traveler,

*D*uring a survival course I remember that one of the instructors used the term 'Self-Correcting Behavior' every time a person in the course made a mistake. He would look at the other instructor knowingly and they would smile. As the course went on I saw the wisdom of what he was saying. The instructors were trying to impart as much knowledge of the wilderness as possible. We had the choice how carefully to adhere to what we had learned. Some people were very self-assured and found it hard to follow explicit instructions to the letter. Others were very attentive to every detail of what they were learning. Even the most attentive people would still make mistakes and get things wrong. Part of the process of learning was just perfecting our skills. The potential for failure went up dramatically for those who would not take instruction.

The consequences of any mistake or failure can be called 'Self-Correcting Behavior' because the consequences will make us want to avoid that behavior in the future. I cut my thumb with a roofing knife about four months ago, severing a tendon. God was gracious to me and the tendon was reattached. I have been careful with knives for years but I slipped just that once. I will be all the more careful in the future.

If I wear the wrong footwear in the wilderness I will soon have blistered or hurting feet. If I drink water without boiling it I may soon suffer from dysentery. If I am not sufficiently quiet in stalking my dinner I may go hungry. If I don't watch where I am putting my feet I may fall down and hurt myself. If I carry too much with me I may not be able to travel with comfort. To experience any of these consequences is painful. The pain teaches a person that they do not want to repeat the behavior again. That is self-correcting behavior.

In the wilderness, efficiency and care are more important than in urban settings. One little mistake can snowball into several mistakes. There is no place to catch a cab if you are lost or buy dinner if you are hungry. Your charge card just doesn't work out there. My instructors knew that all of their students would make mistakes. They were trying to drive home the idea that greater care would minimize the misery and instruction of self-correcting behavior.

The very same principle is at play in this present spiritual wilderness. We find ourselves in a very dangerous environment. These are the last days. They are perilous times (2 Tim. 3:1). Scripture gives us a long list of the negative characteristics of people in the last days (2 Tim. 3:2-9). Jesus said that because iniquity will be abundant the love of many shall wax cold (Matt. 24:11-12). As American society moves into systemic evil behavior it will become inhospitable for those who want to live a holy life. Much of the professing church is, more and more, reflecting the attitudes of the society that they are called to reprove (Eph. 5:11-12). In this environment, errors in spiritual judgment bring greater consequences and sin brings reproach on the name of Jesus.

Christians will sin but they will not continue in sin. The Bible's idea is that we should avoid sinning at all costs. We must cease from all behavior that is in opposition to the new Kingdom of which we are a part (1 John 1:7-9). When we do sin we have Jesus as our lawyer to plead our case, as long as we come to God for forgiveness (1 John 2:1). Sin is one of the ultimate self-correcting behaviors. The problem is that in our current spiritual environment there are fewer and fewer 'instructors' to help point out the deadliness of sin. Sin always has consequences. The Bible teaches that sin is like an agricultural crop (Gal. 6:7-8). I may plant a crop in the spring but it will not come up until late summer. If I am planting seeds of sin in my life the consequences may not be truly evident until further down the road. For the true believer this is self-correcting because they will partake of godly sorrow and regret for the hurt they have caused. The true believer sees the consequences of doing wrong because of the injury inflicted upon themselves and others. Because they love God they learn not to do what they have done in the past.

As the true believer grows up in God they will have many eye opening events concerning who they are and what is wrong and right. When we come to Christ we are blind to the depth and extent of indwelling evil. A great deal of the process of sanctification that we go through has to do with discovering how badly we are bent towards evil. When we discover sin, through the means of conviction, teaching, and God's Word we have a sense of godly grief and want to change. We see the need to confess and tear down Satan's strongholds (2 Cor. 10:3-6). To continue in discovered sin then becomes quite a miserable practice. Sin brings to our hearts an abiding knowledge of disobedience to God. There is also a sense of internal discord the Bible calls condemnation. The only way to rid one's self of the condemnation is to receive forgiveness and cease the offending behavior by God's grace (Romans 8:1-3).

When we struggle against sin by human effort we will experience what I call the **try-hard cycle**. The earnest believer has been given a new heart by God so that they want to do His will rather than resist it (2 Cor. 5:17; Eze. 36:26). I know that was the case with me. I really wanted to change my behavior. At the beginning of my walk I didn't have any mentor, home church, or instruction but my heart had been profoundly changed. I realized through personal conviction that I shouldn't swear, drink, masturbate or run after my old party crowd. These things became quite simple for me. God took the swearing out of my mouth in two weeks and I only fell into the party crowd circumstance once. That was enough for me. I thought of God, the saints, and all the angels watching me and that was a quick cure for sexual immorality (1 Cor. 4:9). For the first few months things were easy to deal with and there was no struggle at all.

Then God started dealing with my lustful thoughts. It seemed the more I tried, the more I struggled, and the worse things seemed. I complained to God and prayed. I did my best and failed, day after day. I came to a place of real personal despair. I asked a spiritual friend and he told me not to worry, that some day it would be like water off a duck's back. I was not comforted and rather resented his glib response. Then one day I just gave up and suddenly God took it from me. I grew stronger and stronger in my thought life. I have repeated this try-hard cycle many times in my life with many different sins that Father has pointed out. It has never gotten any easier but I have come to understand that it is a process to bring me around to a greater over-riding truth: that I am a complete and utter failure and have no hope without His salvation.

I think we miss what Paul told us several different times: that if any person could have pleased God through human effort Paul would have been the one to do it. As a practicing Pharisee, Paul probably tried harder to be good than any man in history and made it part of his testimony (Romans 11:1; Phil. 3:1-8; Acts 23:6, 26:5ff). I have boiled Paul's Gospel down to its essence. Paul believed that any contribution that any human being could make at any time to their salvation came to the sum total of zero. To state it plainly, Paul records his own pre-salvation failure in Romans 7 as both complete and utter. By his own testimony Paul was the worst sinner to ever walk the face of the earth (1 Tim. 1:12-16). Paul goes on to tell Timothy God's logic for saving him. God displayed to everyone that if a rotten fellow like Paul had been saved that they could also be saved.

This is what really **bugs** people about the Gospel, even many Christians. Succeeding in the Christian life is predicated upon admitting failure. It is a great paradox. Using our own human effort to try to live the Christian life brings the consequence of failure. Even if I can manage to handle a few things that I am inclined to do, I will fail in other areas because my human flesh is not inclined to do all of God's will. The very core thing being corrected by each failure is our own self-effort.

Thus, when we try to do God's things on our own, the human effort becomes a self-correcting behavior. We know we are supposed to do good and find we cannot do so. Our failure causes us to cry out like Paul did with misery, *"O wretched man that I am! Who shall deliver me from the body of this death?"* (Romans 7:24). Romans 8 is Paul's answer to the question: God the Holy Spirit delivers us from sin. Romans 6-8 is really a logical representation of the try-hard cycle that we go through until we really learn to rest from our own works and let Jesus live through us (Heb. 4:10-12). Our labor is to continually enter the 'rest' of the Holy Spirit.

I think it is safe to say that most people do not embrace their failure. Failure, however, is our friend. Too many professors of religion are afraid to fail, so they are always playing it safe. Just to get started in this Christian walk we have to be willing to admit that we cannot make it without God. Then God will call us to try things that we are not able or qualified to do. We will sometimes fail. Sometimes we will honestly be trying to do God's will and we will fail anyway. We often learn more from failure than we do from success and we are certainly more humble after a failure. As we try to do God's will with our own strength, it is the cycle of failure that persuades us that we need Someone Else's help.

I remember telling a couple of deacons who were disgruntled with their new Pastor that he would probably make at least three major blunders before he succeeded. I don't find that offensive. Pastors often find themselves with people who need to learn their own strength is useless. God will send such congregations setbacks so that they will learn to rely on Him. It can be a real curse for a congregation that needs to grow up to have apparent success because success will often fuel pride. God is a good Dad. He wants His children to grow up by giving up their righteousness for His.

Somehow it has become a terrible thing for leaders to make mistakes or even admit that they make mistakes. Yet some of the most successful ministries in our day have been built from the learning process of their leaders. In fact, the whole enterprising nature of reaching out to the whole world with the Gospel has a lot more to do with holy determination and persistence than with always getting every particular direction right. We often discover the greatest ministry from what did not work. Show me a stagnant church and I will show you a group of people who quit taking risks or trying new things.

The Bible is full of people who utterly failed. God made them into successes. It seems that God often chooses underdogs to receive His calling and to do His will. As well, God often breaks with societal norms in the people He chooses and how He does things. God chose cowards, sneaks, murderers, the speech impaired, the shy, the arrogant, adulterers, people who were too young, impulsive people, big mouths, doubters, and religious maniacs. The logic, of course, is that if such persons are successful in their ministries that God must receive the glory.

God also called people to do very unusual things such as: kill their only child, marry a prostitute, lead three hundred rude drinkers into battle against an army, or lay on their side for weeks at church prophesying to those who were going by. These approaches to serving God would generally be regarded as failing enterprises. Under God's direction they were successful and pleasing in His sight.

That is why Jesus regarded self-reliant religious people with such low esteem. The one person that God cannot work with is the person who doesn't know that they are a complete and utter failure. If a person is convinced that they are pretty good or that they are essential to the purposes of God, they really are in need of the consequences of their own self-correcting behavior. If they don't learn from their consequences then it may be that the light which they think they have is darkness (Matt. 6:23). They will surely miss the purposes of God.

It really riled Jesus that religious people were never content to just be religious on their own. Religious folk are always propelled by their assurance of their own righteousness to go over 'land and sea' to convert people to their particular way of thinking (Matt. 23:15). This present spiritual wilderness is no different. These 'perilous times' that we live in are full of try-hard believers. They spend all of their time and energy teaching their brands of religion to people.

Abraham is the prototype of the nature of Christian faith (Romans 4:16-25): believing God's promise and having it put into our account for God's righteousness. Like us, Abraham's standing with God had nothing to do with his own goodness or righteousness. It appears that Abraham did not do particularly well or have any particular worldly gifts to qualify him before he met God. God took the initiative and called him. What is clear is that when God called, Abraham followed. This was his initial act of faith. The Scripture records that having faith, rather than doing some human work, is the means of human justification before God (Romans 4:3; Gal. 3:6). Most people have no problem with this until you frame it in the context of failure. Every person will continue to fail until they admit they can't make it without God. The Bible is faithful to record each giant of faith's failure and Abraham is no exception.

If we follow his story closely it kind of seems like Abraham was a wimp. He was willing to be deceptive about his wife being his sister (she was his half-sister). This caused her to be given up to the harem of Pharaoh so that Abraham could save his own skin (Gen 12:12). This was done after Abraham had already heard from God. He should have known that God would take care of him. After all, a lot of brave men have lost their lives protecting their wife's virtue. This was apparently a pretty deeply ingrained cowardice since Abraham repeated the mistake much later. He told King Abimelech of the Philistines that Sarah was his sister again (Gen 20:2). Somehow this behavior followed down to his son, yet unborn, who repeated the same behavior with his wife, Rebekah (Gen. 26:7).

Abraham wimped out again when he had sexual relations with Hagar. Sarah had urged Him to do so, in order to produce an heir without God's help. Such an action was culturally correct at that time but Abraham knew that God's promise was for him and Sarah. Abraham just could not resist the power of plan B. **Plan B** refers to all cleverness and devising of man to make God's will come to pass, just in case God doesn't do what He said. In other words, plan B is my idea of how to make God's will come to pass—the **try-hard cycle**. The greater sin for Abraham was not his actions or their consequences. It was his unwillingness to let God work things out, come hell or high water. Abraham leaves a pretty good record of failure for us to learn from.

Eventually we see Abraham reach his personal pinnacle of faith. It is clear that all of the self-correcting behavior which had resulted in failure brought him to an exhaustion of human means. When a person has reached a hundred, they pretty much give up any idea of new additions to the family. Abraham passed a major test, not at the beginning of his life, but at a time of devastating hopelessness. Only God could make His promise of Isaac come true. He passed this test at one hundred years of age. Everything he had tried had failed. He eventually had to send plan B (Ishmael) away; another act of faith.

By the time God called upon him to sacrifice Isaac, Abraham had the faith that God would raise him from the dead, if necessary. Isaac was a miracle in the first place. We often miss the complete failure of human means in this story. It is Abraham's appropriate response to his own failure that is important. He learned that he could trust God for his very life and all of his future hope. That lesson is what God took a lifetime to teach our father Abraham. It is the same lesson of faith that He teaches his children over and over again, until it is perfected in them.

Moses is another case of self-correcting behavior (Exodus 2). He was a miracle child. Moses was nursed by his mother for years. This may be the time he learned about his heritage. He was raised as a prince of Egypt. He had the equivalent of a university education and had become used to exercising power in the manner of an Egyptian leader. Moses had some sort of growing awareness of the need for his people to be set free. Finally, he felt compelled to go down to see the children of Israel and investigate their living conditions. Moses was absolutely outraged to see the abuse heaped upon his people.

This man, who enjoyed the pinnacle of training and advantage, looked around to see if anyone was looking. He then impulsively killed an Egyptian taskmaster. What a stroke of genius! He couldn't even pull off this little act of terrorism without being front-page news by the next day. His attempt to help his people ended in complete and utter failure. He had to flee the country just to save his own life. The Scripture account does not really belabor the report of Moses' failure but it is clear that Moses had failed. He had no hope of helping his people at all, let alone delivering them out of Egypt.

God used the wilderness to help Moses face his failure and learn to depend on God. Moses married and raised a family in this rural setting. The bitterness of his heart over his failure and flight may be revealed by his name for his first son, Gershom, which is translated 'banishment' (Exodus 2:22).[1] A change in his attitude is reflected in the naming of his second son, Eliezer, which is translated 'God is help' (Exodus 18:4).[2] Somewhere between his first and second sons, Moses had worked through his failure in Egypt and had come to understand that his only hope was God.

Moses did not receive his burning bush call until the end of his forty years in the wilderness. As we have before noted, he learned alone in the school of silence. There seems to be little evidence that he understood the full nature of his call until he was eighty. This is just like God. He calls a man who is over the hill, washed up, and out of the mainstream. Moses had become so conformed to God's ways in the wilderness that he made few mistakes from that point on. He had abandoned his own ability and became one of God's greatest servants. Out of the ashes of a man's failure God can bring greatness.

Recently, a friend of mine told me that I was a failure as a Pastor, a failure as a husband, a failure as a father, and a failure as a man. Doesn't that sound horrible? He actually said this in the context of a very low point in my life and ministry. My church had dwindled down to a very few people and I had resigned. It may have appeared to an outsider that I did not understand my wife. None of my children were serving the Lord yet. I had very few positive prospects as a man in my late forties. My friend went on to say that I had some real potential to do something for God. I was not insulted or bothered by his comments because I learned many years ago that I could not really succeed in this life without God. My friend was absolutely right! People looking at my life would know from that point on, any success or blessing was truly the Lord. Obviously, success will not come from any cleverness or wisdom that I have.

This could be a very depressing letter indeed if not for two little words in the Bible: "but God." I love "but God." When men are down, out, and defeated there is always "but God." For the sinner: *"**But God** commendeth his love toward us, in that, while we were yet sinners, Christ died for us"* (Romans 5:8). For the person who has a hard time understanding spiritual things: *"But as it is written,*

*Eye hath not seen, nor ear heard, neither have entered into the heart of man, the things which God hath prepared for them that love him.* ***But God*** *hath revealed them unto us by his Spirit:"* (1 Cor. 2:9-10). For those who feel alienated from God: *"**But God,** who is rich in mercy, for his great love wherewith he loved us, Even when we were dead in sins, hath quickened us together with Christ, (by grace ye are saved;)"* (Eph. 2:4-5). "But God" is repeated many times in the context of human insufficiency.

King David of Israel put this term in some of his songs. He contrasted negative circumstances with what God did in the midst of them (Psalms 49:15; 73:26). King Solomon used "but God" to contrast what men were planning to what God would allow the outcome to be (Prov. 21:12). Jonah's "but God" was a worm; a cure for his worldly attachment to a gourd (Jonah 4:7). Like us, Jonah had grown attached to something of little value and didn't care about souls. God was faithful to take Jonah's little worldly attachment away so that he would learn to think like God. Can you think of times when God has sent a worm to eat the gourd of self-effort in your life? The failure of our temporal planning always makes us look to God again.

Jesus used the term "but God" to contrast the way that worldly men were attached to the things of this life with eternal perspectives. He illustrated God's perspective of mankind's puny little plans by showing God's reaction to human retirement plans (Luke 12:20; 16:15). Stephen pointed out the fact, "**but God** was with him" as the difference for Joseph after he was sold out by his brothers (Acts 7:9).

Peter got a revelation about the Gentiles. He said, *"but God hath showed me that I should not call any man common or unclean"* (Acts 11:8-9). The mission to the Gentiles came from a "but God." Paul contrasted our sinful state with what we have become with a "but God" (Acts 13:30; Romans 5:8; 6:17).

Admitting failure as a consequence of our self-correcting behavior is an upsetting idea for many nowadays. The Corinthians despised the Gospel of a weak God and weak men. So do many Christians today. In the mind of the Greek philosophers it was a real insult for God to become so weak that He would die on a cross.

This is why the Bible speaks of the preaching of the Cross as a **scandal** (Romans 9:33; Gal. 5:11; 1Pet. 2:8). The Greek mind was scandalized by such a concept. The Corinthians wanted a more success oriented Jesus, a triumphant Jesus, so they had a theology that they were in the 'kingdom now': ruling with Christ. Does this sound familiar? Paul's detractors felt that he was a loser. They didn't believe that God would use somebody so small and unassuming for His ministry (2 Cor. 10:10). Paul rejoiced that God used what men regard as weak and foolish to propel His Good News forward (1 Cor. 1:27). This was the preaching of the Cross to spread God's message and save men's souls from sin.

Paul encapsulates the contrast between the failure of men and God's intervention in his letter to the Ephesians 2:1-5:

*And you [hath he quickened], who were **dead** in **trespasses** and **sins**; Wherein in time past ye walked according to the course of this world, according to the prince of the power of the air, the spirit that now worketh in the children of **disobedience**: Among whom also we all had our conversation in times past in the lusts of our flesh, **fulfilling the desires of the flesh and of the mind**; and **were by nature the children of wrath**, even as others. **But God**, who is **rich in mercy**, for his **great love** wherewith he **loved us**, even when we were **dead in sins**, hath **quickened us** together with Christ, (by **grace** ye are saved)*

What a God! What love! The Bible speaks of us as being without hope or God in this world (Eph. 2:11-13). If that doesn't describe humans as failures, I just don't know what does! Look at the above description. Paul argues that by our very nature we are children of wrath. Do we really believe that we are failures? Have we embraced the fact that only a fantastic rescue mission from heaven, spearheaded by our Savior Jesus, could save us? If so, shouldn't we be a lot more humble and grateful?

That's why I love "but God." The good news is that if we can get off our high horses and admit the truth "but God" comes into effect; but not until then. So many teachers stress aspects of living the Christian life without teaching the need for a constant admission of helplessness to do it on our own. Paul loved this truth. He said that, *"most gladly therefore will I rather glory in my infirmities, that the power of Christ may rest upon me. Therefore I take pleasure in infirmities, in reproaches, in necessities, in persecutions, in distresses for Christ's sake: for when I am weak, then I am strong."* (2 Cor. 12:10). This is the realization that all self-correcting behavior will bring us to.

It is important to interpret events properly. Paul didn't take the multitudes of difficulties, trials, temptations, and even failures as an evidence of God's disapproval or rejection. He had learned to properly interpret the events of his life. He realized that the very things the world rejects out of hand (infirmities, reproaches, necessities, persecutions and distresses) were the things that made Paul so weak that he had to depend on Christ's strength.

The lifelong process of sanctification encapsulates this central truth. Without Jesus living through me I can never please God. All of the failures, errors, and mistakes bring me back to this "Anchor of the soul" (Heb. 6:19). He forgives all of my iniquities and heals all of my diseases (Psalm 103:3). This is where all true Christian assurance lies. The same Father who disciplines His child will always forgive and enable that child for further service and fellowship (Heb. 12:5-10).

I have had it both ways. The Lord has allowed me to partake of the fullness of the sorrow and consequence of sin. He did this when I needed a deep impression of my need for Him. At other times Father has picked me up, delivered me out of my circumstances, and set me on His pathway. **Our God is the perfect Dad that nobody ever had!** He does all things well. Therefore I can assure my heart before Him whether my heart condemns me or not. I have the Spirit of adoption which cries out within me, "Father" (Romans 8:15).

So my friend, do not think that you are so unique. If you have failed or God has disciplined you, don't be so astonished. If you have severe limitations or persecution do not be cast down. If you are struggling, you are not alone. God is working in you. He will cause you to triumph! Embrace the trial and trust that God will bring you through, for His strength is perfected in our weakness. The key is to learn the right lessons from our self-correcting behavior. Admit you can't do it alone and God will bring it to pass in you.

Fellowshipping in His Discipline,

Henry

# CHAPTER 12

# *Tools*

Dear Fellow Traveler,

My father was one of the most talented mechanics and builders I have ever met in my life. As a boy I remember sneaking downstairs late at night to watch him work. He had all kinds of shortwave radios, electronic equipment, saws, lathes and tools of every description. Dad could fabricate items in metal, fiberglass, wood, and any other material necessary. One year, he built a boat in the basement and later he started to build an airplane. He was a master mechanic and when he died in the early eighties his shop tools alone were worth nearly one hundred thousand dollars. Dad believed there was a tool for every job and a job for every tool. If there wasn't a tool for the job he would invent one. What a gifted man he was.

In the wilderness it is extremely important to have or to be able to fashion the appropriate tools for survival and convenience. If you don't have a lighter or a match to make a fire you will need to be able to fashion a well proportioned bow and drill. A good four inch knife has so many essential uses. With just this knife a person can make fire tools, bows and arrows, all manner of traps and snares, and small wooden implements. A knife is essential for dressing and skinning an animal or cleaning a fish. A knife makes it easy to cut and prepare vegetation for eating and to make rope from other plants. A piece of plastic can allow you to condense water under arid conditions. It is very nice to have the luxury of a light tent, a mini cook stove, a good sleeping bag, proper clothing, and good footwear. There is nothing like a little first-aid kit when you need to dress a wound or disinfect a cut. The wilderness wayfarer is careful to take along a kit of essential tools.

God has left us some very simple but useful tools to stay alive and do His work in the spiritual wilderness. I will tell you which tools I have in my tool kit and how I use them. It is important to remember these are not physical tools. God has already provided them for us through Christ's sacrifice but we must allow them to work for us by His grace. Most of God's tools for our salvation walk are quite simple. It is only required that a child of God pick them up and use them. I am sure you have discovered many of God's tools already. God's entire remnant are students of the Word. They know where to find God's tools. They are recorded in the Bible.

Our first tool is the **Cross of Christ**. It is a great tool for both standing and moving ahead in the spiritual wilderness. Many suggest that Jesus had to do something more than to die on the Cross. They suggest He wrestled with the devil in hell or the like. The Bible clearly states the opposite. Jesus completely defeated and made a public spectacle of the devil on the Cross. He atoned completely for our sins there (Col. 2:13-15). The use of the Cross in daily life is absolutely essential. The devil has a ministry of accusation and condemnation that he would love to heap upon the believer. When we have faith in the work of the Cross, have repented of our sin, and are committed to Christ's lordship, none of the accusations or claims of the devil have any standing. The arrest warrant for crimes against God has been cancelled since Jesus nailed it to the cross.

That is why Paul was committed to bragging about the Cross (Gal. 6:14). To Paul, the Cross was his means (or tool) to overcome the world day after day. The finished work of the Cross means that all the power of this world, our flesh, and the devil cannot compel us to displease God any more. Paul 'took up his cross' with joy because he wasn't having a sorrowing funeral for his old sinful life. Instead he was rejoicing that he was crucified to the world and the world was crucified to him.

We need to join Paul in reckoning ourselves dead indeed to sin but alive to God through the Cross of Jesus Christ (Romans 6:11-14). We need to bring this tool into our lives on a daily basis as part of a mindset for victory. We will find that the Cross is invaluable for our survival. We will reflect the attitude, thinking, and ways of the world less and less when we regard ourselves as crucified to the world and the world crucified to us.

Another great aid in living our daily lives is recognition of the indwelling **resurrection power** of God. Paul did not just preach Jesus' death on a Cross. Along with the Cross Paul preached Christ's resurrection from the dead. He viewed this as the beginning of a 'crop' of resurrections (1 Cor. 15:20, 23). Although he looked forward to his own resurrection in the last day, Paul did not relegate resurrection power just to the future. Paul regarded the dynamic power of the resurrection that dwelt in him as an ever present empowerment. He credited the indwelling Holy Spirit with Christ's resurrection and said that this Spirit would make us alive day by day as He dwells in us (Rom. 8:8-14). Although some regard Romans 8:11 as a Scripture relating to healing, the context has a lot more to do with **daily** victorious living. The same Spirit that raised Christ from the dead makes us powerfully alive to God day by day.

The resurrection power of Jesus is the other bookend to His Cross. Jesus rose from the dead! This validated all of His claims and set into motion all of our ability to live the Christian life. Jesus died on the Cross which purchased our right to be forgiven. The Holy Spirit raised Jesus from the dead. Paul made an appeal to the Spirit's indwelling as our 'seal of approval' as children of the living God (Rom 8:14; 2 Cor. 1:21-22; Eph 1:13, 4:30). We have the very heart of children who call Him Father (Rom. 8:15).

Quoting Scripture or having a good confession is of little value if you don't know the power of the Holy Spirit that dwells within. We may be positive minded as much as we wish but it will not be a substitute for having the third Person of the Trinity dwelling inside of us. We may reasonably expect the Holy Spirit to empower us every day. He will inspire the words of truth we both speak and believe. His creative power in us will also make the words of Jesus reality in our lives. That is why our lives will move "from glory to glory" (2 Cor. 3:18). Our profession and confession must be inspired by Christ's resurrection power. Our responsibility is to **allow** the Holy Spirit to do this work in us.

The **name of Jesus** has everything to do with God's Kingdom authority on planet earth. I am amazed that Jesus could send out unregenerate men with just His name. The name of Jesus gave such astonishing and consistent positive results (Luke 10:1, 17). His disciples used Jesus' name and did all of the works that He did. Many speak His name and profess to be His friends today with little or no results. What is the difference? Is it possible that many are speaking His name in vain—using it in an empty way? Perhaps we need to mix faith with our profession. That was Israel's problem (Heb. 4:2). They had the Gospel but no faith mixed with it. Thus, they had a word but not a living Word. As we speak the name of Jesus and allow God to impart His faith to us, we will see situations change.

We are promised an ability to do the works of God in the name of Jesus (Mark 16:17-20). This promise is not for fearfully whispered prayers in a corner somewhere. Such works will be accompanied by a loud and bold enunciation of faith in Jesus' name, out in the public market place. A reason for the great success of the disciples of Jesus in the first century Church is that they boldly used Jesus' name in the way He prescribed. They healed and drove out demons in Jesus' name. They preached bluntly and boldly in Jesus' name (Acts 4:29-30). They had faith because Jesus' name had all the authority of Heaven behind it. His name still has the same authority and we need to quit waiting around for an impartation of power from somebody else. We have the name of the One to whom all power has already been given (Matt. 28:18). We have already been encouraged to work in Jesus' name.

Just give me a momentary aside of crabbiness, if you please. I hate to hear people publicly pray and finish with, "In your name, amen." Use the name! It is the name of Jesus that will propel our prayer to the throne of God. It is the name of Jesus, and that name only, that is heard and respected in the prayer room of God where Jesus ever lives to make intercession for us. Use His name! There is no other name given under heaven whereby we must be saved (Acts 4:12)! All the power of heaven is marshaled in Jesus' name. Be proud of the name! Love the name! Wear the name of Jesus as your only crowning glory! If you do, you will absolutely change the atmosphere wherever you are because Jesus still dwells in the praises of His people.

Our next tool is the precious **Blood of Jesus**. In the Older Testament the blood of the Passover sacrifice was sprinkled on the doorposts with a hyssop bush (Ex. 12:22). Jesus' Blood is more than symbolic and must also be applied to the doorway of our heart. Our confession of sin and request for the cleansing of the Blood of Jesus can be compared to the physical action of applying the blood of a lamb with a hyssop bush (Heb. 9:19-22; 10:21-22). John assures us that if we walk in the light of God we have a continual cleansing of the Blood of Jesus (1 John 1:7). Whenever we see sin in our heart we can go for cleansing since Jesus' Blood paid the complete price for our sins. What a neglected tool the Blood of Jesus is. What a close account we ought to keep with God since this cleansing is integral to enjoying life with the Father.

Some people are very superstitious where the Blood of Jesus is concerned. They 'Plead the Blood' of Jesus as a sort of cure-all to keep the devil away. I do not discredit this practice and will occasionally do it myself. I understand pleading the Blood of Jesus as pleading both the atonement for my sin and protection from the enemy of mankind, the devil. It is most important to understand that you are invoking your Covenant rights which have already been purchased by the Blood of Jesus. By pleading the Blood of Jesus we gain nothing more than a reminder of the finished work of Christ, for ourselves and against the enemies of our soul. The important part of such a process is that we have faith that God will act on our behalf because of the shed Blood of Jesus. This is what will dislodge the devil and his strongholds whether in our own life or in the lives of those around us.

In the last thirty years much has been made of a **positive confession**. I believe that this is quite a simple truth. Every believer should speak out loud about the things that the Bible clearly states are already theirs. This is a very useful tool for changing the way we live, what we expect from God, and many difficult circumstances that will arise. Too much emphasis has been put on receiving material things by the 'gain is godliness' crowd (1 Tim. 6:5). It is much more important to positively confess the simple truths of the Christian walk and character. This will release the power of God to transform our lives into the likeness of Christ. So much of a good confession has to do with simply stating things as the Bible has already stated them. To not have the Bible's truth on our lips would be to lie about the goodness and salvation of God.

As I mentioned above, it is essential to mix faith in with a Biblical confession. For instance, when a believer feels like sinning they should confess that they are dead and their life is hidden with Christ in God (Col. 3:3). They could confess that it is no longer their life but Christ's life that lives in them (Gal. 2:20). If a person feels condemned they should confess Romans 8:1, which states that there is no condemnation for the believer. If a person doesn't feel like they can pray they should confess that they have, "*boldness and access with confidence by the faith of Him*" (Eph. 3:12). The Word of God needs to be confessed often in prayer. This is where the Holy Spirit can mix His gift of faith with our confession to bring it to fruition. So many people are caught up with the idea that if they just keep saying things over and over again they will get them. Confession is not so much about getting from God as it is about becoming like God. God wants our lives to be a workmanship that is a sweet fragrance of heaven (2 Cor. 2:15: Eph. 2:10).

One day, Jesus was transfigured before three of his disciples on a mountain—a profound spiritual event. Meanwhile, the 'boys' who were 'minding the store' at the base of the mountain ran into a huge surprise (Mark 9:1-29). They ran into a manifestation of the devil that they could not remove in Jesus' name. It is important to understand that they had not yet experienced failure in Christ's name. This failure must have been an astonishing event for them. The whole story contrasts Jesus' faith with everyone else's unbelief.

I think we miss the riotous nature of the scene. People were coming and going. Scribes were fussing and arguing with disciples. A crowd had gathered and was growing. A faithless and heartbroken father expressed his doubt that anything could be done. Jesus quickly dealt with the situation and moved to the quiet of someone's house. The disciple's question should ring in our ears: "*why couldn't we cast him out*" (v. 28). It should bother us because there are many who speak in Jesus' name today who do not have the power to dislodge the devil.

I have named Jesus' answer to their failure the **'fasted lifestyle'**. If you are reading a more modern version you will notice that the reference to fasting is eliminated. That is not surprising because the devil hates the tool of fasting very much. Jesus was not just recommending fasting when we come upon a difficult spiritual case. He was really commenting on the lifestyle difference between Him and His closest followers. The disciples were quite happy to trundle along behind Christ's spiritual wake. They had not put together a connection between the self-denial of Jesus, in long hours of prayer and systematic fasting, with His great power. Jesus lived an entirely different lifestyle than His followers. They loved the parties and the praise. They did not understand it was the lonely protracted times of spiritual discipline, fighting the devil in advance, praying through resistance, and self-shattering fasts that caused Jesus to always triumph. Jesus used their abject failure to illustrate to them their spiritual bankruptcy. They had only to avail themselves of the same means that Jesus used to obtain the same results.

Much has been written in our day about the wonderful Spirit-filled life. However, it doesn't take much examination of the walk of Jesus to recognize that the One who had the Spirit without measure sought the quiet and lonely place often (Matt. 14:23; Mark 6:46-47; John 6:15). He was a man of sorrows and acquainted with grief (Isaiah 53:1-4). It is clear that Jesus is inviting whosoever will to come and fellowship with Him in His sufferings (Phil. 3:7-11). So many people want a quick fix or a party. Most people do not want to pay the price to see the manifestation of God's power.

The price is taking on the sin of the world (2 Cor. 4:6-12). The price involves pruning away all of our sin along with the strongholds of Satan in our lives. We do this by cutting them off with Christ's Blood, Cross, resurrection, and Word. Jesus took up His Cross to take away the sin of the world and He commands us to take up our cross and follow Him (John 1:29; Matt. 10:38). As we come to Him in prayer and fasting He fashions our hard, stony old hearts into soft gentle hearts (Eze. 36:26-27). Then we are able to finally see people the way Jesus sees them (Mark 8:24-25).

The fasted lifestyle is bondservant cooperation with God. As we yield to our Father, He allows our hearts to be enlarged (2 Cor. 6:11ff). The bondservant served his master from a motive of love, not because of necessity. Although there was a point where he could leave, the bondservant would avow himself to serve his master for the rest of his life. The servant would then be marked appropriately. Paul knew that people become more like their heavenly Father and less like a rebellious and lost world as they allow God to fill their hearts with His love.

Paul the apostle had a desire that I can't imagine having. He wished that he could go to hell in the place of the lost Jewish people who didn't know Jesus (Romans 9:3). What love was in Paul's heart! He called the motivation for his ministry to the Gentiles the "terror of the Lord" (2 Cor. 5:11). For this reason, no sacrifice was too great. Rather than boasting in his great spirituality as a sign of service he boasted of his sufferings (2 Cor. 6:3-10). The mark of maturity for Paul was that there were no impediments to his service. Nothing would be held back from God. Paul had a holy indifference to his own desires. This is the essence and result of the fasted lifestyle.

As a believer allows God to rule their legitimate freedom, they start to move into the fasted lifestyle. Eating, sleeping, and relaxing are legitimate. To bring these most basic needs into subjection to Christ is to tap into the power that Christ displayed on this earth. There is no virtue in skipping food. However, if you set aside eating for the Kingdom of God the Bible states that this will somehow build your faith (Isaiah 58:1-12). I like to demystify this by referring to fasting as a simple spiritual tool. It is not the self-denial or lack of self-denial that affects answers from God. It is faith which is enhanced by a physical activity both practiced and recommended by Jesus.

Praying and fasting are some of the ultimate denials of the self-life. Praying as God moves you to pray, whether day or night, long or short, develops your spiritual inner ear and builds your faith. It may be even simpler than this. As a man, I am more inclined to favor people who seek me out because they love me and want to be with me more than those who do not seek me out. Although God is no respecter of persons with regard to salvation, He does speak of rewarding those who diligently seek Him (Heb. 11:6). Maybe the fasted lifestyle is that simple. I don't know. What I do know is that it is a powerful tool in a disciple's tool box.

There are some wrenches that need two people to turn them and some tools that need more than one person to efficiently operate them. The **corporate prayer life** of the church is such a tool. We are given 'Presence with Power' as two or more of us gather together, in the unity of the Holy Spirit, for prayer. Any time that believers gather together there should be an electric anticipation in faith for a visitation of God. This is the dynamo of the church that has been given to us by God. We can expect powerful results as we yield the prayer meeting up to the great Administrator, the precious Holy Spirit of God.

One of the great tragedies of our day is the anemic corporate prayer meeting. If a church has one hour of continuous, protracted, Spirit-filled prayer in a week, it is an exceptional church. If there is more corporate prayer than an hour, the church is a rare jewel. Some churches have much prayer but it is a powerless event because the meeting is not controlled by the Holy Spirit but by man. The Mind of Christ is not revealed and prayed through by the people present. If long prayers could get God's attention the Muslims would win. Corporate prayer **MUST** be empowered by the living God.

What a subversive little tool true Christian prayer is. No minister or group can control or regulate it. Any small group can pray anywhere. This is the weapon of the remnant. I am not likely to find fifty people that really agree with me in the Holy Spirit but I may find five or six. I can fellowship with them at my home or theirs. We can pray as much as we want, wherever we want. The devil hates this tool because it smashes his kingdom and his plans. He loves a dead old prayer meeting or a church administered prayer soak that is lifeless, powerless, and useless. He hates a few people turning the wrench of Holy Spirit-birthed prayer. The remnant doesn't just know this fact. They are seeking others of a like mind to practice Spirit-filled prayer and receive water from the wells of salvation (Isaiah 12:3).

This was the great practice of the first century Church. Follow the story in the Book of Acts and you will see the continuous practice of daily corporate prayer. They knew when they were together that Christ was in session. They had no greater desire than to continue 'instant' in prayer, together (Romans 12:12). This generation of religious experts needs to cast aside their 'Saul's Armor', the armor that is not God's armor (1 Sam. 17:38-39; Eph. 6:11ff). If they would drop their programmatic and organizational religious practices, instead humbling their hearts before God, it would truly change the spiritual landscape. Unfortunately, such simplicity is an insult to grandiose intellects and powerful multi-media presentations. It is too simple to think that God waits for His people to really get it together in the humble place of prayer.

Over the years we have been able to have some profound visitations of God during many of our prayer meetings. We have taken the Lord Jesus Christ presencing Himself with us in a 'feelingly near' way as the seal of approval and the acid test of the quality of the prayer service. We have enjoyed the satisfaction of His witness and direction during the prayer meeting. The only proviso we have found is that there have to be other people in the room who understand the goal and will 'go for it'. We have seen that just a few people in agreement are able to move a very resistant room full of people into the presence of God.

When Christ is in session during prayer, the meeting takes on a miraculous air. Suddenly the **gift of faith** is present. Progress is made against infernal spirits in heavenly places. The atmosphere of the community and the whole region is changed. The Holy Spirit brings more conviction into people's lives in the surrounding community. The church services become an extension of the prayer meeting. Of course, falsely religious people, often motivated by the devil, will rise up and resist. Leaders will want to take control. Those praying in the Holy Spirit will be tested and tempted. Nevertheless, the presence of Christ is a powerful inducement to endure such minor difficulties.

False religion will always resist the simple tool of corporate prayer as an overly simple approach. This is the acid test of false religion. They take up the Galatian complaint. The Galatian error was to start changing the simple relationship with Jesus into a rule and wisdom-oriented religion. In their case, they took up Judaism along with Jesus. Again, it really bothers people that knowing God can be so simple and requires no human intervention or assistance. You can have vital corporate prayer wherever you have a few who want God more than anything. Do not let anyone sucker you into empty religion when you can revel in the presence of God day after day.

I believe that these vital encounters with the presence of Christ are what produce the tools of **worship and praise**. Many associate the song service at church with worship. It is my observation that the more refined and performance-oriented we have become, the further we have moved from worship. Praise and worship are the day by day responses of the human heart to the presence and goodness of God. Worship and praise are deeper than emotion, although they are certainly emotional. They flow from knowledge of a Person and that Person is Jesus. Worship is the reverential awe that we experience from the privilege of knowing the Most High. Praise is the natural outflow of gratitude for all that He does for us day by day.

Just do it. A friend of mine praises so loudly in public that it gets everyone's attention. He says he is just cleaning up the atmosphere. He really means it. I have been with him in coffee shops, restaurants, churches, and the like. Wherever he goes people respond positively to that very bold kind of praise. It dispels the wrong spirit and allows God's presence to be released. It is not hard or complex. I am sure that it delights the heart of the Most High God. Praise and worship are immediate mood changers. Praise and worship cause demons to flee. Praise and worship are beautiful and no church, leader, or music is required to give God pleasure (Psalms 33:1; 147:1). Again, be wise and do not let anybody steal the simplicity of worship and praise from you.

Finally, the devil is a liar and the father of lies (John 8:44). In fact, when the devil lies he is speaking his native language. It is therefore imperative that we use **honesty** as a powerful tool against him. Some people prefer to call it transparency but the Bible calls it speaking the truth in love (Eph. 4:15). Every true thing should not be spoken because to do so may not follow the law of love. Nevertheless, a general policy of honesty will save us all a lot of sorrow and reproach.

This honesty is two-fold. First we must be honest with and about ourselves. This includes both our strengths and weaknesses. This will help us avoid pride because all of us have profound weakness that we need God's help with. When we get honest we start to acknowledge our sin. We will cut off and expel that which is not of God. While we live in this world the result of our salvation is for us to be holy as He is holy (1 Peter 1:15-16). As we break the bondage of the devil we will truly start to represent the Kingdom of God as ambassadors (2 Cor. 5:20). Our transparency about having dealt with sin makes us able to truly represent the Kingdom of Heaven. Our testimony of God's deliverance will give hope to all those who here us.

Secondly, we also need to tell others the truth. If our heart is motivated by love we will kindly stand against evil in the church. Besides, honesty makes our personal relationships easier. By being clear what we think and believe we leave a lot less room for misunderstanding. We will confess our faults one to another and pray one for the other that we may be healed (James 5:16). Transparent honesty opens the door for deep and loving Christian relationships. Soon we will start to realize that we really are in God's family.

I am sure that you could add some tools to this kit. Many of you could add insights to their use as well. Tools are no good to us unless we pick them up and use them for the purposes that they were created for. If you use all of these tools, by the grace of God, you will thrive in this present spiritual wilderness. God will set a table for you right in the presence of your enemies (Psalm 23:5). May God lead you forward to His best and happy trails to you,

Your Friend,

Henry

# CHAPTER 13

# *Camouflage: Accidental &*
# *Intentional Pretenders*

Dear Fellow Traveler,

*A*fter you have learned the basics in any wilderness course you will be taught about camouflage. Camouflage is the art of covering your presence in the wilderness from the animals that you wish to stalk or that may wish to stalk you. Camouflage includes many aspects of changing visual cues to blend in with the surrounding terrain. Clothes may be camouflaged for wilderness or desert situations. A traveler can blank out flesh-tones with clay, soot, or vegetable pigments to hide their face and hands.

The general principle is to break up the appearance of your form from the terrain. As well, care is taken to move slowly and in harmony with the activity of the wilderness so as not to disturb your natural surroundings. Smoke from your fire is used to mask the human scent from detection. These and many other techniques will enable the wilderness traveler to move through the forest undetected by man or beast. Philosophically, the wilderness wayfarer wants to disturb as little of his environment as possible. His goal is to move undetected.

The military has also had a great deal of interest in camouflage over the years. If soldiers can hide themselves from their enemies they may pass right by them without being detected. Most of you will be acquainted with the forest or urban camouflage clothing that is standard issue in the military. The Bible states that we are in a war with the forces of evil and warns that our enemy is a master of camouflage (2 Cor. 11:14).

The spiritual wilderness wayfarer has little interest in camouflaging who they are. In fact, the true saints of God are very transparent with all of their motives and dealings in this world. I do not mean to suggest that they will be foolish. We are told that the mature follower of Christ knows how to say the right thing at the right time. They do not utter their whole mind but are discrete and have conversation that is "seasoned with salt" (Col. 4:6). In all of their dealings with both the church and the world they have no secret agenda. Therefore, God's children have no need to hide their true intentions.

There are three general groups who use camouflage in the church. I will deal with two in this letter—the unintentional and the intentional pretender. You may ask, "Why do I need to discern pretenders?" Proper discernment saves time, effort, and disappointment. As part of the remnant it is essential to be able to discern the genuine believer from those who pretend. It is hard to truly identify with people who do not really share your faith. It is impossible to help someone who is not committed to obey God. God does not want His remnant 'spinning their wheels' with individuals who are really not part of His body and have little interest in becoming so.

In an earlier letter I spoke of shelter in the wilderness. Imagine the reaction that a family would have to the sudden appearance of new people in their home claiming to be members of the family. It is easy to imagine that such pretenders would be evicted rather quickly since both parents were present at the birth of all their children. They know who belongs and who does not. This analogy also works for every one of us that has been **adopted** into the family of God. It is clear that children adopted into a family still treat the parents as their own. As well, they regard their brothers and sisters as their own. Both parents and siblings have an intimate interest and knowledge of the time and place of the arrival of each adopted child. Naturally the adoptive family would be very wary of anyone trying to join the family without the endorsement of the adoptive parents. The question would arise, "Who is this stranger?"

It is clear to me that such scrutiny is absent in many places of worship and has become warped in many others. Many churches do not believe they can grow if they risk offending people. They may ask about a newcomer's background but will not press too hard for clear evidence of conversion. As we have become more seeker-sensitive it has been increasingly regarded as impolite to probe into people's beliefs when you first meet them at church. This hesitancy comes from a philosophy that espouses cultural relevance. Many people feel that it is impolite to vigorously delve into people's backgrounds. Nevertheless the question remains, "Should the life of the church be dictated by increasingly profane cultural norms?"

Some other groups have criteria ostensibly based on the Bible. A **salvation formula** is used when attempting to lead a person to Christ. Then the convert is encouraged to stand on the Word or **try to be** a good Christian. They may attend a class on the basics. There is often little scrutiny or interest in whether a person has been truly regenerated. This presents an extra-Biblical problem. The remnant finds themselves fellowshipping with people who are not part of God's family. They either have no intention of meeting His terms or think they have been inducted into the family already. More and more often, you will find church groups who are overwhelmingly made up of people who are not born again. Others may have had some sort of touch from God but have long since given up any interest or belief in a day to day walk with Him. Understandably, this presents a profound challenge to those who are zealous followers of the Way.

Most believers that have been in the church for awhile have been confronted by hypocrisy. Hypocrisy can be a huge stumbling block for thoughtful and vulnerable people. Yet hypocrisy is most often expressed by those who profess but do not possess the living God—accidental and intentional pretenders. One coping mechanism people use to deal with hypocrisy is to make a kind of treaty with themselves not to be the person who is in charge of exposing hypocrisy and sin. The truth be told, the honest saint is often much taken with their own inconsistencies. Experience has taught them that mercy rejoices against judgment (James 2:13). Furthermore, it is clearly the job of those in authority to deal with discipline in the church so the average congregate will leave it to leadership.

Jesus truly detested hypocrisy of every kind. A word study on the word for hypocrisy yields much light. The Greek word *hupokrites*[1] is best translated role player, pretender, or actor, in our present vernacular. This is fascinating since such veneration is given to actors in our culture, even in the professing Christian world. It is interesting that people who make their living by fooling us into thinking they are someone else or who convince us that they believe something differently than they really believe command such attention, status, financial remuneration, and credence in our society. It is clear that people with such talent should be doubted in everything that they say and do. These are the ultimate camouflage artists, the great pretenders. To Jesus, such talent was to be carefully avoided by believers. They were to abhor pretense of every kind.

As I mentioned in an earlier letter, believers go through a process of becoming real. We have learned all the phoniness that society teaches us in the name of politeness and societal norm. Jesus presents a small child as an example of humility, weakness, honesty, and uncamouflaged behavior and attitude. Jesus' anger against hypocrisy stems from the fact that it imposes external pretensions upon people. Jesus prescribed humble admission that we are sinners as the beginning of our walk with the Father. Paradoxically, we can only have righteousness imputed to us if we contritely admit we are sinners. If we plead guilty, then human pride, effort, or pretension is rendered redundant. Paul states, *"Where is boasting then? It is excluded"* (Romans 3:27).

A very common type of person using camouflage is what I have called the **accidental pretender**. This kind of person may be found in almost all evangelical, charismatic, independent, and main-line churches. In fact, they may well be a creation of well meaning evangelicals. Although he did not use my terminology, A. W. Tozer[2] spent a great deal of time in the late fifties and early sixties examining the degeneration of the Gospel presentation and the resulting conflicted so-called 'convert'.[3] His main concern was reflected in many of his essays which dealt with people professing to know Jesus who failed to successfully live the Christian life. In fact, Tozer was very concerned that in many parts of the evangelical world that new converts were not even **expected** to experience profound change. He also mourned the fact that so many displayed little interest in the rigors of the Christian life. If the problem was bad when Tozer was writing it is certainly much worse now.

In this present day we have produced what is tantamount to a 'magic formula' to deal with people who want to 'accept Christ'. This formula is what is called the **'sinner's prayer'** and has somehow become the standard approach in dealing with seekers. At its core, this prayer has the confession that Jesus is God, the confession that the person praying has sinned, the confession that Jesus died for their sins, and the invitation for Jesus to come into the person's heart and be their Savior. Some of these prayers will have something about living for Jesus; fewer will express sorrow over personal sin. The need for repentance is usually completely ignored.

Very often the sinner's prayer is prayed at the end of a service and sometimes at an altar call, if an altar call is even given. Very often there are no preparatory comments before the prayer. Many times, after the prayer is finished, individual attention, explanation, or diligent personal follow-up are not given to the seeker. The person leading the sinner's prayer may just tell the congregation that all who prayed that prayer are now Christians and have new life in Jesus Christ. How can the person leading possibly know that? Where does the Bible tell us that? Besides, only a moron would say 'no' to the question, "Do you want to go to heaven?"

It is clear to me that such an approach lacks any means for measuring the level of concern an individual may have for their eternal soul. Unless a person is profoundly convicted that they are a rebel against God and desperately need salvation, their conversion will lack depth. I think it is wrong to use this prayer without some appropriate introductory explanation. In addition there must be an exploration, on an individual basis, of a seeker's conviction. If we do not challenge a person to completely repent of their sins they will not be saved (Matt. 4:17; Acts 2:38; 3:19; 8:22; 17:30). The seeker must understand that to pray such a prayer is to invite Jesus to be their personal Lord for the rest of their life.

When we do not press home God's absolute claim on their lives, we are setting seekers up for failure and accidentally pretending to be Christians. It is reprehensible indeed, for us to pronounce people Christians (by the power invested in us as churchgoers or ministers) without them even understanding the magnitude of their deeds or the cost of their commitment. Does it really surprise us we have so many who quit so quickly and others who display no understanding of the Christian life? How can they? They have never been born again!

What help can we offer to an individual who prayed the sinner's prayer without any understanding of its ramifications or commitment required? Many people now believe that they are saved, when in fact they are not saved at all. You may approach them and explore why they have not really changed (we used to call this change conversion). You may point out that living in habitual sin is a symptom of not being born again. Generally, unintentional pretenders are quite unconcerned about such matters. They will protest, "Who are you to judge me?" or, "I accepted the Lord many years ago!" What they don't know is the Lord is not interested in being accepted, for He is God. He never asks to be accepted. One may easily accept Him by intellectual assent. Jesus is interested in being **received** intimately as the only Lord and resident of the human heart (John 1:12). What a horrible place to be—deceived into thinking you are in the family of God when you are not.

Very often accidental pretenders are given a warped idea of what being a Christian is. Since they have not experience the power of salvation by faith through grace, they will usually be involved in certain behaviors they believe are Christian. Very often they will closely reflect the unbalanced views that are presented in their church or on Christian TV as the center of the Christian life. These may be activities such as going to church, attending meetings, paying their tithes, and some system of trying to be good. Many American churchgoers now reflect either an obvious or covert expression of the prosperity message. This is very appealing to people who live in a culture of greed and pleasure. Any message that promises something of a material nature will be popular with the accidental pretender.

Amazingly, many accidental pretenders enjoy church. They like a good song service and enjoy music or drama in the service. They may even like and understand sermons or study the Bible. Some can sense God's presence and may have been touched by His Spirit in the past. Since they believe they are already saved they often become inoculated to the conviction of the Holy Spirit. Because they have not experienced new life in Jesus they are kind of like people at a buffet—they will take what they like and leave what they do not want.

The accidental pretender can be diagnosed by a lack of inclination for the rigors of the Christian life. They will do the right things that suit them and justify the things that they want to do that are wrong, even though the activities may be diametrically opposed to the Bible. Many religious churchgoers do not believe that you can live a victorious life. For this reason, when they are confronted with accidental pretenders they are not bothered by habitual sin in another professing believer.

When I was in Bible College I met a most remarkable accidental pretender. To speak to this young man you would be persuaded that he was a fervent believer. He had persuaded his Pastor and the entrance committee for the college that he was both a believer and leadership material. His mother was a godly Christian who had raised him in a Bible-based church, with good ministers who preached the Gospel. He asked a lot of troubling questions in class and I enjoyed his questioning outlook.

In his second year at college he was taking a class on the Book of Romans. As he went through the weeks and studies he came to realize that he had never actually **received** the salvation that he had **accepted** most naturally at his mother's knee as a child. He took me aside shortly afterwards and told me the whole story with wonder on his face. With all of the input into his life he had missed the Person of Christ. He had prayed the words but nobody had ever diagnosed his problem. It finally became obvious to him that he had no experience of the Lord. Finally he found himself in Bible College. How in the world could such a pedigree not be regenerated? He had flown under the radar with, I might add, many others.

I do not believe accidental pretenders have to end up as the weeds in God's garden spoken of by Jesus (Matt. 13:25-30). They are more a product of the shoddy or even ungodly practices of many present day churches. In so many places the invitations are so general and generic that a person may not even understand what to do to become a Christian. They will have no idea how to check to see if they are really saved. In relation to the Parable of the Sower they are perhaps the path-ground where the birds of the air come and eat up all of the seeds (Mark 4:4, 15). We are so conditioned to thinking in terms of church buildings that we don't comprehend that bodily location has little to do with knowing God. All over the world people go to church buildings but do not enjoy or draw from the life of God.

What I do know is that the longer the accidental pretender is left to languish in the prison of their delusion, the harder it is to deliver them. There are many examples of bacterial infections that are simply and permanently cured if immediately treated with antibiotics. If these same diseases are left unchecked they will eventually destroy and even kill the body. In the wilderness even a simple scratch can be dangerous unless it is disinfected. We have the cure for folks who are not really regenerated. It is the continuous and pointed presentation of all the major Bible truths that pertain to our salvation. Unfortunately, many ministers spend a lot of time on minor truths that they often present in an unbalanced way. Nothing will awaken an accidental pretender to their need more quickly and thoroughly than pressing the rigors of discipleship and the wonderful Spirit-filled life upon them. This needs to be done firmly and often to awaken the pretender to their need.

The ramifications of having all kinds of accidental pretenders in the church can be very far reaching. As accidental pretenders gain seniority in the church they are accepted to teach Sunday School, lead ministries, head committees, become deacons and even become ministers. There is no doubt that they learn the internal lingo and often are quite sincere, in their own mind. The problem is that they have climbed up another way (John 10:1). Once they are accepted as a member of the church body people look for other explanations for their 'quirks', 'personality clashes', 'problems', or 'besetting sins'.

Wrap this up in the bow of the culture of acceptance, tolerance, and plurality and you create a disastrous internal church culture. It is little wonder that we can have some amazing problems with harmony and agreement. Many churchgoers do not have the Holy Spirit in them—they are not part of the family of God.

The intentional pretender is a completely different kettle of fish. There are two types of intentional pretenders. The first type is the person who has attached themselves to a church or group but **never made** a personal **commitment** to Jesus Christ. In the case of these individuals, they know that they are not saved but have some personal motivation for being with Christians. There are as many specific reasons for pretending to be a Christian as there are actors but they usually fall under a few general categories.

The most obvious category is children that **grow up** in Christian homes. I think it is only normal and good that a parent will want their children to receive Christ. It is natural for people to want the best for their children. Going to heaven would generally be considered to be in the category of what is best. A lot of parents, though well meaning, have little understanding of Who will really save their children. Often parents will only know their children after the flesh. They will not make an effort to discern what their children's spiritual gifts and calling are or whether they have been awakened to their need for salvation. This is often because the parents have little spiritual life to share and are barely maintaining their own walk with God. Often there will be no family Bible reading or prayer time. People in such a state may be great parents but lousy spiritual leaders. Many children are pressed to get saved before they are convicted of a need to get saved. They have not realized that their lives are in opposition to God's will. They may secede to their parent's desire for them to make a commitment. This may be just to please the parent rather than because of a conviction that it is the right thing to do.

A powerful motivation for many younger adults and an increasing number of older adults to pretend they are believers is **sex**. I say sex instead of marriage because there is such a breakdown of morality in many churches that churchgoers have a tendency to be much bolder to engage in pre-marital sex than ever before. Let's face it; church is a great place to find nice people. It is also an easy place for predatory individuals to find naïve prey. It is not uncommon for some of the nicest people in a fellowship to take up with some of the most unsavory individuals. I never cease to be astonished at the approval many obvious pretenders get if they speak loudly about loving the Lord and go along with the church program. There has clearly been a breakdown in outrage over such wolf-like behavior occurring right before us in the household of God. Some people in the congregation may disapprove but will not feel that it is their place to say anything. Often leadership will not take bold public or even private disciplinary action.

Even in the more conservative groups more and more professing Christians are **marrying unbelievers**. Even if the individual Christian has the integrity to want to be married before participating in sexual activity many are still deceived into thinking the unsaved person will change their ways after they are married. The more honest pretenders leave soon after they receive their prize and will often discourage their spouse from continuing Christian fellowship. Those who do attend put on the camouflage and head to the building. They smile and make nice but remain unconverted.

Sometimes these pretenders will become involved in the life of the fellowship and gain credibility through their spouse, time, and association. These people are like time bombs just waiting to go off. In their business or social life they may bring reproach on the fellowship and they can see nothing wrong with it. Business is business and church is church. One thing is for sure, this intentional pretender can be counted on to bring a worldly perspective to every situation. Their association with the believing spouse makes it very hard to discipline them since leadership is often loath to bring trouble upon the spouse.

Another intentional pretender is the **social type**. They have religious inclinations and may also enjoy aspects of the church such as music, preaching, social events, and helping the community. Their main platform is to do good works. Unlike the unintentional pretender they know they have not made a commitment to God. They think they are good enough. They are sure that their good behavior will earn them salvation. This type of camouflage may run deep. They may have the lingo down for your little group and only by extensive prying questioning can it be learned that their faith does not lie in Jesus for their eternal salvation. They may have even prayed the good old 'sinner's prayer' but through lack of light or just pure unbelief, feel that Jesus' atonement alone is insufficient to save them—they must do something! Their works-oriented salvation comes from a misunderstanding of the Source of Christian 'doing'. The religionist 'does' to earn merit or reward. The Christian 'does' because God's Spirit has come to dwell in them and changed their stony heart into a heart that is after God (Eze. 36:26). The trouble is that diagnosing an individual's motives by external observation alone, is difficult. Later, I will give a few diagnostic hints for pretenders.

The second kind of intentional pretender is the **backslider**. Scripture states that, *"The backslider in heart shall be filled with his own ways"* (Prov. 14:14). This statement is very interesting. It does not say a backslider is filled with ravening evil. The diagnostic is, 'Who are you working for?' The believer is walking in God's ways. Jesus said, *"If ye continue in my word, [then] are ye my disciples indeed;"* (John 8:31). It is amazing how many sins, goofs, and blunders I committed the first few years of my walk with Jesus. We do grow up. It is essential that we see the Christian life as a series of commitments to Jesus Christ rather than just one. As we walk in His light, He cleanses us and reveals more things that need to be committed to Him. We grow in the grace and the knowledge of Jesus Christ. A Christian will show progress to the point of the last time they said, **"No,"** to God.

At some point backsliders have said no to God. They have experienced an inner conviction to do something or not to do something. Those who have said no to God may have researched it in the Bible. They will often seek other people to confirm their opinion. Nevertheless, given light, they have chosen their own way. Satan said, "I will" (Isa. 14:12-14). Self-will is the heart and essence of sin. In contrast Jesus said, *"Not my will, but Thine be done"* (Luke 22:42). When a person chooses to do things their own way, God deals with them like people are supposed to discipline children. Our Father uses circumstances to bring correction to us (Heb. 12:6-11).

If a person persists in sin God has ordained a process of church discipline. If an individual remains rebellious, they must be removed from the sphere of the family of God (Matt. 18:15-17). Once excommunicated the rebel has placed themselves in Satan's sphere. They receive the consequences of living like an unbeliever (1 Cor. 5:1-8). God's motive is always to bring the rebel back to a place of full appropriate fellowship.

Of course these Biblical actions will not be taken in most churches, even under the most blatant and persistent violations of God's Word. Most backsliders are ashamed or afraid of exposure. They wear all kinds of camouflage so as not to be discovered. In some places the majority of people in attendance are backsliders. Many people are habitually persisting in the more acceptable sins of the middle class that are often never spoken of from pulpits. These sins are gluttony, white lies, greed, selfishness, rejoicing in evil through entertainment and music, cowardice, and spiritual laziness just to name a few. When was the last time you heard a sermon on deliverance from gluttony? Be clear, I am speaking of persistent lifestyle sins, not the occasional sin that earnest believers quickly deal with. The backslider is often ignored or even not detected in the church today. They are very often the easiest to detect because they will often talk about the very issues that are holding them back.

Some will say, "You are too harsh. Why do you need to find fault? Let God deal with it in His time." What many do not understand is that where sin is concerned, **God's time** to deal with it is **right now** (2 Cor. 6:2). I do not advocate remnant people start condemning or publicly exposing the sins of others. Most of us are not in a place of authority to do such things. My concern is the effect pretenders have on our personal zeal and work for God. I have seen many remnant people laboring to 'revive' pretenders who do not wish to be revived. It is a complete waste of their time in the economy of God. Our time is too short! Many in America have never had an appropriate presentation of the Gospel.

We do not want to become suspicious of others or harsh in our thinking towards others. I highly recommend that we be very careful in diagnosing people's spiritual state because it is spiritual business. The Bible recommends that only those of the most mature spiritual stature should be dealing with the sins of the church (Galatians 6:1). Nevertheless there are times and places where we have to call things as we see them for our own good. The basic principle is the ironic Scriptural question: *"Can two walk together, except they be agreed"* (Amos 3:3)? In this portion of Scripture God is reasoning with Israel. He tells them that unless they are in agreement with Him and His Word they will never be able to walk with Him.

This is true with people, as well. If you are part of God's remnant you have to know the layout of the wilderness that Father has called you to walk in. Many commit the 'Ostrich Error' by refusing to look at problems honestly and assessing things by God's Word and His Spirit. If you are submitting to camouflaged leadership you will be disappointed and possibly destroyed. If you are laboring with a group who are mostly camouflaged unbelievers how will you bring forth godly fruit?

Remember to learn the Bible for yourself. If you are honest and love Jesus best, He will open the Bible up to you. Start by reading the Gospels over and over. Jesus is the Word so He is best able to shed light on the rest of the Bible. Stick with the bigger picture topics rather than worrying about minor questions. Memorize God's Word so He can bring it back to you again and again. Take time to be quiet and meditate on His Word and He will grant you insight. As you do so, you will be conformed to Jesus' will and an alarm will go off in your mind when people say things that are not quite right. Sometimes, these alarms may just indicate a person's spiritual maturity but other times they will reveal that the person is a pretender of some sort.

Listen to what is really being said by people. The person who speaks in a personal way about Jesus and what He is doing will always have vibrant new reports. The defining aspect of those who know God will not be sinless perfection but steady transformation into the image of Jesus (2 Cor. 3:18). The unintentional pretender will often turn to subjects that are not spiritual: politics, sports, weather, and family; anything but God. The intentional pretender will also turn to worldly subjects or stick to their pet religious topics. The backslider knows the lingo but is looking back. They will be revealed by efforts to justify themselves. Their conversation will reveal the objects of their own stumbling such as their own backsliding habits or negative events that occurred in the past in the church. Our words are the indicators of our spiritual condition to the world at large and also to ourselves.

Finally, God has placed gifted people in the Church to strengthen and protect the Body of Christ. Gifts such as discerning of spirits, word of knowledge, word of wisdom, and prophecy can reveal the contents of a person's heart. We need to love deceived people enough to both diagnose and cure their spiritual maladies. In my experience many do not want a cure but some do. We can only benefit people by bringing their true spiritual condition to light with the love of God. Let us respect and hear truly gifted leadership who has our best interests at heart.

A personal word to you beloved reader—I am writing this letter to you to help you to see your world as it is. If you are in a place where leadership does not discern camouflaged unbelievers of all kinds, your church life will be difficult indeed. There may be worldly order in your church but there will never be spiritual order. Many churches are largely made up of camouflaged persons who are either unintentionally or intentionally fooling those around them, for their own personal reasons. You cannot expect such groups to ever function in a healthy way.

These 'churches' may succeed, have great music, grow, collect money, and support missions. Nevertheless, they will never provide the fellowship that believers require to be fulfilled. If you are called to such a place make double sure it's not your own idea or desire. If you are not, get out and search for Christian fellowship. God will not honor that which does not reflect His will. Jesus said, "Beware of men" (Matt. 10:17). While sending forth his followers He warned that religious people would be the persecutors and there is nothing more religious than a camouflaged unbeliever.

Walk Safely Loved One,

Henry

# CHAPTER 14

# *Wild Predatory Animals*

Dear Fellow Traveler,

Quite a few years ago I lived in a small town on Vancouver Island in British Columbia. Lake Cowichan was walled to the north and the south with mountains forming two rows around two thousand feet above sea level. You could walk up any logging road just a few hundred feet and find yourself in the wilderness. One day I took my young son for a walk with me. We parked the car at the gate and started hiking up the road. Just a couple of hundred yards up the road I saw a black bear. Just as importantly she saw me. I could have continued up the trail but it was springtime and she might have had a cub. I decided to go back. Black bears are not usually predatory but a female will protect her young ferociously.

At that same time there was a young fellow who lived in a small community down the road. This community was even more remote than our town. This guy loved to ride his bike to work. One morning two, one year-old cougar cubs started to chase him down the road. He pedaled away as fast as he could and just barely escaped. He still has the cougar claw marks to prove it. When the people in the community heard it you can bet that everyone was surprised. There are animals that can really hurt you when you are in their territory. In the wilderness you have to know what will hurt you and what will not.

In the wild there are animals that will defend themselves against you. If you happen upon a venomous snake and surprise them, they will bite you. In Asia and Africa there are certain kinds of cobras that will aggressively seek to bite you. There are all kinds of wild cats, bears, and wolves who, under certain circumstances, will view you not with fear but with hunger. The wilderness wayfarer is trained to listen carefully and read the tracking signs that warn of predatory animals. They know that these types of animals have to be treated with respect. It will be the same for you, fellow traveler. As you make your way through the wilderness or desert landscape, you will need to be aware of dangerous predators.

You may already be aware of dangerous predators that are running rampant within the church in North America. These kinds of people are nothing new. Ever since Jesus' day they have been with us. Unlike the actors in my last letter, who primarily wear camouflage for their own personal reasons, these pretenders masquerade in order to deceive and destroy as many people's lives as possible. Jesus calls them ravening wolves and deceivers (Matt. 7:15-16). Not content to fool you, their wish is to destroy you. The apostles Paul and John call them dogs and wild beasts (Phil. 3:2; Rev. 22:15; 1Cor. 15:32). Both Jude and Peter call them brute beasts (1 Peter 2:11-22; Jude 1:10). The writers of the Bible used animal metaphors to describe dangerous people who come right into our shelter, if we let them. Their weapons of destruction are lies and deceit. The animals in the wild are one cut above these spiritual animals because wild animals have been made the way they are by God. The ravenous spiritual animals have created themselves after the image of their father, the devil. The Bible breaks these dangerous predators down into a few easily identifiable groups.

The first predator was and is the **Judaizer**. Judaizers (**rule-keepers**) cropped up as soon as the Gospel was taken out to the Gentiles. Preachers of 'Moses' followed the apostles and evangelists around. They used a pitch that sounded something like this: "Now that you have become a Christian you need to show your faith in God's covenant with Moses and be circumcised. This means you will try to obey all of the covenant laws to show your faith in Jesus." A lot of Paul's writing was meant to counteract this insidious perversion. He was very frustrated with the Galatians because they had become good little 'try-hard' Christians instead of letting Jesus do the work for them. Paul told them that their addition of religious work as a condition of justification before God constituted a fall from grace (Gal. 5:1-4).

The idea of grace seems to be very difficult for believers to grasp until they start to understand what grace really is and what grace really does. Every world religion is, in some way, based on the work of the follower to commend them to God. Believers in Jesus trust in Christ's work of substitution alone for salvation. The work of God is to believe on the one who He sent (John 6:29). This saving faith changes a person's heart and gives them the inclination to follow God. We cannot do anything in our Christian life without God's help (John 15:5). Everything I will ever do or be has to do with His imparted ability; not any human effort that I can put forth. Therefore, grace is unmerited favor from God, unmerited ability to do His will, and unmerited reward because God has provided all of the power to fulfill His will in our lives.

Today, most Gentile believers are not tempted to try to be Jewish. What has been handed down through institutional church history is rule-oriented religion. The Roman Catholic Church added many sacraments, traditions, and extra-Biblical rules. The Protestants rejected some of the rules and practices of Roman Catholicism. Protestants have kind of picked and chosen what they would keep and what they would reject. A lot of the service and ministry in the Protestant church today still looks very Roman Catholic. In our day, we see all kinds of priorities that are unbalanced and extra-Biblical. Different groups have added different rules. If any person believes in following a set of rules for Jesus instead of receiving Christ's salvation power personally, they become a rule-keeper. If a leader promotes Jesus plus the church rules, He is a Judaizer. It is the same problem, just different rules.

What still remains the most insidious kind of rule-keeping is the notion that you receive Jesus and then make every effort to serve Him. In other words you **imitate** Christ. The work becomes one of **human effort** to try to modify personal or group behavior to be more and more like Jesus. Songs are sung that express our desire to be more like Jesus. Prayers are prayed that ask to be more like Jesus. Sermons are preached about God's law, which is good. What is powerfully absent is the thorough recommendation of God's **means** of obeying His Law—Christ's salvation and the indwelling power of the Holy Spirit.

Followers are often exhorted week after week to follow lists of 'does' and 'don'ts' without reference to Christ's enabling power. Leaders use Scripture to prove that their followers need to reform and to do their best. The Bible states that 'our best' is 'filthy rags' (Isaiah 64:6). This belief system ends up recommending Jesus for salvation **plus** a set of duties a person must try to fulfill with personal effort. Yet God's enabling grace is the only means of keeping what we have committed to Him against the final day of judgment (2 Tim. 1:12).

Why do leaders resort to such lowly tactics? For the same reason they did in the first century. They misunderstand and despise the simplicity of God's indwelling power. There is an underlying arrogant assumption that to just lean on Jesus for everything is too easy. There must be more in life and it must have to do with knowledge and rules. Leaders who promote human effort want to be important and to exercise their authority over their followers for their follower's own good. This kind of leader tends to think of themselves as a good person. They wish for others to learn from their goodness and become good like them. They are proud of their knowledge of the Bible and feel that they can impart their wisdom to others. They are most like the Pharisees, who felt that their position and separation from all types of evil gave them authority over other people's consciences. After all, the Pharisees felt that they knew best.

I struggled with the difference between Law and grace for years. Nobody tried harder to be good than me. I failed a lot and the only time that I was able to change was when I got fed up with myself and called on Jesus. Every positive change in my life has come from Jesus. I see no other way to be like Him than to yield to Him. I think this was why Paul was so riled about rule-keepers. Of all people, he felt their influence was the most evil. He was the living example of a guy who tried super-hard to be good and failed miserably. He chronicles his failure for us in chapter seven of the Book of Romans. In Romans 7:5, Paul stated that the struggle he was describing occurred during the time before Christ had come into his life. As a Pharisee he was trying to be the best rule-keeper in the world. Romans 8 describes Paul's victory. This victory was not obtained by his effort but by his surrender to Jesus.

Rule-keepers want to make Romans 7 the epitome of the Christian life. This is how they explain to people why they are failing all of the time. Paul warned the Galatians that, as rule-keepers, they would fall into bondage to sin every time. This is the case because the flesh desires against the spirit and the spirit against the flesh so that we end up doing what we are trying not to do (Gal. 5:17). Paul clearly rejoiced that God's Holy Spirit had set him free to live the life of Christ (Romans 8:1). He saw the Gospel as something quite separate and distinct from the human effort he had put out to keep the Law. He saw the Law as his teacher. God's Law let him know that he was a sinner and needed salvation (Gal. 3:24).

That is why Paul hated what the Judaizers were doing. He knew first-hand that it would never work. It still doesn't work! I am appalled that there are many churches whose first set of instructions to people who have just received Jesus ends up being: "Come to church, pay your tithe, and try to do your best for Jesus." Such advice has no root in the Gospel and following such advice will destroy people. It is not wise to have sympathy for people or allegiance to churches that cling to any type of 'good works' point of view because they end up preying on people's best intentions. Law-keepers are very hard to convince to change since they trust their works so implicitly.

What rule-keepers often purport that they are trying to guard against is **lawlessness** or **license**. Leaders who promote license are the next type of predatory animal. The lawless position is best answered by Paul in Romans 6:15, *"What then? Shall we sin, because we are not under the law, but under grace? God forbid."* The leader who promotes license does not say 'God forbid', he says 'God forgives'. The argument for license sounds like this: "Since Christ has died for me, I am now forgiven for my sin. I now can live the rest of my life with little concern about departing from sin because I believe that I am cleansed as I go." A leader promoting this form of 'greasy grace' does not see the need for the Blood of Jesus to deliver them from sin. To them, the Blood of Jesus is like a giant eraser that just keeps erasing their sin while they go. They see no need for repentance or continual confession for they believe their sins are remitted in advance.

I ran into my first preacher of lawlessness when I had been a Christian for only a few weeks. He was a teacher at my high school. He was excited to hear that I had made a commitment to Jesus and wanted to give me some guidance. We met several times over coffee or lunch and discussed the nature of salvation. This man was adamant that once you had made a commitment to Christ, you could never be lost, no matter what you did. I had taken the opposite view. [By the way, it is interesting to me how many people who promote Reform Theology believe in this perversion of it. Calvin never would have believed that an elected person would be able to persist in sin because of the doctrine of **perseverance**. Yet today, so many use this belief as a justification of a life of sin.]

During a heated argument he pointed to a woman and said, "You mean if I lusted after this woman and had an automobile accident that I would be lost?" (One of those ridiculous 'what ifs' that people put forth). I was young and ignorant and responded, "Of course." I didn't have the sophistication to understand that this man was enslaved by lust. He had a two-fold belief that ensconced him in his point of view and practice. First, he believed he could never overcome his sin. Second, he didn't see a need to since he believed that his sin had no bearing on his relationship with Jesus Christ. He was a committed sinner for Jesus. He was eventually criminally prosecuted for habitually fornicating with under-age high school girls.

There are other obvious cases of license on a much larger scale. Whole denominations tolerate or even promote gambling, social drinking, divorce, abortion, perverse political figures, and homosexuality. They use the Bible to back up their beliefs and extend their influence via inter-denominational and inter-faith fellowships. Many evangelicals have profoundly watered down their core values. In the name of unity they try to reach out and connect with people of either profoundly liberal views or even completely non-Biblical outlooks. The byword of all such groups is enlightenment and tolerance. All such efforts express corporate license since their proponents must set aside the truth of the Gospel for such unity.

The Bible and history clearly teach that you cannot reach those who are committed to a life of license and lawlessness. They are heretics bent on promoting their own views for their own purposes that are alien to the purposes of God. God does not want us to waste our time trying to change people and groups who are antichrist. Their father is the devil. Indeed I have seen many well-meaning crusaders converted to a lifestyle of license by the very people they were trying to convert. Flee their fellowship fellow-traveler, for they will devour you!

Lawlessness and license were necessary to promote the doctrine of Balaam and the Nicolaitans (Rev. 2:6, 15). Both Balaam and the Nicolaitans overthrew believer's faith with the introduction of sexual immorality and alien religions as acceptable practice along with the real faith. They taught that people could sin because they were forgiven anyway. Jesus said he hated their deeds. Today, all such tolerance is presented in the name of **luv**. I use the word **luv** because we need a word other than love to properly represent the phoniness of the proposition that we can live in continual sin which Jesus will forgive.

**Gnostics** are the next group of dangerous predators. Gnosticism caused a lot of grief in the first century A.D. They believed that Jesus had not come in bodily form; that He was some kind of spirit man. They mixed their intellectual ideas about God in with faith in Jesus. Since they believed that bodily flesh was evil they taught that whatever you did with your body would not affect your salvation. The consequence was that their followers were emboldened to commit sexual immorality and drunkenness. They loved human wisdom and education and made the simplicity of Christ complex. This caused their followers to mix Eastern religion with the real faith of God. I am using the term Gnostic in a broader sense that extends to any group who think they have the special, secret, and exclusive knowledge of how to be saved. Many different groups promote themselves as the only true church or group.

Today we have many expressions of this old scourge. Most of the cults come from somebody's special revelation or special understanding of the Bible. Many mess with the divinity of Jesus. The apostle John made it clear that anyone who denies that Jesus came in the flesh has an antichrist spirit (1 John 4:2). It is more popular today to attack the fact that Jesus was God (John 1:1; Heb. 1:3). Some groups use baptismal formulas as their distinctive and deny the Trinity through the 'Oneness' of God. Each group claims some special revelation of knowledge—they are right and everyone else is wrong. If you don't join up you will go to hell or oblivion and lose out. Cultish behavior is always expressed by individuals or groups that make their special knowledge or group the go-between for salvation.

America may have spawned more cults than any nation in modern history. What is fascinating to me are the numbers of people who attend or lead conservative Christian churches who deny aspects of Scriptural orthodoxy. They deny the virgin birth, the existence of the devil, the existence of heaven or hell, the divinity of Jesus, the existence of the trinity, or God's eternal judgment. Their denomination may proclaim orthodoxy but individual church leaders do not adhere to or teach the denomination's orthodoxy. For this reason, some of these churches become cult-like.

Early in my walk with Jesus I had a friend who was saved and transformed from a terrible life of sin. He was of above average intelligence and very earnest in his walk with the Lord. He and I used to spend a lot of time with our spiritual parents because we were both very hungry for God. One day Mom and Dad informed me that my friend had joined a new church and had been baptized over again in the name of 'Jesus only'. He was taught new things about God. He was told to break his friendships with all who did not agree with this church group. Apparently, the group had worked on some doubt or fear about his salvation and he wanted to be sure he was 'saved'. After a few years he came back out of that error. He is one of the few that I have seen come out of this type of Gnosticism and re-establish his walk.

In the past two decades we have seen a move to multiple **teachings** on **faith**. These alleged 'faith' teachings usually involve external actions by their followers such as **confession** of certain Scriptural texts and denial of the possibility of failure. The goal is usually to get something material from God or to receive healing. This teaching has been around for quite some time. As a result **extreme positive confession** seems to be ingrained as part of many churchgoers thinking. This doctrine has been emphasized by many TV evangelists who have strong followings.

Many preachers know that they had better not get too negative. The average pulpit man now thinks it is bold to give a balanced rendering of the truth. He knows that it is much more important to keep away from 'negative' preaching about the need to repent and give up backsliding. Many churchgoers can no longer bear to hear the full council of God. They seem to resent a strong and persistent message of repentance from dead works and faith towards God (Heb. 6:1). This kind of underlying pressure to keep it positive is a reflection of mixing worldly positive thinking in with the Gospel. The Gospel is the most positive thing in this world but you don't have to continually talk yourself into it. All who believe are in a relationship with God which does not depend on our work but upon our Father's goodness (Romans 2:4). Believers do not have to make themselves believe.

Within this faith movement there has risen a **'gain-is-godliness'** crowd. This group reflects the other half of the sin of Balaam. Balaam was making a living being a shaman. He spoke on behalf of a multitude of gods. As well, he had become aware of the God of Israel. Balaam was for hire. The idea that God's main purpose is to make His followers rich, especially the leaders, is one of the most prevalent errors of our day. Those leaders who are construed to be non-prosperity and preach against avarice can come in for a lot of criticism. Many churchgoers will not attend a church where this prosperity doctrine is questioned. Even if you know how unbalanced the American church has become in relation to money you had better keep it quiet. We have heaped up teachers to ourselves who tell us it is God's plan that we should be rich (2 Tim. 4:3).

This subject gets me riled. The wanton waste of God's money and the greed of His purported servants should bother any true believer in Jesus. Such waste was a first century problem. Paul talked to his spiritual son Timothy about it (1 Tim. 6:3-11). He classed all who promote the doctrine that Christianity is about acquiring money and possessions as perverse, contentious, and devoid of truth. His response to this lie was to warn believers to get away from greedy teachers (v. 5). Paul further counseled that believers need to be content with what God has given them (v. 6). Paul drew perspective by observing that we have brought nothing into this world and we can take nothing with us when we die (v. 7). This statement raises the question, "Why would any believer worry about money?" (Matt. 6:25-34). Paul then pushed the envelope by telling us not to want anything more than food or clothing (v. 8). Clearly, Paul was a traveler of the first order in the spiritual wilderness. He realized that it is hard to go trekking with an overloaded pack. He predicted that all who seek riches would encounter nothing but snares and evil desires. Eventually they would drown in perdition (v. 9). His conclusion was that **loving money** is the root of all evil (v. 10). Finally, he reiterated that Timothy should run away from all kinds of temptation to be greedy (v. 11).

I can count the number of TV preachers whose message is not obviously warped on one hand. I thank God for the few who are faithful! Add to this the flagrant merchandising and money grubbing, and it is little wonder that so many reject their message of Christ. The question may be asked, "What message of Christ?" On many shows, the unsaved never hear the Gospel. If they do, it is presented at a financial cost. We have supported this, my friend. The scourge of the half-truth telling, heretical, Bible-distorting gang that is beaming over the airwaves could be stopped in a few short weeks. If people would quit letting themselves be manipulated into giving money to teachers of lies, these teachers would be gone. All people have to do is a little bit of research. If they find the individual is a millionaire, living lavishly, or unwilling to disclose their expenditures, it is proof that they are not of God, period.

A Gospel of prosperity is an enticing presentation. The legitimate concept of sowing and reaping is twisted to mean the support of the ministry of the TV personality. They promise that benefits will accrue in a multiplied manner to the person who 'sows' into the ministry. There are many books on prosperity which are compelling unless you just sit down and read one of the Gospels yourself. Jesus usually promises that the treasure you will receive will be in **HEAVEN** (Mark 10:21; Matt. 6:19-20)! The money sown was to be given to the poor, needy, widows, and so on. The magnitude of the giving was to be all the possessions, not out of an overflow of abundance (Luke 12:32-34).

The reason for delayed reward may be obscure to prosperity people but is obvious if you read the Bible. The people enquiring after Jesus needed deliverance from the **hold** of the things that they possessed. They needed to cease to continuously work in order to acquire more possessions (John 6:27; Matt. 6:19-21). We need to find our security in God. Hey preachers, try pressing this kind of message on your hearers and see what happens! It is probable that you will get Jesus' results—many will depart from hearing you.

It is wise to avoid any teacher who is mustering a group to follow him. There are many new 'charismatic' leaders with 'revelations' of all kinds. These leaders are like wilderness guides who have no experience. Imagine yourself walking across a desert with a person that claims to be a wilderness guide. After three days you find you are out with a person who has no knowledge of survival at all, he just thought he did. How will you make it? You now know that he lied but what good does it do you? You're still going to die because of that leader's delusion that he was a guide. It is obvious to me that we do not need a new revelation today. We do need to return to the simplicity of obeying the old revelation which is salvation by grace through faith. This faith brings the results of obedience to God's Word and hearing the voice of the Holy Spirit.

Finally, I would like to share something I have learned about the concept of **anointing**. I have heard many people recommend people by saying they are very 'anointed'. I am always glad when someone has the Holy Spirit's anointing. It is interesting that the word 'anointed' has the same root as the word Christ, which can also be translated Anointed One or Messiah. The direct inference is that Jesus was anointed with the Holy Spirit. In fact Jesus was identified by John as the One who had the Spirit without measure (John 3:34). In reality we are paying a high compliment to an individual when we call them anointed. We are saying that they have the same power in their lives as Jesus—the Holy Spirit of God.

Jesus warned that as we came to the end of the age that there would be individuals who called themselves Christ or 'Anointed One'. They would become famous and people would invite you to go hear them (Matt. 24:5, 23-34). Jesus said that they would have false anointing and be able to do false signs. There is a false anointing. Eschatologically speaking, I do not believe that we are at the very end, yet. Jesus warned us that falsely anointed Christs would crop up to the point where they would fool the very elect if it was possible (Matt. 24:24). Again, we cannot always trust our gut. We have to take the record of His Word as an unemotional guide. In spite of any attachment we might have to a person or their ministry we must use God's Word to measure the truth of what is being said and done. If they make a practice of evil, they are not of God.

I have to admit that when I hear about 'anointed preachers', I regard such reports with godly skepticism. I think this is because the Lord allowed me to encounter so many different haywire types as a young Christian. I remember going to all kinds of meetings in my first couple of years as a believer. These traveling preachers really could speak dynamically. Many claimed great power and divine healing power. They were adept at appealing to their listener's emotions. I started to notice that they took up a lot of offerings and used unusual methods.

One preacher had pasted paper footprints all over the platform area. During the offering he said that God had told him that seventeen people were going to stand in the footprints and pledge to give one hundred dollars each to his ministry that night (that was a lot of money in 1975). He waited for seventeen people to go forward. A teenage friend that was with me felt compelled to go forward. On the way home he wondered where he would ever get one hundred dollars. I knew him well. He was fortunate if he had one hundred cents on him at any one time. I had many such experiences. I look back now and see that these preachers were the precursors to the gang of hucksters that travel around or come to us today on television.

A pocket full of money is of little value when you need to live off the land. You understand quickly that the basic rules of survival have little to do with the artificial construct of so-called civilizations. You need to know the rules of the wilderness. You can't buy a shelter there; you have to know how to build one. In the spiritual wilderness you realize that the Bible is true. Possessions will hinder your freedom and liberty to move around and do what God wants. Just as the camel could not get through the eye of the needle when laden down with possessions, neither will we enter heaven when laden down with possessions (Matt. 19:23-24). You can bet that the camel in the parable did not mortgage his house and borrow money to load himself up with the weights that he was carrying. I am sure the camel would want to be free of the weights. Who wants to carry around extra weight?

There is a great danger that comes with identifying error. You can take it personally or internalize the realization in a negative way. It is disillusioning when a leader, a TV personality, or a friend moves into error. This can excite the strongest kinds of passions in our hearts. The enemy of our soul will try and move us to hate the individual or to even blame God. We have to listen to what Jesus said in the garden: *"Watch and pray that ye enter not into temptation: the spirit indeed [is] willing but the flesh [is] weak."* (Matt. 26:41). If we enter into the temptation to be bitter we will surely lose our spiritual vitality. In the wilderness, we may survive the attack of a wild animal, but we then must take time to heal. Fortunately loved one, we know the Source of all healing. Remember, the animals we come across in our spiritual wilderness are wild, so be careful! 'Do Not Feed' the wild animals.

Be Wise,

Henry

# CHAPTER 15

# *Parasites, Varmints & Dirty Birds*

Dear Fellow Traveler,

*I* remember several years ago when I first started surfing the internet that I came across my first website trying to sell me something to get rid of intestinal parasites. As I viewed different sites on the subject, I saw all kinds of magnified pictures of worms, flukes, and single-celled animals that could have potentially been living in my body. The pictures were both terrifying and horrifying because these magnified creatures looked like monsters. My first reaction was to go into denial but curiosity kept me reading the testimonials and learning more about the problem of parasitic infection.

Many websites asserted that parasitic infection is very common in America. I learned that improper food preparation and cooking, household pets, and inter-human contact, both casual and sexual, could cause infestations of parasites. As well, I learned that my diet could produce an atmosphere where single-cell parasites would breed in my bowels, vital organs, and joints. The inclusion of single-celled organisms as part of the parasitic threat raised the statistical infestation claimed by these websites to be well over eighty percent.

I learned later what great care was needed to avoid parasitic infection in the wilderness. A person need only drink parasitically infected water one time to learn the need for boiling water. If you improperly prepare and eat meat or vegetation in the wilderness you may not destroy all of the parasites that may be living on or in them. I remember a young man that I worked with who went on an extended vacation to India. When he left he was a body-builder's picture of health. In India he contracted a very intractable parasite that took Western medicine about six months to kill. He had shrunken down to skin and bones and was unable to work for months. I have contracted water-born parasites myself and suffered the convulsing pain they can cause.

As with many of my discoveries in life I shared my new information about parasites with my wife and friends. You can easily imagine the horror I was greeted with. Not only are parasites an unpleasant subject to most people but will often make it right on to their 'rude' lists. People do not even want to know that they may be infested with these nasty little beasties. Somehow, I had stumbled onto something deeply ingrained into our culture. We find the discussion of parasites very unpleasant.

I have observed the same behavior in the spiritual wilderness. In this day there seems to be a true revulsion when people are confronted with the possibility of a **spiritual parasitic infestation**. Jesus had the troubling habit of identifying such infestations and naming their source, the devil. Human rebellion and satanic influence are behind all sin. Denial and unbelief were the greatest obstacles in the way of people who needed the deliverance of Jesus. In this day, professing Christians seem to refer to persistent and habitual sin as a 'problem'. There seems to be some hesitancy to face it for what it is: soul-damning wickedness. When a believer sins and dismisses it as just a problem, they set themselves up for becoming infested with spiritual parasites.

I wonder what we would look like if we could see our spirits instead of our bodies? Would we look all nice, tidy, and fashionable or would we look dirty and disheveled? Would we see all kinds of nasty looking spiritual parasites all over us as we looked in the spiritual mirror with horror? I remember different scenes from the movies when people found themselves covered with leeches.

While they were in the water they were fine but when they came out they found blood-sucking leeches all over themselves. What horror they expressed and how quickly they picked all the leeches off their bodies. There is a natural revulsion to seeing something that is drinking our life blood.

What are the spiritual parasites that plague so many? They are the habits and tendencies that reveal themselves in behavior or thought but are brought forth by the hindering spirits of the devil. I am not talking so much about what we still think is sin in the church. I am speaking about the practices that we now commonly allow as acceptable Christian behavior. There are many things that were unacceptable to truly regenerated Christians thirty years ago that are now ignored or accepted. Church-goers watch TV programs that influence them to think with a worldly mindset. Many cannot quit watching the television. Worldly entertainments of all kinds bring unseen spiritual parasitic infection to those who partake of them. Many couples use pornography as an aid to their sexual pleasure and find themselves in bondage to the parasites of perversion and sexual addictions.

Social drinking, prescription drug abuse, tobacco and other addictive substances once abhorred by believers now bring people into bondage to the spiritual parasite of addiction. One third of the church is obese and one third is overweight. Many who suffer from such conditions are hopelessly in bondage to the spirit of gluttony. The desire to own more and more has brought the spirit of greed into many homes. Families find themselves discontented with what they have. These, and many other **culturally acceptable bondages**, are still viewed by God as sin. They have the same potential to damn the soul as the sins we really hate if we do not go to God for deliverance.

When a believer persists in known sin they separate themselves from God and set up a cycle of asking forgiveness and then falling for the same thing again. Each failure creates a stronger hold for the sin and accompanying wicked spirits. The sin and evil spirits suck the very life and vitality out of their victim. People become settled into an ever hardening state that used to be called 'backsliding'. Unfortunately, backsliding isn't a little problem but a life and death struggle. The spiritual parasites of condemnation, bondage, and spiritual oppression take hold. The human heart is deceitful in these circumstances (Jer. 17:9). Any number of explanations and justifications are used. The bondage is described as a **problem** or a **disease**. The stories we tell ourselves seem both reasonable and good. Once overcome, people spiral downward to a spiritual crash that is sometimes seen and other times invisible.

To survive in this present wilderness we must identify and remove spiritual parasites. This removal takes two things. First, we must be **brutally honest** with ourselves. We have to look in God's spiritual mirror, the Bible, and apply it ruthless to **ourselves** (James 1:23-25). Secondly, we must want to rid ourselves of **everything** that would hold us back, not just the things that we don't like. This is the process of sanctification that is so little spoken of or talked about today. We must not allow our values and outlooks to be formed by the current spiritual atmosphere which is so licentious in our day.

Neither are we to become the spiritual monitors for others. We need to heed the saying, "Physician, heal thyself!" Jesus said that I should leave the speck-picking for the time when I was well advanced in taking care of my own planks (Matt. 7:3). It is very important that we focus more upon our own growth and less upon what wrong is easily seen in others. Somehow, when we spend most of our time looking at other's sins we tend to excuse ourselves. It is clear that the only person I have a hope of changing is myself.

It needs to be understood that the enemy of our soul is very persistent and will not give up the ground he gains unless we mean business. It takes quite a bit of time and attention to kill and remove physical parasites. Their life-cycles make it quite easy for their offspring to come back. Spiritual parasites cling to any person who has allowed them access. These wicked spirits know that unless they are recognized and rejected with the Blood of Jesus that they will not have to leave. Any person who wants to get rid of the devil can easily do so but only if they want to do it with all of their heart. Half-hearted efforts will always fail in these matters.

There are times when the devil gets too much credit for something and other times where he does not get enough. I do not want to get involved in the controversy surrounding the exorcism of believers. I think that most of the controversy around this subject comes from a wishy-washy definition of what a believer is. People do not want to admit when they are backsliders today. A person who once made a commitment to God may be profoundly overcome by evil and yet be called a believer today.

It really comes down to honesty and labeling. If a person is in bondage to evil, the devil has gained ascendancy. To discuss, in ignorance, whether this is oppression, possession, or something else, is fruitless. It is clear that such people are usually not possessed in the way that those who were insane or infirm in the Bible account. Nevertheless, bondage is bondage. We must deal with it. Trust me when I tell you that when there is a large leech attached to your body, sucking your blood, you do not really care to define whether it is 'in you' or 'on you'. You just want it gone! That's what Jesus did. He exposed and defeated the devil wherever He saw him with little fanfare or discussion.

The Bible continually contrasts people who have a theory with those who have power. It is interesting to note that where there is no power and deliverance there will be a Bible teacher offering his theory. As Jesus came down from the Mount of Transfiguration he was confronted with the scene of the failed exorcism (Mark 9:14-29). The cast of characters included the defeated disciples, the unbelieving father, the growing crowd, and the **religious guys**. The religious guys were the scribes, apparently doing an official investigation. There are all kinds of theories and writing in our day about deliverance and spiritual oppression. It is amazing to me how complex teachers want to make this subject. To this point in Christ's ministry the scribes had little to say because they were confronted with the awesome power of God. They took their little spiritual potshots but had nothing of substance to say. Their cue came as soon as things didn't work. Notice that after the deliverance there were no more questions asked or answered. God's power silenced the religionists.

I submit that the devil is no harder to dislodge in our day than in Jesus' (Heb. 13:8). Our problem is the age old problem, faith. Few who have spiritual parasites recognize them as such. Just as we can't see physical parasites we really can't see spiritual parasites. We have a symptom but are not willing to face the cause. Since it was Jesus' stated purpose to destroy the works of the devil we can call on Him today. He will still destroy the works of the devil in our lives (1 John 3:8). All of the complexity that man may add to this issue only serves to cloud the issue. In the name of Jesus demons must give up their hold and leave. The key is to **want** what you are asking for with all of your heart. When we seek God with all of our heart we will find Him (Jer. 29:13).

There is little doubt that ridding ourselves of parasites is an uncomfortable task. If we use herbs it can really cause an upheaval in our intestinal tract. If we change our diet we will no doubt feel old desires and discomfort. If we use other cures there are other discomforts. During the Vietnam War American POW's sometimes used kerosene to get rid of their parasitic infestations. They did this because of the severity of the infestations. The human body likes kerosene about as much as parasites do. The POW's were in wrenching pain but felt that it was worth it to get rid of the parasites. In the same way, we must ruthlessly kill all infestations before they take hold. In this spiritual wilderness this is a matter of life and death—not physical but spiritual. If you don't deal with the devil he will take you with him to his eternal fate.

Jesus promised us that He was giving every believer power over all the power of the devil (Luke 10:19-20). Let God be true and every man a liar (Romans 3:4). This is one area where we have been moved away from the simplicity of the Gospel of Jesus Christ. We have Christ's warranty that He will deliver us. The cure is before us and it is an easy cure. When we believe God to deliver us we can be sure that He will not fail.

Another challenge in the wilderness is what some people call **varmints**. Tom Brown Jr., the ultimate wilderness teacher of our day, talks about his childhood brushes with packs of wild dogs in the New Jersey Pine Barrens.[1] These dogs, which were bred to be domesticated, had been abandoned or became lost. They roamed the wilderness in packs. They had reverted back to a wild state. Even as a child, Mr. Brown knew that an unexpected encounter with such a pack could be deadly.

Any animal that deviates from its natural purpose can be called a varmint. The definition of a varmint is: **troublesome person or animal:** a person or an animal regarded as troublesome, unpleasant, or despicable.[2] The varmint becomes pestilent to others when it invades their space and robs their sustenance. If you have ever had a squirrel, a rat, or bats in the attic of your house you may have an idea of what I am talking about. Varmints get in and are hard to get out. In urban society most people hire pest professionals to remove them.

In the wilderness, if you store food improperly or discard your trash carelessly you will turn perfectly benign wildlife into varmints. They will do what comes naturally and infest your campsite. I remember one wilderness trip where someone was careless with food. What a night we had as many field mice came looking for an easy meal. It is quite distressing to have those little critters crawling all over you. The main thing about varmints is that they can really take the enjoyment out of a situation.

In today's spiritual wilderness there seem to be more and more varmints. Some of the remnant has not recognized the waste and even danger that spiritual varmints can carry with them. In fact, people's efforts to love others will often prevent them from calling a varmint a varmint. It is interesting that the definition of a varmint extends to the human species.

The saying, "The enemy of the best is that which is good or better," has almost become a cliché in our day but we would do well to bring this principle into our personal relationships. The enemy of our soul knows our weakness well. He is only too happy to bring people across our path to cause us to stumble, suck out our energy, or simply waste our time. These people become the varmints in our spiritual wilderness. They may suck the very strength from our being. It is very important that we give our best, in the best way, to the people that God wants His best given to.

The Bible clearly teaches that evil associations can corrupt righteous people (1 Cor. 15:33). It is better to be lonely than to find comfort in the fellowship of people who are not committed to the truth. The **stumbling-block** varmint may be nicer to you than the religious crowd but the spirit behind them will not be content until you are overthrown. Unfortunately today, many such people spend their lives in the fellowship of a church. They have a form of godliness but deny the power of God which delivers from evil (2 Tim. 3:5). I can count a number of times in my life when my efforts to help people or my need for friendship were turned wrong by association with wrong-spirited people. There have been times where the very people that I assumed were looking out for me were thinking of ways to get me to go along with their compromised lifestyle. When the situation comes to light, these varmints may even blame you for their own evil circumstances and behavior.

Sometimes, those who are part of God's remnant can find themselves very lonely. They find themselves without sufficient fellowship and encouragement. At such times they can be very vulnerable. The next thing they know, someone from work, a leisure activity, or a chance meeting will strike up an association with them. Soon these new friends take more time and attention than they should. Although they may be very nice, if they are not saved, their father is the god of this world. It is amazing how many fine people of God get carried away by these varmints into a life of worldliness and conflicted loyalties.

The enemy of our soul has a hierarchy of priorities for our defeat. He starts with separation from God's fellowship. He then works toward separation from fellowship with true believers. What follows are a loss of joy, a loss of vision, a loss of separation from the world, a loss of sanctification, a loss of fruit, and a loss of the use of gifting. The devil's ultimate goal is always the loss of our souls. He starts at the top of the pyramid and works down as far as we will allow him to go. Spiritual varmints are one of his favorite tools.

I want to add just a word about friendship between members of the opposite sex. The enemy of our soul is an expert in persuading susceptible people that they love someone they really cannot legally have. The devil wants to turn righteous relationships with members of the opposite sex into varmint relationships. If a person causes you to step out of appropriate relationship with them or vice versa, the offender really becomes a spiritual varmint. The words exchanged are always 'I love you' but it can never be true. I have come to see that the devil will speak to otherwise nice people that they just have to have somebody they shouldn't. It is always the devil. People want to think it is love but it is never God's love. We have so many varmints in the professing church that the divorce rate is no different within the church than in the world. Take care not to listen to a varmint or be one yourself.

Everyone who has ministered to people has run across this next kind of varmint—the **energy sucker**. This is the person who takes up a great deal of your time with their problems but never really shows any signs of improvement. There is usually a chip of anger, self-pity, or inferiority on this person's shoulder. They will play on your sympathies but will always eventually revert back to their particular self-destructive behavior. You may spend years sincerely working with such persons with little result. Many churches deal with this kind of behavior by simply saying, "That's the way they are, there's no changing them. We'll just have to accept them the way they are." Those churches that confront such behavior usually see the individual move on to another church where they will do the very same thing over again.

It is not mean or unkind to understand that such people are varmints. They are not Kingdom people because Kingdom people always grow. The Kingdom of God is full of life; not death. Kingdom subjects will experience real positive growth and change, over time. Those who do not grow may be the people that Jesus warns us about (Matt. 7:6). They are the aggressive swine who turn to attack you or the hungry dogs that turn upon you. Perhaps they are the passive servant who buries his one talent (Matt. 25:24-27). The time you spent trying to help brings forth no fruit because the person you spent it on was not really interested in growing or changing. Every experienced minister can remember people that they put time, effort, care, and means into that did not respond.

I am by no means recommending that we become hard or unkind but there are moments where God will make it very clear to us that we are spinning our wheels in our efforts to help an individual. God does not turn us into do-gooders but His children that do His good. Once we understand that somebody is behaving like a varmint we need to stop wasting our efforts because our time belongs to God (Titus 3:10-11).

Remnant people are prone to help this kind of person. Remnant people are the people who are willing to go the extra mile and to love the unlovely. It is no crime to face the truth about a person. There is an absence of sentimentality in Jesus' ministry where it relates to varmints. Jesus was quick to dismiss excuses because He knew that if the person was sincere and honest that God would always deliver them (Luke 14:18ff). We need to have that same faith in Jesus. He will save to the uttermost those who come to God through Him (Heb. 7:25). It dishonors God to waste so much time and so many resources upon those who just take and want more. Even baby believers are discernable by whether they are givers or takers. Don't waste your time on this kind of varmint or you'll have nothing left for those who really need you.

The other kind of varmint is the **time-waster**. This may be a believer or an unbeliever who just takes up time. The time-waster from the church may be the well-meaning individual that solicits you to do a job or a ministry that God really doesn't have for you to do. They may be the social butterfly churchgoers who will invite you to their home or will come over to visit you at your home. While visiting they talk about nothing but the things of this life and this world. The church time-waster has nothing better to do than to become a varmint in other people's spiritual lives. Either they have the time to waste or they have a need for social contact that they just want to have fulfilled.

The worldly time-waster can be a boss with extra work and assignments that have to be done in order for you to climb up the ladder of promotion. They may be all of the different people asking you to volunteer for clubs, boards, school events, and sports for kids or adults. Many of these activities may be worthwhile but the people influencing and asking can become varmints because they are used by the devil to steal the best of your life with activities that are merely legitimate. They can be friends who draw you away to a myriad of lesser activities that take the time that the best activities should have taken.

Don't miss the metaphor here. People are people. We will be held responsible for how we react to every individual. The enemy of our soul knows that we already have too much on our plate. If he can not seduce us into living a carnal, worldly life he will bring out the varmints. He will have people who he uses to tempt us to do evil. If we will not do evil, he will use people to bring us down and wear us out. If that doesn't work he will use them to waste our time on lesser things. Our main task as believers is not to be nice but to be obedient to God (Matt. 7:21ff).

God allows varmints as temptation, in order to strengthen us against the fear and influence of men. God may lead us in unusual pathways but they will always be His pathways. Many people have let the varmints steal their best so that they are either disqualified or too busy to answer the greater purposes of God. The remnant needs to run every varmint out of their spiritual house so that nothing is stealing their strength and substance for God's service.

In America the Canadian goose has been a protected species. In my lifetime I have seen them grow from a rare to a rather common bird. In the Northeast they just kind of hang out in fields and parks and leave their little 'goodies' for people to step in. Since they are not hunted anymore they are multiplying like crazy and may soon be off the endangered list. Another major challenge in American cities is the pigeon. They really tend to attach themselves to cities and live in any nook or cranny that they can find. People have become very squeamish about eliminating what used to be regarded as pest birds so their numbers have swollen. Extraordinary and expensive solutions are sought in protecting property from their abundant feces. The European starling was successfully introduced to North America in New York's Central Park. They have spread and multiplied all over America and Canada. There are hundreds of millions of them. They are truly an annoying pest, as many farmers can attest. In the wilderness, an absence of predators or an introduction of a foreign species can cause huge imbalances that cause a lot of difficulty from birds that would not otherwise be a problem.

In the spiritual wilderness we need to be aware of the devil's **'dirty birds'**. In Revelation 18:2, the demonic world is compared to "every unclean and hateful bird." This is not a knock on birds but a description of the nature of our unseen spiritual enemies. The specific context is the end of Spiritual Babylon. The world's

Babylonian system has corrupt evil spirits striving to drive its agenda. There are three Babylonian systems that continually manifest themselves in the world. They are Political, Religious, and Economic Babylon. The Revelation of Jesus Christ gives His prescription for success to God's people. His solution is that God's people come out of the Babylonian systems (Rev. 18:4). We are to do this so that we do not partake of their sin or their judgment. That is, we are in this world but not of it (2 Pet. 1:4; 1 John 2:15-17).

But how does this relate to little old you or little old me in our little, tiny, worlds? Revelation 17 & 18 give us three general devices of the enemy of our soul. In his kingdom he exerts power and pressure through these three basic realms to bring individuals and whole nations into bondage. In America's realm of influence we see all three of these realms of spiritual influence coming together in a rare and powerful convergence. We need to be able to recognize and separate ourselves from their spiritual control of our lives.

The evil birds of **Political Babylon** hold many professing Christians in their sway. The Bible clearly states that, although world politics may be influenced by God, they are an expression of mankind known as the kingdoms of this world (Rev. 11:15; 1 Cor. 2:5-8; Matt. 4:8-10). Those who hope to bring lasting and true change to this current society will suffer the fate of all who have gone before them. Political activism will do much less than people think. Even if you can impose your 'morals' on people you have not really given them the means to become moral. Government may legislate Christian values upon others but laws do not change people's hearts. Besides, since when did the Church move from principles to values? We see no such activism or approach given in the New Testament.

The pervasive and threatening aspect of Christianity is revealed when the living Christ is presented with the power of the Holy Spirit. This is not the pallid nonsense often presented as the Gospel today but a power encounter with the living God. Paul was preaching in a semi-democratic empire. His approach was to present the claims of Jesus Christ with a powerful demonstration of power. His goal was the transformation of as many individuals as possible (1 Cor. 9:19-23). Rather than trying to promote Christians into places of power and influence Paul simply attempted to win those who were already in power or places of influence (Acts 13:4-12). He understood that Christ's Kingdom, though not yet fully revealed, held the ultimate power to transform individuals. He was changing society one person at a time. Near the end of his ministry he was called the man who "turned the world upside down" (Acts 17:6).

The reason that there is little persecution in America may be that the alleged Christianity is not subversive enough to our Political Babylon. It constitutes no kind of real threat to the worldly power base. Countries like China have a real problem with true Christianity. The Chinese understand that the Christianity being presented in word and deed by the non-institutional Church is transforming individuals. In the government's mind this poses a real threat to their totalitarian regime. God is calling His remnant out of political lobbying and into the kind of lobbying that changes society: lobbying God by prayer and fasting. Such people will not be subversive with guns or political dissent but with the true transformation of lives. Now that is dangerous!

I believe that Evangelicals, Pentecostals, and the rest of the Born-again crowd have been simple-minded about discerning **Religious Babylon**. They have pointed to the cults, the Roman Catholics, or the Muslims as the Harlot Church and missed the point. Religious Babylon in America is reflected in the smorgasbord of religious options available to us. These options are revealed by denominational interests that work against the unity of the Body of Christ. These religious substitutes dim the reflection of Christlike character in their adherents. The Body of Christ is not discernable with human eyes or organizational titles. It is very disconcerting to professing religious people when they cannot appropriately label the group that is 'right'. In my earlier letters I have gone to some extent to explain that the remnant will be found all over but will adhere to no group which proclaim that they are 'right' or 'most right'. The true Church is always made up of every believer, known by their Father in Heaven, who listens to the voice of their great shepherd, Jesus. The rest constitute Spiritual Babylon.

These are shocking statements and very insulting to every human who is building a human religious kingdom. We see a lot of this kind of activity all over America. Although we have the common mission to win souls and preach Jesus, we can barely get along. The bulk of television preachers and teachers are building ministries, missing essential truth, lining their pockets, and promoting personalities and showmanship. We now see mass-marketed solutions that claim to help grow churches. Others are actually mixing the prayer practices of Eastern religions under the banner of Contemplative Prayer. George Barna comes to this conclusion in his "The State of the Church: 2005":

> Related to this lack of laudable direction and courageous initiative is the failure of ministries to measure the outcomes that matter. Churches—and, by extension, the people associated with them—continue to evaluate the success or failure of a congregation and of individual lives according to factors that do not do justice to the life, death, resurrection and teachings of Jesus Christ. Churches measure attendance, donations, numbers of staff, numbers of programs and square footage as their primary indicators of spiritual health and growth. Jesus did not die on the cross for such incidental outcomes. Individual believers, taking their cues from their church, measure their spiritual vitality on the basis of the frequency of their church attendance, whether they donate money to ministry, and their general sense of personal "goodness" on a day-to-day basis. Again, such measures insult Christ. The axiom "you get what you measure" is certainly true for the Christian body in the U.S. Until we start to think about, pursue, and measure genuine Spiritual transformation in individual lives, we will continue to get what we've been getting, as unsatisfying as that is, for years to come.[3]

The American Church is caught in a quagmire of competing religious interests that make it difficult for most of its members to fulfill its very simple mission.

Although I have already mentioned this, I must repeat for emphasis. To continue in a place or with a group that you are not fully sure that God has placed you with may be placing yourself in

Spiritual Babylon. Many Evangelicals, conservative Born-again groups, and Pentecostals seem confused about their core beliefs. It seems to me that many are in a very defensive posture. It takes more than a theological statement to stay alive. It takes properly applied theology. Any fellowship that boasts His presence must resemble His glorious likeness. To the rest Jesus says, "Come out of her, my people" (Rev. 18:4). Dead religion is an insult to God and has the spirit of Antichrist. Do not let an evil bird of false religion take nest in your life, beloved.

The love of money is the root of all evil and its pursuit will destroy the pursuer (1 Tim. 6:10). Wow! I think we might have to take that Scripture and paste it in front of our eyes until it is seared into our brains. I wonder if there is one house in America that has this Scripture posted on the wall! All of us have to make a living. Yet, we see the Bible presenting **Economic Babylon** as the eventual lever to renounce Christ. Although the Mark of the Beast is associated with this aspect of Babylon, financial survival has always been a favorite snare of the devil. He loves to take the legitimate needs of life and exalt them as a god over us.

What great danger we find ourselves in today. The dirty birds of greed want to roost in the lives of the Remnant Church. I have seen so many potential heroes of faith reduced to grubbing when faced with the claims of the faith life. Many of the finest saints that I have known have let providing the needs of their family become the reason they never launch out. Many of us have an inflated idea of what we need. Then we spend a great deal more time working to get it. We become susceptible to the suggestion that we cannot do things because we don't have the money. God will and does provide but not for fancy cars and homes. God provides the means for us to stake our ministry. It is a commonly promoted idea that church members are supposed to go out and make as much money as they can, come and sit in church on Sunday, and throw their money in the bucket. People that live this way naturally expect others to do the work since they are using their time to earn money. This contravenes the Biblical concept that we are all called to be His ministers.

Every dirty bird will roost in one of these three general ways. Paul states that God's people are not ignorant of the devil's devices

(2 Cor. 2:11). John presents His vision with these themes. In John's Revelation, Jesus is revealed as the great conquering Christ who will soon return with power. What will happen on the earth in the mean time is more sinister. The devil is revealed as the great end-time deceiver.

The devil cannot get you unless you let him my friend. He would love to infest you with dirty life-draining parasites but the blood of Jesus can remove each one. He would love to defeat or distract you with all kinds of varmints but the Holy Spirit can reveal each one to you. He would love to deceive and destroy you with his dirty birds of Babylonian deception but all authority is given to us through Jesus' name. The Revelation of Jesus Christ gives us an insight into how it will go for God's American remnant church. The record states that believers will win because of the Blood of the Lamb, the word of their testimony, and not loving their life in this world even to the death (Rev. 12:11). These are the simple keys. A lot of our troubles and tests will bring us around to being stripped of all but these three empowering keys. The remnant will be part of the Glorious Church without spot or wrinkle or any such thing (Ephesians 5:27). Maranatha!

Your Friend and Fellow Traveler,

Henry

# CHAPTER 16

# *Teachers And Teachability*

Dear Fellow Traveler,

**M**ost city dwellers would quickly acknowledge that for them to survive in the wilderness they would need someone to teach them the basics. Most of us are so far removed from wilderness skills we probably wouldn't last a week out there. There has been a proliferation of wilderness teachers as people seek to reconnect with nature. You can find many teachers by searching the web for available wilderness courses. There are also many books on the subject readily available in book stores. As you learn about the wilderness, you realize that living comfortably there has many more facets than I have used in my letters. The educational task is so overwhelming that you will quickly realize you need hands-on training.

If a person wanted such training they would need to take the initiative. They would need to contact a teacher, cooperate with their timetable, pay the appropriate fees, and dedicate themselves to learning the material being taught. A great deal of care would need to be taken to investigate the ability and qualifications of the teacher. As I already mentioned, gaining expertise in wilderness wayfaring will take a great deal of hands-on training. The teacher would need to be a mentor. A person would need to understand the motivating philosophy behind their training as well as the general strategies for success. The teaching relationship would allow the student to hone and perfect their skills under personal supervision.

I am just a dilettante when it comes to wilderness wayfaring. I have read a bit and had a bit of instruction on some very basic skills. I claim no expertise at all. Once I had taken a basic course, I immediately realized the cost and attention that would be required to become an expert would be more than I was willing to pay. Unfortunately, the vast majority of professing American Christendom would likely be regarded as dilettantes by God when it comes to traversing the spiritual wilderness landscape we now face. We have explained some of the basics of spiritual survival but how do we become proficient in our spiritual survival skills? God's answer is two-fold: Teachers and teachability.

I am proof that you cannot become a wilderness expert by reading books. Books can give me the information but I still need the instruction. It is fascinating that there is no record of Jesus having formal sit-down classes for His disciples like the other Rabbis did. Jesus taught His truth in the context of ongoing life situations. He took the events that developed and taught within them. He lived with His disciples. They viewed His example and criticized Him when they thought He was making a mistake. Jesus was teaching them a whole new way to live. The supernatural power of God was guiding the agenda and was manifested as the Word of God was being preached. Jesus gave unprecedented accessibility to His students so that they could learn a whole new type of life in this world: Living with the Father.

I have been reflecting upon the reasons that I am even here today to write to you. It has occurred to me that I have had one benefit that most people in the Church have not enjoyed; New Testament-style teachers. I have enjoyed several different relationships that have transcended the Rabbi-style classroom approach often associated with teaching today, let alone the distance of television teaching. I have not just experienced a transfer of information but an exchange of life and vision. In reality, I have hardly appreciated the privilege that has been mine. As I hear the lonely stories of others I have realized how fortunate I have been.

In the realm of discipleship there is a necessity for a commitment between the teacher and the taught. We must trust the providence of God to bring us our instructors. The fact is, we need to be diligently looking and praying for those who would instruct us. I am amazed at the low expectations of students in the professing church of God. We have already examined the puerile, worldly reasons that people often use in choosing a church fellowship. Very few are looking for a relationship that involves discipleship with the Biblical scrutiny that Jesus gave His disciples. If you are seeking to be a Disciple of Christ it behooves you to seek someone who exhibits the purity of life, wisdom in the Scriptures, and practical experience to assist you in your quest to partake of the life of God.

As well, the person taught must make a commitment to the person teaching. I have never lost my desire to learn. This turned out to be a great benefit to me because I would seek out the most spiritual people I knew and attempt to establish a relationship with them. Most of them were not ministers, so little formality was required. What was required was to meet and learn from them on their terms. I can't imagine being a demanding student. True submission is sometimes no more than recognizing someone's superior agenda and following it. The reverence for a teacher must be kept intact when that instructor has to discipline and correct us. Any teacher worth his salt will deliberately make it difficult to be his student from time to time. This will test and prove the commitment of the person the teacher is discipling.

Finally, the person teaching must agree to teach me. They have what I need. It is a privilege to receive both knowledge and experience from them. They are on the high ground. Their authority comes from both tried experience and God Himself. When a relationship is well-defined more learning will take place because everyone understands their role.

People have come and gone from my life as God has ordained. One mentor will teach their out-living of truth and the next will often teach the flip-side without even knowing it. So much of Kingdom living has to do with what seem to be extreme contrasts. God's love and His wrath, God's grace and practical obedience, living in the world but not being of the world, the Kingdom of God is in our midst and is yet to come, are all examples of the contrasts that we have to reconcile into everyday living. I have noted several common characteristics that identify a true Christian mentor/teacher.

The foremost characteristic that I have observed is ***agape*** love. This simple term has fallen out of favor lately. *Agape* love is the love that God's Spirit imparts. No human can produce it. It is nothing like brotherly love, friendship, emotional ties, or human sexuality. Agape is the pure and divine love imparted from God. When a person has walked in obedience to God for a long season they become infused with God's Spirit and this Spirit fills them with the love of God (Romans 5:5). When Jesus loves somebody through us, our natural prejudices and preferences are placed on the sideline. We are then loving somebody with the love of the LORD.

I have been loved this way. Besides at least six teachers, I have had a few of my peers love me with the love of Jesus. While accepting me for who I was, all of these people had my better interests at heart. They wanted to see me mature into a spiritual adult. They made space for me in their lives and poured in whatever I could or would receive. They all cared enough to correct me and tell me the truth, sometimes at the risk of our relationship. These relationships were based on the love of God and not on the impetus and desire for mere human friendship.

My spiritual parents, Mom and Dad Gillespie, probably showed me more of this kind of love than any other people. I was welcome at their house anytime. They always were welcoming and loving no matter how inconvenient my timing was. They were truly interested in my life and my concerns. In retrospect, some of my concerns must have been quite banal and simple for such mature people. An interesting aspect of this relationship was that they rarely contacted me. They demanded no accountability or control. When I wanted or needed them they were simply there. During times of struggle or waywardness they simply waited and prayed. No matter how much my behavior disappointed them they just embraced me and pointed me back to the Cross of Jesus for healing and deliverance.

God's mentors **love His Word** very much. They are people who have both taken and eaten God's truth into their very being (Matt. 4:4; Luke 4:4). The Bible will change your character if you let it. That is what I observed in all of my teachers. Some of them had come from very evil past lives and were profoundly changed. They all embraced the truth they learned. It was evident in their lives. They were not simply hearers of the Word but doers (James 1:23). They were all committed students of the Word of God. This allowed them to look at my complex problems quite simply and prescribe the appropriate cures. Their credibility came from their experience with God's Word.

Jesus laid down a very simple standard for being a teacher. In John 3:11, Jesus stated the obvious. We can only really impart spiritual things to other people when we have **experienced** those things ourselves. Nicodemus was purportedly teaching the nation of Israel. He found that he was strangely lacking when he came under the scrutiny of the Son of God. The Pharisees had a lot of rules and theories to impose but were sadly lacking in their experience of God. Jesus taught that one must experience truth in order to impart it to others. Today, many are trying to present concepts and ideas in a primarily academic way. My mentors were more academic than most ministers but their power to impart Bible truth came from their submission to it. They were 'living letters' that required no book or instruction to understand (2 Cor. 3:2).

My teachers had **healthy** outlooks and healthy souls. If you met them you would want to be like them (1 Tim. 4:12). There was just a vibrancy and conviction about them that made them spiritually attractive. I admire those people in whom God is truly manifested. Over the years I have come to realize the great personal expense involved in having Christ live His life through me. When a person is finally yielded to Jesus' agenda the life of God starts to be represented through their life. The characteristics of the Perfect Son of God start to manifest themselves.

Jesus makes us well. We are not just forgiven but effectual. That is what I saw in my mentors. Their yielded lives gave them inner health. They loved life and enjoyed living it. Such personal zest for life is just infectious. It is not the product of academic endeavor but of personal relationship. Many people have stated that, "To be much for God you must be much with God." A true teacher does not just 'know the Lord' but is 'known of the Lord'. They have experienced being "accepted in the Beloved" (Eph. 1:5-7).

Closely associated with this spiritual health were the byproducts of **zeal** and **joy**. We spoke about fire already. My mentors all had a fire and passion for God. To be with them was to be strangely warmed and encouraged. I remember Jim speaking with great conviction about what the Bible taught and the need for obedience to it. I have experienced the exquisite desire to represent the Kingdom that my spiritual parents constantly displayed. I have enjoyed the merriment of my friend Clare that accompanied his committed life to God. He had absolute confidence because he knew that he knew the truth. I remember how Alex harassed me to constantly pray with him to be filled with the Holy Spirit. I remember the presence of God that visited while Diddi and I prayed on the phone over three thousand miles apart. I remember hundreds, maybe thousands, of passionate conversations and prayers that all centered around Jesus. What zeal they all had. What joy it brings my soul upon every remembrance. How I am warmed right now to represent God's Kingdom.

And oh, the **stories**! All of my mentors and teachers had stories to tell about God's dealings with them and the people who influenced them. God was not a distant task-master demanding His due but an imminent Friend teaching and guiding them into all truth. All of them had a connection to true revival and renewal. Clare's stories of his father's faith while pioneering churches still inspire my faith. Jim told stories of the giants who influenced him to become a man of prayer and spiritual warfare. Alex talked constantly about Sister Durell, his spiritual mom, who had been saved during a season of revival. She had prayed through with him again and again. He never tired of listening to the stories of revival days. Mom and Dad Gillespie spoke of all of God's dealings with them through the loss of their only daughter and the hope they received. They always had a report of some answered prayer which was impossible for man to have done.

There was a common thread in all of my spiritual friend's and mentor's stories. They all spoke of what **God had done**. They all shared the miraculous interventions of a merciful Father and Friend. The stories were all about a Personal God who was involved in their lives. God was no impersonal power or force to them. All of these stories aligned with the truth of God's Word. They were current, experiential examples of what God could do in **my life**. What hope these stories give me to this day.

All of my teachers believed that to know Jesus was to cultivate a walk and life of **holiness**. Holiness is one characteristic that we rarely see displayed in this present wilderness. Matthew 1:21 clearly states, *"And she shall bring forth a son, and thou shalt call his name JESUS: for he shall save his people from their sins."* Jesus saves us from our sins, not in them. These exemplary people all lived lives of exceptional purity. They were not perfect and made no such pretensions. They clearly desired that Christ would come and make His home in their hearts. They knew that anyplace that Jesus lives is holy, because He is perfectly holy. They did this because they loved the Lord and wanted to let Him have His way. They were not motivated by some external set of rules that they felt they needed to obey.

Above all, my teachers **could pray**. That is, when they prayed, the presence of God quickly came upon all present. To be able to pray and call down the presence of God is central. My teachers didn't just say prayers but had vibrant conversations with God, under the influence of His Holy Spirit. The cumulative effect of all my mentors and close spiritual friends placing such importance upon the presence of God in prayer has profoundly affected me. As we experience God's presence we are more and more adept at discerning what is and is not of God. The glory of group prayer is the special attendance of the Holy Spirit. I find myself dissatisfied with any prayer that does not involve the unction of the Holy Spirit. Prayer is not just conversation but interaction with the King of the Universe.

How I remember the prayers! I remember Dad Gillespie praying late into the night after the house was asleep. Groaning and crying, he wrestled men out of the hands of the devil. Hour after hour he would fight on alone, until he was satisfied that the answer was on the way. I remember a sweet hour of prayer with Clare. He prayed in English and I prayed in the Spirit. Then he prayed in the Spirit and I prayed in English. What a Presence with power. I still can taste the air as Jim and I wrestled against infernal local powers.

I learned to discern the gift of faith in those seasons. I especially remember learning one of my most important lessons with my friend, Alex. We learned that if two people abandoned themselves to God and 'went for it' that they could always break the heaviness on their lives in short order. Oh the difference between knowing God and knowing about God! I learned it all in the place of prayer.

Where are the teachers; the mentors? You will find most of them **hidden** away in the humble and quiet place. Most will never have great position or recognition in the institutional church. Their lives are too strange and troubling to externally religious people. All of the people that have had input into my life were very hard working people. They worked with their own hands and provided for their own families (1 Thes. 4:11; 1 Tim. 5:8). This type of person has no need to rule over people or have them follow. They are identified by the character and nature of Christ dwelling in them. Unfortunately, this kind of individual is becoming more and more rare. You will have to really want to find them because they are not seeking to be found. Once you have found them, you will have to practice the discipline of **teachability**.

The word disciple means learner. The New Testament gives us a simple picture of the way that Jesus taught and the way that He expected people to learn. Jesus chose twelve **'learners'**. These men were to live with Him to learn how to live the life of God. Implicit in the acceptance of the invitation to follow was a commitment to follow. There was no great discussion when Jesus said, "Follow me" (Matt. 4:19). They would or they wouldn't, it was their choice. There were a lot of questions raised, a lot of troubling events, and a lot of misunderstandings but there was little room for disputing the authority of the Leader. This, in a nutshell, is the duty of the learner—to follow and learn. Something essential is imparted from one person's life to another. This was the method Jesus used. He was so successful that the men that he taught influenced the whole known world in their generation.

It is clear that Barnabas used this approach with Saul (soon to be Paul). Barnabas first introduced Saul to the apostles and stood up for him when the Christians were, understandably, afraid of Saul (Acts 9:27). He went and brought Saul back from Tarsus to assist in

God's work in Antioch (Acts 11:22-26). Eventually the Antioch church sent Barnabas and Saul out as missionaries to the Gentile world (Acts 13:1-4). All through those years Barnabas was the leader. There is no doubt that he recognized the blessing and calling of God on Saul's life. Barnabas was used by God to assist in Saul's encouragement and growth. It seems that Saul became the lead speaker after he started to use his Roman name, Paul. Later, Barnabas and Paul parted company. Barnabas found another 'learner', John Mark (Acts 15:37-40).

What do you need to do to obtain a teacher and mentor? Foremost, you must **see your need**. A characteristic of mature believers is their recognition of how far they fall short of God's glory. A characteristic of more immature believers is their oft dependence on their own ability and strength. As a younger believer, you will avoid a lot of trouble by placing yourself in the seat of the learner. If you have been on The Way for some time, and have not humbled yourself to be a learner, this process may be very humbling. There seems to be an independent spirit in this generation of church adherent. Many people do not want to endure the rigors of a learning relationship. Many are very content to 'go' to church. It is imperative from the start that we see our need for instruction in the most holy survival skills. To carry on with the Christian life without a teacher-learner relationship is very similar to walking into the woods without supply, instruction, or experience. Such behavior in both realms is tantamount to arrogance or insanity.

It takes a great deal of **personal honesty** to admit that our experience may be sadly lacking in essentials. God's teachers have studied and learned His Word. They have learned the ways of the indwelling Christ and have grown to a healthy state of spirituality. It is very interesting that the early church members *"continued steadfastly in the apostles' doctrine and fellowship, and in breaking of bread, and in prayers"* (Acts 2:42). The credential the apostles had was that they had been with Jesus. Their doctrine was not just dissertation on the Scriptures but the practice of allowing the indwelling Christ to rule in them (2 Peter 1:1-8). Their teaching was the same as they later delineated in their letters which became our

Scriptures. We have a very deep need to see this kind of life honestly displayed. We also need to hear the stories of how such believers learned and grew mature. Many people will not acknowledge their great need. They thus disqualify themselves from God's methods and means of growth from the start.

Teachability is **hard**. A new or carnal believer is dominated by their senses and their self-life. The teacher will start to challenge the lifestyle practices of the learner. The learner has to be able to take the repeated criticism and correction of the teacher. It is very **humbling** and can feel humiliating. We see that the disciples were continually being corrected—hearing Jesus say 'wrong again'. It is interesting to do a study on all of the times that Jesus rebuked them. They hung in there with Jesus when the crowd could not take what Jesus was saying.

The learner must have a commitment to learn. The Christian teacher will follow the method of Jesus in continually challenging for a total commitment. Sin is easily discerned when we see that its roots exalt the individual over the will of God. God will continually show us practices to cease and new practices to start. How do we apprehend His grace? How do we do things the easy way instead of learning every lesson the hard way? What can an experienced believer add to our life? It is only as we discover a commitment to be taught that we will avoid the pitfalls of our own ability to delude ourselves. A well balanced mentor can be as important to an inexperienced believer as a parent is to their child.

I have observed that a lot of people are not very desirous to learn. Jesus said that those who "hungered and thirsted after righteousness" would be filled (Matt. 5:6). If you observe that you have little desire for spiritual things and little interest in being corrected and taught, you might do well to ask God for such a hunger. I have noticed that it is very useful to ask for new fire and desire when I have grown a bit cold. Once I have received new motivation from God I do not find it such a chore to submit myself to the rigors of being taught His ways. When God humbles me I find myself rejoicing instead of complaining for I see such humiliation as very useful in keeping myself in the learning mode (Luke 14:11; 18:14).

As I look back, I am amazed how I just kept **coming back for**

**more**. In fact, I find it hard to imagine most of the people that I have met subjecting themselves to such constant and repeated correction. All of my mentors were brutally honest. They never seemed to apologize much for their candor. Something inside of me knew that my very survival depended on hearing what they had to say and learning what they had to teach. I really have seen the Scriptures fulfilled that speak of loving instruction and correction (Prov. 9:8-9, 14:16, 17:10, 27:5; Eccl. 7:5; Matt. 7:24-27). By this time of my life I have seen so many fail and fall. I am more persuaded than ever that it was the drive to come back and be accountable to my teachers that kept me humble. I do not remember one of them claiming any authority over me. Their character as well as their love for me made me want to give an account and make things right.

The teacher-student relationship, as taught in the Bible, is so different than what is so often presented today. The Biblical model has so much to do with family relationship. There are fathers, mothers, and children in the Body of Christ. Ultimately, it is love that motivates people to both give of themselves to teach and to humble themselves to learn. Paul the Apostle expressed his fatherly concern and authority in his first letter to the Corinthians (1 Cor 4:15-16). Since Paul had won the Corinthians to Christ, he felt emboldened to claim fatherly authority and express fatherly concern concerning their sin. Paul knew that sin was not a 'mistake' or a 'problem' but a cosmic disaster with devastating consequences. Like any parent, he lovingly brought correction to save his children from harm. As well, Paul set forth such an example that he could say, "Just do what I do and you will be fine" (1 Cor. 11:1-2).

It is to the credit of the disciples that they hung in there with Jesus. I'll bet Jesus' rebuke just cut like a knife. He rebuked Peter as Satan's helper (Matt. 16:23). He continually expressed exasperation with their slowness, hardness of heart, and wickedness. He hated unbelief and rebuked them often. There currently seems to be some fascination with the smiling, happy Jesus. This may mask from us the rigors of what it was like to try and please the absolutely perfect Son of God.

In a way, it couldn't be done. A large part of the process they went through was for the very purpose of exposing the disciple's personal bankruptcy. Jesus knew that their self-confidence was the very thing that would block the flow of God's love and power in their lives. When Jesus had offended everyone else to the point that they left Him alone with the disciples he asked, *"Will ye also go away?"* (John 6:67). When most of the crowd dissipated Jesus' disciples hung with Him in the hard times. Why would we think the program is any different today?

Above all, the disciple has to be a **Student of God's Word**. God states that He has exalted His Word above His name (Psalm 138:2). All men and women are fallible. They will make mistakes. Even the best of my teachers have, at times, had views that did not seem to jive with the Word of God. These were usually minor things or matters of personal practice and preference. Ultimately, we will not be able to point at anyone else on the Day of Judgment. God will judge **us** for what we have both said and done in relation to His Word. Whether we are a seasoned veteran or a rookie in the Kingdom, we need to continually hold up every area of our lives to the scrutiny of God's Word and the conviction of the Holy Spirit.

If you have a faithful mentor, have **mercy** on them. They need to be loved and cared for. Every good child loves their parent and looks up to them. There are few things more satisfying in life than the gratitude of one's child. All of us are susceptible to failure and sin. That is why the Bible teaches that when we think an elder has sinned that we should handle it with the "spirit of meekness" and apply the scrutiny of God's Word to our own lives as well (Gal. 6:1). Sometimes younger Christians can misunderstand their leader and think that they have done something wrong when they haven't. We are all human and are susceptible to temptation, frailty, and weakness. We can sometimes learn a lot from other's failures. That is why it is important to love and forgive those that are over us in the Lord.

Inquiring minds want to know. It is really important to **keep pursuing** an understanding of God's Word and plan. Jesus is our ultimate and perfect example. The Bible can stand the scrutiny of man. Jesus was the impeccable son of God but He never crushed sincere inquiry into what His Father wanted. He was patient and kind. He put in a lot of overtime with 'the boys'. The Bible is by far the most fascinating book in the world. The best teachers I have known are still looking into apprehending the truths in it for themselves and a lost world. That is the key. Bible truth is not just known but incorporated into a person's life. That means that the mature and the babies are all 'in process' while they travel through this world. Keep inquiring and never give up.

My hope for you, my friend, is that you will find both teachers and parents 'in the Lord'. It is God's plan for His family to reproduce and bring children to maturity so that they may also reproduce. Purpose in your heart to find the relationships that God has for you in this present wilderness.

Your Brother in the Family,

Henry

# CHAPTER 17

# *The End Of The Trail*

Dear Fellow Traveler,

We are coming to the end of our journey together. Every journey has an end. Some journeys are long and some are short. Sometimes we are very aware of the end of a trip, like the day we get home from vacation. Other times we don't know we have finished a journey until we look back at a portion of our life and realize that it had a theme to it. Each day and each season are journeys. People react to the end of different journeys in accordance with the quality of the journey and the temperament of the individual. It takes wisdom to **rightly interpret** the meaning of every journey.

I remember a canoe trip I took as a teen in Barclay Sound, on the west coast of Vancouver Island. The weather was rough and it rained every day but one. I had food poisoning just before I started the trip and felt about as poorly as I had felt in years. My canoe partner was not into the trip and we found ourselves in some real danger in choppy waters because he wouldn't paddle the canoe. He just sat in the bow and cried. Our bedding was wet and starting a fire was unusually hard. I couldn't eat for three days and when I did I was nauseated by the seventies-style freeze-dried food. The last day was sunny and I was so grateful just to finish the trip.

Immediately following this trip we traveled the West Coast Trail, in Pacific Rim National Park. The trail started a few miles from where the canoe trip ended. We had beautiful weather every day. I felt better. We had some fresh food to supplement the freeze-dried food. The hiking was hard but the whole tone of the trip was different for me. I loved the scenery and appreciated the rugged wildness of my surroundings so much. I actually had mixed feelings as I left my friends and headed home. What a contrast to the first trip.

In this present North American spiritual wilderness there seem to be some journey endings that people are conflicted about. These are the inevitable endings that must happen. Each one represents a good thing, although it is clear that many would disagree with me. Because God's people have an eternal inheritance, their perspectives are truly different than those who live only for this tiny little journey called life. Let's see if we can bring a little perspective to three important endings.

A human life can seem so long at the beginning and so short as it draws to a close. To the unbelieving person **death** is the great, inevitable, and terrible conclusion to all they have and hold dear. How sad it is to think that men could, as my father used to say, "Die like dogs" (I refuse to broach the subject of doggie heaven). Paul the apostle answered those who denied an afterlife: *"If in this life only we have hope in Christ, we are of all men most miserable"* (1 Cor. 15:19). For the person who denies any life, other than this flesh and blood present life, there is only sorrow ahead. For those who have a vague, undefined idea of death; the end of life is a terrifying and miserable prospect. Since our society dreads death, people choose not to speak of death in concrete terms. There is a tendency to think that a long life is the best you can expect and a shorter one is a tragedy. This is the sad outlook of the unbeliever.

At this juncture in time I find the attitude of the majority of professing believers toward life and death astonishing. This dread amongst professing American believers may be caused by the abundance of our possessions. Any Medieval or Third-world person would think that they had gone to heaven just to live as we do. Perhaps this is why the professing church is such an earth-bound, secularized bunch when it comes to the subject of death. I am sure that secular society has had an influence as well. So much of the focus of our culture has to do with what we are doing and building here on earth. Many lack a joyful anticipation of the glory of heaven.

Unfortunately, this earth-bound mentality is reflected in what excites so many in the institutional church. They love big ministries and large successes. They measure the nickels and noses. They care about buildings and programs that they hope can catch the attention of people in this frenetic society. The unchurched and nominal believer is savvy enough to know that these things do not reflect what is important for eternity. The concerned soul is looking for assurance of eternal salvation.

In contrast, the recent theologies of Reconstructionism, Kingdom Now, Amillennialism, and Postmillennialism, which deny Christ's physical return to the earth before the Millennium, have become popular in certain quarters of the church. All of these theories relegate Jesus' Second Coming to something related to what humans will do for God here on earth. The return of Jesus is interpreted as a figurative return within the Body of Christ. Only within the context of such a worldly and hedonistic society could such an end-time outlook flourish. Somehow, these outlooks glorify their teachers and their idea of a new 'church' much more than they do the Coming King of the universe.

The important facts of heaven and hell are lost in the shuffle. Nevertheless, these facts are very important to Jesus. In fact, Jesus clearly taught that our eternal destiny was the major matter to be dealt with in this life. The nagging question, "where will I go when I die and how can I be sure?" still needs to be answered. This is why Jesus became a sacrifice for sin (Eph. 5:2; Heb. 9:26). Careers, families, possessions, and the like have their place but all of them are temporary. What is permanent is what we do by Christ's grace. Paul recommended cautious use of even the most basic privileges of life because, *"the fashion of this world passeth away"* (1 Cor. 7:31). To get caught up in the politics, family, business, or pleasure of the present system was generally regarded by the New Testament writers as catastrophic behavior. Loving the world would destroy the life and eternal reward of the believer (James 4:4; 1 John 2:15-16).

Even a very long life is such a small drop in the bucket of eternal time. Meditation on this fact can be very beneficial. For the young this can draw perspective. When the legitimate plans and ambitions of youth are brought under subjection to what God desires, they can take on a whole new meaning, direction, and focus. An individual's career will then be used for God's Kingdom rather than earning money. One's spouse will be chosen on the basis of their heart of faith rather than on the basis of simple attraction or romance. An individual's money will be spent as heavenly chattel.

For those who are older, who might feel that they have squandered their best days, there is still the use of the rest: 401k or the Kingdom today? Will there simply be a retirement or will there be a career change, as a minister of Jesus? It is very helpful to remember that Samson's last effort was his best (Judges 16:30). Moses really got going at eighty. Abraham finally passed the big test at around one hundred and twenty.

I love to officiate at the funerals of those who have lived well for Christ. I have never led such a funeral that was not well attended. I have simply used the person's life and testimony to preach the Gospel. I remember the eulogies and testimonies of strangers to the goodness and usefulness of these obedient servants. The term 'salt of the earth' has often been used for such people. Their 'salt' had become synonymous with goodness expressed by the glory of Jesus in their lives. Without variation, these kinds of funerals follow people who spend and have been spent for the glory of God. Such people have not 'tried to be good' but have yielded each day to the indwelling Christ. When Jesus is allowed to live through an individual, that person will leave a legacy of blessing behind them that they could never have procured by human means.

It is clear that every professing believer wants to go to heaven when they die but few live as if death were an imminent event. For much of history, much of the world has lived under the shadow of death. Wars, pestilence, famine, accident, and disaster have been the norm rather than the exception. These events have kept the appeal of heaven pointed in the minds of those who lived through them. Most of the current population of the world struggles to survive day by day. When you live in a war zone, a famine zone, or you have no medicine to treat simple diseases, death looms large. Each day must be lived. Human relations are more precious. A person may not have tomorrow. At such times there is great comfort and testimony while living with imminent assurance that heaven is our home.

In contrast, American society has many comforts and protections. The entertainment industry gives constant diversion from reality. This definitely anesthetizes us to the imminence of death. A lot of the professing church has fallen for the cultural taboo that inhibits plain talk about death. Many do not firmly press the imminence of death upon those in society because it is not 'sensitive'. Yet the writer of Hebrews teaches that without Christ even the most diverted people live their whole life in the "fear of death" (Heb. 2:15). Those who have received Christ are not to live as the rest of the world does, yet I see and hear so much that points to the fact that professing believers are living their lives ruled by the fear of death. Is it possible that this fear is a symptom of the diseases of unbelief or love of this present world?

Finally, the **quality** of our whole eternity is determined by this very short space called life. Ultimately the minimum reward of obedience will be eternal life (Matt. 20:1-16). The reward comes because we are chosen and because we continue (Col. 1:23). There are further rewards for those who yield themselves to God, thus making them more perfectly faithful (Romans 14:7-12; 1 Cor. 3:8-15). Paul attributed his ability and calling to the grace of God (1 Cor. 15:10). As well, he took pains to point out that he cooperated with the grace of God (Gal. 2:21; Col. 1:29). It is clear that the quality of our eternity is somehow affected by the quality of our obedience to the will of God in this life. This boggles the mind. A mere blip in time, in all of eternity, will determine both our location and our vocation. It is therefore of the utmost importance to do all that we are directed to do, by His grace. Only a fool would ignore the means and direction of their eternal salvation, wouldn't they (Heb. 2:3)?

For the obedient servant of God, death is the happy conclusion to their redemptive journey. Every true believer who leaves this world leaves the world poorer but makes heaven richer. So why should we fear? Why should we behave anything like this world? Heaven is our hometown. We are part of a temporary embassy team commissioned on earth and subject to recall at the Governor's request (2 Cor. 5:20). Death has no sting for us because we will never die (1 Cor. 15:51-57; John 11:25-26). I am sure the remnant will have the opportunity to illustrate these facts in the public forum. Death is a happy ending for a believer and Psalm 116:15 gives God's attitude: *"Precious in the sight of the LORD [is] the death of his saints."*

Our next ending has to do with the idea that **America** is a Christian nation. Those who believe this have also concluded that God is therefore in some way aligned with America's political decision making. This point of view seems to be an amazingly prevalent world-view for many professing believers. This idea seems to have been intensified by the political and philosophical polarity in American society. There is a cultural battle between a largely secularized left and a multi-religified right. It appears that many on the religious right (claiming to represent all 'good' Christians) are using diverse political and sociological resources to champion their idea of God's point of view for the nation. Politicians feel a need to portray the appropriate religious beliefs and champion the appropriate causes to get elected. Much is made of America's religious heritage to prove that we are still a nation under God and that we need to legislate godly principles for the populace.

The Old Testament records the children of Israel's lack of obedience to God's laws. The present professing church in America could learn a great deal from the punishment of Israel, given from the very hand of God. Although we should be active in the privilege of free democratic expression this will not stem the ever increasing flow of evil in our society, even if we could create all the laws needed to prohibit that evil. The Gospel has always been primarily about transformation, one person at a time. Rather than praying for some obscure 'revival' in the future we may find that revival occurs as each individual is revived. Once revived, they will profoundly influence their sphere of life with the Gospel.

There is little doubt that the faith and sober living of past generations has brought blessing and help to America. The thrift and hard work of past generations have benefited all of us to this present time. The churches, mission related ministries, and financial aid ministries that have risen up in America over the past one hundred and fifty years are likely unparalleled in human history. The generosity of present day Americans is astonishing. I am amazed at the funds given to victims of natural disasters, terrorist and military attacks, and world hunger. America has been a force for many good causes in my lifetime.

Unfortunately, many professing believers have equated these past actions as a sort of insurance policy that God would never allow a change of America's prominent place of power and influence in the world. What is clear by simple observation is that America has suffered a profound moral decline. Since many fine Christians have authored works that chronicle and bemoan this decline I will just state it as an obvious fact. Yet many professing believers are hostile to the idea of any change in America that might profoundly affect their lives.

This denial of the basic life-principle of sowing and reaping reflects the spiritual and moral decay that is rampant in the church (Gal. 6:7-8). It is very normal and human for us not to want to have changes come that threatens our comfort and security. Nevertheless, human history is full of changes. Every worldly kingdom rises and falls. Every righteous government eventually is corrupted and is replaced by graft, fear, and favor. The joy of the believer is that God transcends all earthly kingdoms and will bring them to an end, setting up His own perfect and permanent government.

I am calling the fundamental shift that is coming for American society '**The Change**'. The remnant knows that the change has already started to happen. America owes too much money to its creditors to ever pay them back. This is a violation of God's command to stay out of debt. America kills over a million unborn children every year through state-sanctioned abortion. America is coming under profound pressure from illegal immigration. There are too many people who want what America has without obeying the rule of law. America's politicians do not tell the truth to America's citizens or their trading partners. This is lying and cheating. The sanctity of Biblical marriage and the nuclear family has been desecrated by legal proclamation. The very genetics of mankind is being played with by the scientific community. These are perversions of God's order. But most importantly, the professing American church has fallen into habitual sin, bickering, and heresy. The misrepresentation of Jesus Christ by a majority of professing believers is the foremost reason that America will change.

The Change will bring a profound loss of personal freedom. When Americans are faced with personal losses that rival or exceed those of the Great Depression I do not believe they will behave very well. Society has grown very uncivil and selfish. Hard times will reveal these characteristics in individuals and regions. When people are denied the things that they have come to think are their 'rights', there may be substantial social unrest. The government will have to become very repressive to keep the public order. More and more personal freedom and civil liberties will have to be suspended or society will fall into anarchy.

Because of the misrepresentation made by many so-called Christian leaders, more people may start to view Christians as undesirable fanatics. As well, unrest may cause Christian militias to rise up and further misrepresent the cause of Christ. If militia types succeed they would repress the truly peaceful remnant believers. If militia types fail, they will cause a natural social backlash against the church-going crowd. It does not take a lot of imagination to think of many similar possibilities. The one fact I am sure of is that we will not avoid trouble and persecution.

Many who have put their hope and faith in prosperity will be disillusioned. If their world has revolved around owning things, their losses will be very devastating. I expect that many of the pretenders will quit. A lot of money-making religious enterprises will close down. Many highly funded mega-churches will be abandoned. A lot of the denominations will have to lay off workers, close offices, recall missionaries, and close publishing houses. Scarcity of funds, departure of adherents, and persecution will change the face of American Christianity.

Recently the Lord gave me a couple of pictures that relate to these events. The first picture was of people sitting on a sunny tropical beach. They all were on recliners drinking exotic drinks. Next to each person was a large cardboard box. Just offshore a huge storm was gathering. The Lord seemed to be saying that the people were the current professing American church. They were all at their leisure and enjoying their lives. The cardboard boxes represented all of the things that they had bought, often with credit. They attributed their abundance to God but He never wanted them to get the things they had. The storm was The Change that is coming. Like the houses made on sand, the boxes would be blown away. The people on the beach would be disillusioned and actually blame God for their losses when it was really just their own fault.

The second picture was of a house on fire, just off the beach. People were calling, "Emergency, fire!" The people on the beach didn't hear or they just didn't care. The Lord seemed to be saying that the emergency was the lost and dying in the sphere of influence of each of the people on the beach. Each of us has a particular sphere of influence and acquaintance that nobody else has. We may be the only representative of Jesus that some individuals ever meet. If we do not fully represent His Kingdom to them they will be lost forever. Just as we would think a neighbor was horrible who wouldn't help us in a life or death situation, God thinks professing believers are horrible who won't go to the rescue of their neighbors who are bound for eternal punishment.

The Change will be good! Persecution divides the pretenders from the genuine. Some people who have been sitting on the fence will sell out to God. The remnant will step forward. They will shine and represent the Kingdom of God. Many who have never believed will find God. They will be ripe for something real to live for as their world falls down around them. There will be a final harvest in America but it will be in the midst of difficult times and severe persecution. It will be the end of the trail for the Old America and something we cannot imagine will follow. Whatever follows, the Church will look like the Church again. That is a happy ending.

Our final ending is the **end of the world**. When I was crying as a little kid my mother would comfort me, "Now, now, it's not the end of the world." This was meant to help me draw perspective. My little cut or bruise was a small and temporary problem compared to the end of the world. I suppose for the earth-bound person, the end of the world is about as bad is it can get. There have been all kinds of stories and movies about cataclysms and invasions that would end mankind's reign over this planet. These dramas play on people's deepest fears. I suppose the end of mankind would be the ultimate horror to the natural man. If there is no God, the end of the human race would be the loss of everything.

This is what we should expect from those who regard this world as their only home. They will spend their lives in the pursuit of 'making a name for themselves' like the residents of Babel did in their day (Gen. 11:4). They just wanted to do things their own way rather than God's. This gathering of rebellion will be replayed in a massive worldwide forum during the Great Tribulation. One of the major teachings we can draw from John's Revelation of Jesus Christ is that man is, individually and corporately, a rebel against God's will. Given the choice, the masses will always align themselves with Satan because they have the same self-will as he does.

To those who believe in God, the end of the world is generally regarded as the point where He will 'settle up' with mankind. Two atrocities would occur were God to ignore the rebellion of His creatures. The first would be the loss of ultimate justice. God is the true arbiter of good and evil. Through the Gospel, He has set down the means of mercy and forgiveness through Christ alone. As well, God gives an ultimate standard of justice for those who reject His mercy and do it their own way. Without an end time judgment, life just doesn't make sense. What would be the point of laws, societies, or being good at all? The second atrocity would be to leave men to their own devices. Those who say life is hell on earth haven't seen anything, yet. I am convinced that mankind would manage to pollute, breed, oppress, and war itself to extinction without the intervention of God or the temptation of the devil.

In the spiritual wilderness of America it is amazing how few professing Christians long for or live for Jesus' return. There seems to be little excitement about His return. Jesus associated faith in His return with the activity of the faithful. He warned His disciples that before His return many of His followers would grow weary and start participating in the world system (Luke 12:42-48). Although they may pay lip service to Him their heart's attitude would be, "*where is the promise of His coming*" (2 Peter 3:4-6)? Just as obedience to Jesus' word is an expression of faith in Him; soul-saving and mercy work is an expression of faith in His coming.

Of course we may be thought of as mad. Noah must have been deemed crazy. That was the blessing of being 'right' in his day and will be in our day. I have little doubt that Noah's project was sufficient warning to His neighbors both in time-frame and magnitude. I find it hard to imagine Noah weeping self-pity tears into his sleeve. Jesus said that the end-time would hold the same challenge for those who would live righteous in Him (Matt. 24:37-39). Many people will not understand or believe the remnant in these last days.

I regard the increasingly popular idea of this so-called present church ushering in the millennial rule of Christ without His literal return with horror. As mentioned earlier in these letters, this idea is becoming more and more popular amongst Charismatics, Pentecostals, and even Evangelicals. Ostensibly, the church people would move into positions of political power and religious authority. The whole world would eventually come under their rule. I suppose the leaders of such a movement would be the ones 'called' to lead in this New World Order for God.

Any member of God's remnant will see the idiocy of such an idea. How could such a generation of spiritual pipsqueaks lead anything meaningful? I have no confidence that any of the leadership of this day could bring anything to pass that would resemble what the Bible says the millennium will be like. The Bible-twisting required to promote such ideas is remarkable. This is nothing more than Babel revisited. Religion always tries to emulate the real thing and it always fails miserably.

Fortunately, Christ will literally and physically return to the Mount of Olives (Acts 1:11; Zech. 14:4). This can only be a present comfort to those who follow Him. There is nothing like a father coming home to his family to straighten out any discord or disorder. Our heavenly Father is sending Jesus to set the earth in order during His one thousand year reign before the final judgment (Rev. 20:4-6). This is a truth that believers can hang on to. Anything less would be a disappointing sham. The knowledge of His imminent return will be one of the things that will bring God's remnant through the very hard times to come. In fact, Jesus said that when the terrible signs occur that His follower will look up because their redemption will be drawing near (Mark 13:29; Luke 21:31).

One of the sorrows of the bleak spiritual landscape is the lack of unity about the Second Coming of Christ. At a time when there should be an unprecedented unity of witness to the return of Jesus Christ in the American Church there is either silence or silliness. There is no shortage of theories. Those who have the energy argue and write incessantly about what their best guess is. Often, these opinions are taken as absolute truth by religious 'consumers'. There is a lot of money changing hands but the arrogance of adding details that have not been revealed by prophesy is dangerous and sinful (Rev. 22:18-19). Many thoughtful Christians have decided to simply ignore prophecy in the name of peace and quiet. They just want to concentrate on the Gospel. Many of the sanest voices in American Christendom are quite silent about the abuses of Scriptures that refer to the end times.

The Jewish people who were waiting for their Messiah in Jesus' day were wrong about the manner of His coming. This generation of American churchgoer is missing their opportunity to appropriately represent the coming of their King. A few facts need to be vigorously pressed upon the American public. Firstly, Jesus is about to physically return to the earth, with His saints and angels, to set up God's millennial government. This will be an irresistible event. Secondly, immediately preceding His return great evil will be rampant. A large percentage of the population will perish because of natural and supernatural disaster. Antichrist will appear, demanding worship. To worship him will be an unpardonable sin. Thirdly, every human being will have to give an account for their lives. Finally, people should fear this coming judgment. They should receive God's free gift of salvation through Jesus Christ. Arguing over times or events is fruitless. God's remnant will stick to the pertinent facts since most prophesied events will be kind of obvious when they are occurring.

What a happy event the end of the world is to those who love God. God's remnant longs for Jesus' return to the earth. Our God is a God of justice. He loves judgment (Isaiah 61:8). Just as my dad was able to fix impossible fishing 'snarls' in the bottom of our boat my heavenly Father will sort out all the evil 'snarls' of this present world. He will judge all evil. He will also reward those who did not trust their own righteousness but trusted the sacrifice of His dear Son Jesus, who took their place on the Cross for their sins. What a beautiful, clean, orderly, and happy world is described under the direct rule of God. Embrace and love this truth fellow traveler.

The apostle John speaks of the love of God which can cast out **all** fear (1 John 4:18). Death, political upheaval, and the end of the world are pretty scary subjects. Our society tends to just block out the unpleasant with louder and louder noise. Unfortunately, so do many who profess to know Jesus. Not so, the remnant. God is quietly preparing, teaching, and seasoning those who will fully yield to His purposes. God's remnant is being set free by the knowledge that God loves them. They are learning that whatever comes their way, Father will be with them. There will be a testimony in America of what God's Kingdom is like. These beautiful ones are hidden all over the place. They will not be terrified by disease, disaster, or famine. They will have hilarious joy in the midst of the worst the world has ever seen. The remnant will be a taste of heaven to those who meet them (2 Cor. 2:15-17). This will be the true representation of Christ to those looking for real life.

So here we are at the end of our letters, dear one. Although we could send many other letters, this collection would represent the basic core of what I have learned to survive here in the spiritual wilderness. If you are part of this American remnant, you will take what you can and apply it in your life. You will realize that the best truth is what you can apply and practice in your own experience. Even where we have given extensive thought to what is going on in the brick and steel that calls itself the church, our purpose has been discernment rather than criticism. One of the greatest traps we can fall into is taking upon us the ministry of criticism of others. There are plenty who are experts at criticizing already. It takes no genius to find out what is wrong with people. The genius of God is to love them with His love.

Jesus is not merely an answer. He is the very life of every believer. He becomes the appropriate center for all who invite Him to rule their lives. We are just ahead of the curve, loved one. When God sets the earth in order, He will be the whole earth's "all in all"

(1 Cor. 15:28). When Jesus is your all in all, you will do well. May the fullness of Christ be revealed in you, beloved. Until we meet, here or over there, I am,

Your Fellow Traveler,

Henry

# *Epilogue*

*T*he great experimenter Solomon wasted his life pursuing human wisdom. At the end of his quest he was returned to the place of simplicity where he had started. At the beginning of his reign He asked the Lord for wisdom. At the end of his dissipated life he stated, *"Let us hear the conclusion of the whole matter: Fear God, and keep his commandments: for this [is] the whole [duty] of man. For God shall bring every work into judgment, with every secret thing, whether [it be] good, or whether [it be] evil."* (Ecclesiastes 12:13-14). The smartest man in all of history boiled it down to obedience to God; but how?

I have always been a 'boiler'. I need simpler answers not more complex answers. Our wonderful Savior is aware of the vastness of our limitations. In the light of the pit of sin that we each make for ourselves He has extended the simplicity of grace. The grace of God is the means that will enable 'whosoever' to lay hold of all the obedience to God that they desire. We have His righteousness put into our account. We have His ability dwelling in our hearts in the person of the Holy Spirit. We have His assurance of His lavish provision and concern recorded for us in His Word. Our goal is holiness, our task is to spiritually reproduce, and our destination is heaven. God will do the work in yielded vessels.

These letters lay out the basic focus for and hindrances to, life in this spiritual wilderness of America. The hold of organized religion is strong. There are many foreign interests in the professing church. The infernal forces of Satan seek to carry many away into sin and darkness. In the face of such darkness I can simply testify that Jesus is enough. He has a remnant and they will hear His voice.

God will manifest His glory and nature through those nobodies who hear His voice, know the sound, and follow Him. It is as simple as that. I'll see you in our heavenly home.

Your Brother,

Henry

# *Endnotes*

**Chapter 1:**
1. Finney, C. G. *Revival Lectures: Lecture 1,* Page 1.

**Chapter 2:**
1. Nock, Albert J. *Isaiah's Job* (NY: Foundation for Economic Education, 1962, http://mrsdutoit.com/Right/Isaiah.pdf, accessed 9/2005), p. 2.
2. Nock, Albert J. *Isaiah's Job*, op cit, p. 3.

**Chapter 3:**
1. Shakespeare, William *The Songs and Sonnets of William Shakespeare* (London: Lamboll House, 1987), p. 110, Absence, lines 3 & 4.
2. Bull, Geoffrey *The Sky is Red* (Chicago, IL: Moody Press, 1965), p. 171.
3. Rediger, G. Lloyd *Clergy Killers* (Louisville, KE: Westminster John Knox Press, 1997), pp. 6-8.
4. Rediger, G. Lloyd *Clergy Killers,* op cit, pp. 8-14.

**Chapter 4:**
1. Strong, James S.T.D., LL.D. *The Exhaustive Concordance of The Bible* Greek Dictionary of the New Testament, #1577.

**Chapter 8:**
1. Barna, George *The State of the Church: 2005* (Ventura, CA: George Barna and The Barna Group, 2005), p. 17.
2. *The Holy Bible, New International Version* (Grand Rapids, MI: International Bible Society).

**Chapter 11:**
1. Keil, C. F. & Delitzsch, F. *Commentary on the Old Testament* (Peabody, MA: Hendrickson Publishers, 1989), Vol. 1, p. 434.
2. Keil, C. F. & Delitzsch, F. *Commentary on the Old Testament,* op cit, p. 435.

**Chapter 13:**
1. Strong, James S.T.D., LL.D. op cit, #5273.
2. Tozer, A. W. *I Call it Heresy* (Camp Hill, PA: Christian Publications, 1991), pp. 2-3.
3. Tozer, A. W. *The Set of the Sail; Chapter 7: Facing Both Ways* (Camp Hill, PA: Christian Publications, 1986), pp. 28-31.

**Chapter 15:**
1. Brown, Tom Jr. *Tracker* (New York, NY: Berkley Books, 1979), pp. 72-74.
2. MSN Encarta, (http://encarta.msn.com/dictionary /varmint.html, accessed 9/2005).
3. Barna, George *The State of the Church: 2005* op cit, pp. 52-53.

## Suggested Reading

### Physical Wilderness:

Brown, Tom Jr. *The Science and Art of Tracking* (NY: Berkeley Publishing Group, 1999).

Brown, Tom Jr. *The Tracker* (NY: Berkeley Publishing Group, 1978).

Brown, Tom Jr. *The Way of the Scout* (NY: Berkeley Publishing Group, 1995).

Brown, Tom Jr. *Tom Brown's Field Guide: Wilderness Survival* (NY: Berkeley Publishing Group, 1983).

Meyer, E. C. (Ted) *Basic Bush Survival* (Blaine, WA: Hancock House, 1997).

Newman, Bob *Wilderness Wayfinding* (Boulder, CO: Paladin Press, 1994).

Stevens, James Talmage *Making the Best of Basics* (Seattle WA: Gold Leaf Press, 1975).

Wiseman, John 'Lofty' *The SAS Survival Handbook* (London: Harper Collins: USA, Lewis International, 1986).

**Spiritual Wilderness:**

Barna, George *The State of the Church: 2005* (Ventura CA: George Barna and the Barna Group, 2005).

Bonner, William; Wiggin, Addison *Financial Reckoning Day* (Hoboken, NJ: John Wiley & Sons Inc., 2003).

Bull, Geoffrey T. *The Sky is Red* (Chicago, IL: Moody Press, 1965).

Entiknap, C. G. *Every Believer Evangelism* (London: Benhill Church Press, 1963).

Little, Paul E. *Know What You Believe* (Colorado Springs, CO: Chariot Victor Publishing; Division of Cook Communications, 1987).

Lovett, C. S. *Dealing With the Devil* (Baldwin Park, CA: Personal Christianity, 1967).

Murray, Andrew *Be Perfect* (Minneapolis, MN: Dimension Books, Bethany Fellowship Inc., 1965).

Murray, Andrew *The Secret of Power From on High* (Fort Washington, PA: Christian Literature Crusade, 1986).

Murray, Andrew *With Christ in the School of Prayer* (Old Tappan, NJ: Fleming H. RevellCo., 1973).

Payne, J. Barton *The Theology of the Older Testament* (Irving, TX: ICI with the permission of Zondervan Corp., 1962).

Ravenhill, Leonard *Meat for Men* (Minneapolis, MN: Bethany House Publishers, 1989).

Ravenhill, Leonard *Revival God's Way* (Minneapolis, MN: Bethany House Publishers, 1983).

Ravenhill, Leonard *Sodom Had no Bible* (Minneapolis, MN: Bethany House Publishers, 1971).

Shakespeare, William *The Songs and Sonnets of William Shakespeare* (London: Lamboll House, 1987).

Rediger, G. Lloyd *Clergy Killers* (Louisville, KE: Westminster John Knox Press, 1997).

Tozer, A. W. *A Treasury of A. W. Tozer* (Harrisburg, PA: Christian Publications Inc., 1980).

Tozer, A. W. *I Call it Heresy* (Camp Hill, PA: Christian Publications, 1973).

Tozer, A. W. *The Divine Conquest* (Camp Hill, PA: Christian Publications, 1950).

Tozer, A. W. *The Set of the Sail* (Camp Hill, PA: Christian Publications, 1986).